THE DIVAN OF GHALIB

THE DIVAN

OF

GHALIB

Mirza Ghalib

TRANSLATED FROM URDU
WITH
AN INTRODUCTION AND COMMENTARIES

BY

ZIAUDDIN A. MALIK

SKRYCOFT

(Translation)

Copyright © 2013 by Ziauddin A. Malik

ISBN: 979-8-433288-95-9

ACKNOWLEGEMENT

I wish to thank my son, Khurram, who, though not fluent in literary Urdu, was my chief co-labourer in this translation. When two or three equally accurate renditions of a phrase or line from Ghalilb's poetry into Urdu were made by me, he often assisted in making the more feliciltous choice. Together, we entered into this tribute to Ghalib's genius, a tribute of making Ghalib available in English, the entirety of his final version of the Urdu *Divan-e-Ghalib*, a tribute that took us fifteen years to complete.

I also wish to thank my wife, Khalida, for all the support she has given me in the long years of my work on this project.

Introduction

I

Ghalib, Urdu and the Mughals

"If I were asked what are the Mughal legacies to India," wrote Professor Rashid Ahmed Siddiqui (1896-1977), a highly respected Urdu scholar and writer, "I will, without a moment's hesitation, name these three: Ghalib, Urdu, and the Taj Mahal." We may well read in this succinct statement, which has almost become a proverb, that we cannot think or speak of the one without, at the same time, recalling the rest: we cannot speak of Urdu without speaking of Ghalib, or of either without speaking of the Mughals, and just at the mention of the latter flashes before our mind's eye their splendid achievements in the fields of other arts, and architecture, particularly the Taj.

The much celebrated Mughal Empire was founded by Babur (1482-1530)— "the most brilliant Asiatic prince of his age and worthy of a high place among the sovereigns of any age or country"[1] and "a born general"[2] who came to the throne of Delhi after his stunning victory in the famous First Battle of Panipat, fought in 1526 on the plain of a well-known town of that name, fifty three miles to the northwest of Delhi, when the "mighty army"[3] of the reigning sovereign, Sultan Ibrahim Lodhi, "was laid in the dust in the space of half a day."[4] Babur's son and successor, Humayun (1507-1556) had a troubled reign. It was during the reign of Akbar the Great, the son and successor of Humayun, who ruled for forty-nine years (1556-1605), when began that glorious period in the recorded history of India for which the Mughals are known and

---

[1] *The Oxford History of India* by Vincent A. Smith (1919), revised by J.B. Harrison and edited by Percival Spear (1981), pg. 320.
[2] *The Oxford History of India* by Vincent A. Smith (1919), revised by J.B. Harrison and edited by Percival Spear (1981), pg. 321.
[3] *Babur Nama,* ("Babur's Memoirs") by Zahiruddin Babur, translated by J. Leyden and W. Erskine.
[4] *Babur Nama,* ("Babur's Memoirs") by Zahiruddin Babur, translated by J. Leyden and W. Erskine.

remembered and which lasted for one hundred and fifty years till the reign of Aurangzeb (1658-1707), followed by a century and a half of declining political power but undiminished cultural glow, strength and vigour.

It was Shah Jahan, father of Emperor Aurangzeb, and son and successor of Jahangir[1], who built the Taj Mahal as a monument of love of unrivalled beauty in memory of his wife, Mumtaz Mahal, who died in childbirth in 1631. Shah Jahan reigned for thirty years (1628-1658) and it took twenty-two years to complete the Taj, the like of which there is no other memorial in the world raised by an emperor in honour of his empress.

The Taj was built when the Mughal Empire was at the zenith of its power and prestige, but Urdu came into its own as a major Indo-Aryan language (within the Indo-Iranian branch of the Indo-European family of languages) in the early eighteenth century, when the Empire had started showing the first signs of its political decline. However, for Urdu, not unlike other languages of the world, it took time to reach the stage of being a distinguished literary language. The process started with the founding of the Delhi Sultanate by Shahabuddin Muhammad of Ghor in 1192 which introduced a new factor in the development of Indic dialects, and the factor was the Persian language that came with it and which had absorbed a vast Arabic vocabulary in the preceding more than five centuries since Persia became a part of the Muslim world in 641 A.D. during Omar's caliphate. And as the assimilation of Arabic had enriched Persian and enhanced its literary possibilities so did Persian with the Indic literary language. With the shift of the political power and the Delhi Sultanate taking root, the inflow of Persian-speaking people from the neighbouring countries substantially increased and their everyday social, cultural and business exchanges with the vernacular-speaking natives led to the development of a language which in time reached a stage of being the vehicle of expression of a whole range of the most complex thoughts and feelings and emotions and it came to be known first as Hindi or Hindvi, then as Urdu.[2] And this happened

---

[1]Jahangir succeeded his father, Emperor Akbar, in 1605 and ruled till 1628.
[2]For a comprehensive discussion, see *Early Urdu* by Shamsur Rehman Faruqi (Oxford University Press, India: 1999).

in the reigns of the later Mughals. It is because of this background of its evolution that Ram Babu Saksena (1895-1957) characterized Urdu as "the best symbol of Hindu-Muslim unity."[1] Now more than fifty million Indians speak Urdu and it is the national language of Pakistan, a nation more than 168 million strong, the sixth largest in the world. And in many of the major cities of Western Europe and North America, as well as in the Persian Gulf States, one would find Urdu-speaking communities.

The other precious gift of the Mughals is Ghalib and his Urdu *Divan* (the collection of his Urdu poetry); of the latter Dr. Abd-ur-Rahman Bijnori (1885-1918) famously said, "There are two inspired books of India, the holy Veda and the *Divan* of Ghalib."[2]

Mirza Asadullah Baig Khan who first used the nom de plume of "Asad" and then "Ghalib" was born on December 27, 1797, in Agra, the city of the Taj. His grandfather, Mirza Quqan Baig Khan, a Seljuk Turk, emigrated from Samarqand (Samarkand) in Uzbekistan to India in the mid-eighteenth century during the reign of the Mughal Emperor Shah Alam II (1759-1806). He came from a prominent family and was well-connected with the powers that be in India as is evident from the brief facts of his life available to us. Of his seven offsprings we know the names of only two, Mirza Abdullah Baig Khan and Mirza Nasrullah Baig Khan.

Mirza Abdullah Baig Khan, the elder of the two brothers, married Izzat-un-Nisa Begum, daughter of Ghulam Hussein Khan, a retired commander of the Mughal army and a grandee of Agra; three children were born to them, one daughter and two sons: Chhoti Khanam, Mirza Asadullah Baig Khan and Mirza Yousuf Baig Khan.

Both brothers, Mirza Abdullah Baig Khan and Mirza Nasrullah Baig Khan, following the tradition of their forefathers, made the army their career. Abdullah Baig Khan first went to Lucknow and took service with Nawwab

---

[1] *A History of Urdu Literature* by Ram Babu Saksena (Lahore: Sang-e-Meel Publications: 1996) Preface, pg. ii.
[2] *Mahasin-e-Kalam-e-Ghalib*, by Abd-ur-Rahnman Bijnori (Lucknow: Uttar Pradesh Urdu Academy) (2005), pg. 1 [translation mine].

Vizier Asaf-ud-Daula, then moved to Hyderabad in the Deccan where Mir Nizam Ali Khan (Asaf Jah II), the ruler, made him the commander of a force of hundred cavalry. When he lost this post after a few years because of some court intrigues, he entered the service of Rajput Maharao Bakhtawar Singh of Alwar. Soon after, he was killed in a battle; it was the year 1802 when Ghalib was hardly five, and he was orphaned.

Nasrullah Baig Khan, the younger brother of Abdullah Baig Khan, took Ghalib, his sister, and his younger brother under his wing; at the time he was the Governor of Agra representing the Maratha chief, Daulat Rao Sindia. Next year, in 1803, when the British captured Agra in which they were facilitated by Nasrullah Baig Khan, the British commander-in-chief, Lord Lake, gave him the command of a cavalry of four hundred, and a monthly salary of Rupees 1,700. Later, when Nasrullah Baig seized the principalities of Sonk and Sirsa (Sunsa) near Bharatpur from Holker, they were given by Lord Lake to him for life. Thus his income reached a figure of about 125,000 rupees annually which in his time was a huge amount. But soon afterwards a tragedy happened; in 1806 he fell off an elephant and died. Ghalib was then only nine.

Nasrullah Baig Khan had married the sister of Nawwab Ahmad Bakhsh Khan, whose father, Arif Jan, too, had emigrated from Bukhara perhaps with Quqan Baig Khan, Nasrullah Baig Khan's father. Ahmad Bakhsh Khan, who was a darling of Lord Lake and remained "in attendance on him" during the Maratha war of 1803-1806, represented Alwar chief's interest with the British. He was rewarded by both for his services: thanks to Lord Lake he received the principality of Firozpur Jhirka in the Punjab from the British and Loharu from the Raja of Alwar. When Nasrullah Baig Khan died in 1806, Sonk and Sirsa were initially resumed by the British and then given over to Ahmad Bakhsh Khan on the condition that he would provide for Nasrullah Baig Khan's dependents that included Ghalib (Nasrullah's nephew), Ghalib's younger brother and Nasrullah's mother and three sisters (Nasrullah had no child of his own). This decision was to be given effect through a financial arrangement under which Ahmad Bakhsh Khan was given a remission of rupees 10,000 per annum from the quitrent of rupees 25,000 per annum he was required to pay to the British in respect of Firozpur Jhirka that he had received from the British to which was now added Sonk and Sirsa after the death of Nasrullah Baig Khan; the relief of rupees 10,000 so given to Ahmad Bakhsh Khan was to be applied by him towards the payments of pensions to the dependents of Nasrullah Baig Khan. Ghalib's share would have amounted to a monthly pension of rupees 208 and paisas 33. Ahmad Bakhsh Khan was also exempted from the payment of the remaining rupees 15,000 of the quitrent if he kept in readiness a contingent of fifty horses. An official letter incorporating this arrangement was issued by Lord Lake on May 4, 1806 and approved by the Governor-General in Council at Calcutta. This timely and straightforward solution of both the human and the entitlement issues arising from the tragedy of the untimely death of Nasrullah Baig Khan later became a cause of serious, complicated, and long-drawn out dispute to which we will have the occasion to return.

Ghalib's parents, both father and mother, as we have seen, belonged to the nobility and thus, despite the fact that he lost his father and then his uncle, he lived in comparative comfort and luxury. We may also note that because of his parentage and family involvement in the high politics of India which was characterized by wars between the native rulers and between them and the rising power of the British, all of which was a sign of the declining power of the Mughals. Ghalib was, from his childhood, exposed to, and thus became a witness of, the changes of the greatest consequence that were taking place in India; and Ghalib was a precocious child. However, very much in the tradition of his time, for formal education he sat at the feet of Khalifa Muhammad Muazzam who was a well-known teacher of Agra, learned in religion, Arabic and Persian. We know that Urdu was Ghalib's mother tongue but at the same time he had a great passion for Persian and in this respect he was in luck as, in late 1810 or early 1811, there arrived a traveller from Persia by the name of Abdus Samad who, as Malik Ram put it, "had been born in the Zoroastrian faith and through his study had voluntarily embraced Islam ... it was therefore natural that he should have a thorough knowledge of Zoroastrianism and

Islam."[1] He also turned out to be a profound scholar of Persian and Arabic, as well as logic and philosophy. Ghalib and Abdus Samad struck up mutual rapport between themselves and the latter stayed with Ghalib for two years at Agra and Delhi. Apparently, this association when Ghalib was in his early teens proved to be of great benefit to him inasmuch as his natural interest in and sensibility to the beauty of the Persian language received timely impetus and input from Abdus Samad who remained in touch with him through letters for some time even after he left Delhi.

It was at about the same time, in August 1810, when Ghalib was thirteen that he was married to Umrao Begum, daughter of Nawwab Ilahi Bakhsh Khan who lived in Delhi and was the younger brother of Ahmad Bakhsh Khan of whom we already know something as the brother-in-law of Ghalib's deceased uncle, Nasrullah Baig Khan. After his marriage Ghalib's visits to Delhi became more frequent and when he was sixteen or seventeen he permanently moved there. We may recall here that Shah Jahan, after about ten years of his reign (1628-1658), started building the new city of Delhi, called Shahjahanabad. The construction of Lal Qila (Red Fort) was started in 1638 and took ten years to complete in 1648; it extended for two kilometers and rose in height from eighteen meters on the Jumna side to thirty-three meters on the city side, complete with its gardens and fountains and Diwan-e-Am (Hall of Public Audience) where the emperor sat to hear the complaints and disputes of his subjects, and Diwan-e-Khas (Hall of Private Audience) of which the magnificent Peacock Throne was the centrepiece and on which sat the emperor while presiding over his cabinet meetings. The construction of Jama Masjid (Great Mosque), which had begun in 1644 and on completion in 1658 was to become another landmark of Delhi, was still in progress. However, in 1648 when the Fort in all its grandeur was ready for occupancy, the capital was partly shifted to Delhi, 204 kilometers north of Agra, the seat of the Mughal Empire since Babur; complete transfer took place later in the reign of Aurangzeb (1658-1707), the last of the great Mughals and the first sovereign in history who ruled

---

[1] *Mirza Ghalib*, National Book Trust, India (Delhi: 1968), pg. 8.

the whole of India except the southernmost tip. But when Ghalib made Delhi his home in late 1813 or early 1814 it was not the same city as of yore—"a great and imperial city ... with anything between one and two million inhabitants ... the largest and most renowned city, not only of India, but of all the East from Constantinople to Canton. Its court was brilliant, its mosques and colleges numerous, and its literary and artistic fame as high as its political renown."[1]

II

Delhi and Ancient India

Delhi, like Rome, was not built in a day; both rose from obscurity to the greatest eminence and both had chequered histories. It is generally believed that Delhi is a city of great antiquity, the basis of which is the tradition that Indarpat village in its vicinity is the sight where once stood Indraprastha, the town founded by the Pandavas of the *Mahabharata*[2] as their capital and is supposed to have extended up to the Purana Qila (grand citadel of Emperor Sher Shah's Delhi who reigned from 1540 to 1545), on the bank of the Jumna, between Shah Jahan's Delhi and Humayun's tomb. Unlike ancient Egypt and Mesopotamia that are rich in permanent inscriptions, ancient India lacks them and tradition remains the main source for historians who may probably have not much difficulty in accepting the one regarding the location of Indraprastha. However, at the beginning of the recorded ancient history of India, Bimbisara, who ruled over Magadha (c. 522-c. 494 B.C.), made Rajgir in Bihar his capital, a city mentioned by *Mahabharata*, and equally important, for different reasons, to Hindus, Jains, and Buddhists. Bimbisara's son and successor, Ajatasatru (c. 494-

---

[1]*Twilight of the Mughals*, by Percival Spear (London: 1951), pg. 1.
[2]*Mahabharata* is one of the two great epics of India (the other being *Ramayana*). It is a huge work of Sanskrit compositions by different authors of different eras, only one fifth of which constitutes the epic part narrating the Great War between the Kauravas and the Pandavas. Tradition has it that the war was fought in 3102 B.C., but historians incline to place it 2,000 years later in 1000 B.C. The narrative itself, however, is thought to have been composed between 400 B.C. and 200 A.D.

c. 467 B.C.), built a fortress in the strategically secure triangle formed by the confluence of the rivers Son and Ganges at a place called Patali that developed into the city of Pataliputra, Azimabad of the Muslim period and the modern Patna, also in Bihar, and became the first imperial capital in the history of Hindustan in the reign of Mahapadma Nanda, the founder of the Nanda dynasty which ruled from c. 362 B.C. to c. 322 B.C.; it remained the imperial capital of Hindustan during the great Mauryas like Chandragupta Maurya (c. 326-273 B.C.) and Asoka (273-232 B.C.), and the illustrious Guptas (320 A.D.-480 A.D.). In the words of a learned European scholar, "The Gupta period is in the annals of classical India almost what the Periclean age is in the history of Greece."[1] Then came a period of uncertainty, wars, and obscurity till King Harasha appeared on the scene in 606 A.D. at Thanesar and made Kanauj his capital, about three hundred miles south of Delhi. Harasha died in 647 A.D. without leaving an heir and there again followed a rather long period of confusion and obscurity with no central authority to hold the land together. It is not before 993-994 that Delhi finds a mention that has come to be regarded as the most probable historical date of its foundation on a site close to where now stands the Qutb Minar.

III

The Sultanate of Delhi and Harmony

But Delhi shone as the brightest star in the firmament of Indian politics when it became associated with the sovereigns of Hindustan who came to be known in history as the Sultans of Delhi, and the years 1192 to 1526 as the Delhi Sultanate period. All monumental events that have permanently changed

---

[1] See *The Oxford History of India* by Vincent A. Smith (1981), pg. 172, for the quotation from a learned European scholar.

the course of history have been the work of man, nature, or both; this one seemingly was man's and it happened in 1192 on the battlefield of Tarain near Thanesar when Shahabuddin Muhammad of Ghor[1] soundly defeated the mighty force of the confederacy of a multitude of kings under the command of the redoubtable Prithiviraj Chauhan, ruler of Ajmer and Delhi, and founded the Sultanate of Delhi. But 1192 does not mark the date when Islam reached India; it had already been there in 712 when Muhammad bin Qasim conquered Sindh and when later, in 1020, Mahmud annexed the Punjab to the kingdom of Ghazni. In fact, within a short span of eighty years from the death of the Prophet of Islam, Muhammad, in 632, by which time he had founded the Islamic state comprising Mecca and Medina, Muslim rulers became the masters of the entire Arabian peninsula, Persia, Syria, western Turkistan, Egypt, south Spain, Sindh, and Baluchistan. In the words of Vincent Smith, "The rapidity of the spread of Islam ... and the dramatic suddenness with which ... [it] rose to a position of dominant sovereignty constitute one of the marvels, or it might be said, the miracles of history."[2] So it is not exactly the territorial expansion of Muslim rule that makes the founding of the Delhi Sultanate historically important; its true significance seems to lie somewhere else, in the fact that it provided an unique opportunity for experimenting in living in social harmony of two peoples, Hindus and Muslims, who diverged from each other in every particular—ancestry, history, tradition, social structure, culture, custom, manners, morals, language, and, most fundamentally, religious beliefs and practices. It is beyond the scope of this introductory essay to discuss this in any detail; suffices it to say that while it would be unrealistic to expect the experiment to be a complete success, it cannot, at the same time, be gainsaid that it did make significant progress to which more than one factor contributed, the most fundamental being the political unity which the Sultanate achieved virtually for the first time since the fall of the Gupta empire in the 5th century A.D. From the political stability ensued social peace giving birth to fellow-

[1]Ghor was a little known principality in the mountains of Afghanistan to the southeast of Herat. Shahabuddin Muhammad, however, was a Turk.
[2]*The Oxford History of India* (4th edition), pg. 38.

feelings across religious divide which was greatly helped by the nature of the two religions, Hinduism and Islam. Of the latter Arnold J. Toynbee has this to say, "As for the religious pluralism of the original Islamic state and of its successor-states, this has been made obligatory on all Islamic states by the ruling in the Qur'an that Jews and Christians share with Muslims the distinction of being 'People of the Book.' In virtue of this, Jews and Christians … are entitled, according to the Islamic religious law, to remain faithful to their own respective religions and to be protected, besides being tolerated, by the Islamic government, so long as they submit to the Islamic government's authority and pay a surtax. This toleration and protection, to which Jews and Christians are entitled, has been extended, by analogy, to cover the adherents of other higher religions, e.g. Zoroastrians and Hindus."[1] With regard to Hinduism, Percival Spear writes thus, "Sardar K. M. Panikkar, diplomatist, historian, and publicist of the Indian Union … turns Hinduism into an assimilative magic. Its skill is to absorb ideas and customs from all quarters, to assimilate them into a harmonious whole, and to clothe with local colour. Hinduism is not like a sponge, to hold foreign matter for a time and then disgorge; like the Hindu cow it absorbs and assimilates foreign matter to produce the precious nectars of milk and cream."[2] Besides these general characteristics of the two religions which greatly helped the evolution of mutual confidence between their followers, the Sultans of Delhi took specific policy measures to win the loyalty and cooperation of the Hindus, e.g., employing them as officers and clerks in the secretariat, and as revenue collectors in the fields, allowing rajas and the landlords to retain their privileges by becoming tributaries, some of whom even provided auxiliary forces for the imperial army in times of wars. It is a sign of success of these policies and the consequential general peace and prosperity that reigned during at least the first two centuries of the Delhi Sultanate that "north, central, and western India were covered with nobly conceived and

---

[1] *Change and Habit: The Challenge of Our Time*, by Arnold J. Toynbee (Oxford University Press: New York, 1966), pg. 186.
[2] *India: A Modern History*, by Percival Spear (The University of Michigan Press: Ann Arbor, 1972), pg. 39.

brilliantly executed buildings."[1] A new architectural style was also developed which can best be termed as Indo-Muslim. The famous Qutb Minar, one of the landmarks of Delhi, was built in this period—started by Sultan Qutbuddin Aybak (reigned 1206-1210), completed by his successor Sultan Iltutmash (reigned 1211-1236), and named after the great mystic of Delhi, Khawja Qutbuddin Bakhtiyar Kaki (1187-1236). The latter part, viz., the naming of the monument, points to another distinctive feature of this era; some of the greatest sages and saints and sufis, besides Bakhtiyar Kaki, lived and taught and preached in the twelfth to fourteenth centuries, including Khawja Muinuddin Chishti of Ajmer (1141-1235), Baba Fariduddin Ganj Shakar of Pakpatan (1174-1259), Sheikh Bahauddin Zakariya of Multan (1183-1262), and Sheikh Nizamuddin Auliya of Delhi (1239-1325). While they all lived dervish's lives they were all very powerful personalities, and their strength lay in their deep knowledge of religion and philosophy, their personal spiritual experiences, their humility, and, above all, their love for human beings without any distinction. All these factors made them at once highly revered and extremely popular with peoples of all faiths and classes—Hindus and Muslims, elites and commonalties, rich and poor—all of whom were equally attracted by their teachings, which centered round love for man and love for the loving and caring God that gave them a feeling of a kind of touch with the transcendent One. The effect of all this, inter alia, was the infusion of hopefulness and a sense of the intrinsic worth of human beings as human beings—the ultimate basis of mutual respect and fellow feelings.

---

[1] *India: A Modern History*, by Percival Spear (The University of Michigan Press: Ann Arbor, 1972), pg. 107.

IV

The Delhi Sultanate and Mongol Raids

While all of these subtle forces were at work within India, beyond its borders a new power erupted with a ferocity and in a part of the world which not even the wisest of the time would have anticipated: the power was Genghis (Chingaiz) Khan, and the region, Mongolia. Born Temuchin in 1162, early in his life he came to dominate the tribes of Mongolia who elected him as their Chief, the Great Khan; it was then that he adopted the style of Genghis Khan. By the time he died in 1227, he ruled an empire that stretched from the Pacific Ocean to the Black Sea; to build this empire, the vanquished peoples—men, women, and children—were slain indiscriminately, and in millions. Once he came up to Attock on the river Indus, but Sultan Iltutmash acted wisely, handled the situation adroitly, and succeeded in averting an imminent invasion and its consequence, the massacre of his people. The menace did not disappear forever, however, and within five years of the death of Sultan Iltutmash, the Mongols, left behind by Genghis Khan and those who joined them later, raided Lahore in 1241-42, causing great havoc. Sultan Balban (reigned 1266-1290), checked the incursions first by repulsing them and then by the refortification of Lahore, and by appointing his son Muhammad the governor of Multan, and making him the guardian of the frontiers; in 1279, the invading Mongols were completely routed by Governor Muhammad. But by then they had created such a great terror that about fifteen kings and princes fled to Delhi to find refuge in Balban's court. And this fear was not wholly unfounded, for, before long the Mongols regrouped and resumed the raids in 1296 in the reign of Allauddin Khilji (1296-1316), and from then on it became an almost annual feature. In 1305, the Mongols under their leader Qutlugh Khan headed straight for Delhi, overcoming the resistances on the way; just outside Delhi they were met by Allauddin's army under the command of his brother, Zafar Khan, who roundly defeated them before dying of his wounds. Henceforth, Ghazi Malik, the governor of the Punjab who later ascended the throne of Delhi as Ghiyasuddin Tughluq, kept the Mongols at bay.

V

The New Cities of Delhi

Sultan Allauddin, who was fond of building, could now give his attention to constructing a new Delhi called Siri near present day Hauz Khas. Within four years of Allaudin's death in 1316, the Khilji dynasty came to an end, and Ghazi Malik who had stood like an impregnable wall against the Mongols since 1305 ascended the Delhi throne at the invitation of the nobles at the court and took the title of Ghiyasuddin Tughluq. His son and successor, Sultan Muhammad Tughluq (reigned 1325-1351), built another Delhi, Tughluqabad, southeast of the Qutb Minar, and his successor, Sultan Firuz Tughluq (reigned 1351-1388), created Firozabad at the site where the present day New Delhi is situated; he also got moved two Asoka pillars (with original inscriptions on them) to his newly built Delhi—one from Topra in the district of Ambala and the other from Meerut. He founded other cities, too, like Hisar and Jaunpur, and established institutions of learning, such as Firuz Shahi Madrasah.

Sultan Firuz Tughluq died in 1388, and ten years hence in 1398, there descended upon Delhi a calamity; Amir Timur (1336-1405), the Tamerlane of English literature, invaded India with a force of 90,000 cavalry, defeated the reigning Sultan, occupied Delhi, despoiled the city for five days, spreading death and destruction all around, and then left with a booty for Samarqand, his capital city. When he died in 1405 he was ruling an empire that extended from the borders of China at the one end to the Mediterranean at the other.

With Timur's invasion in 1398, the Delhi Sultanate virtually came to an end, though until 1526 it continued in name. Between these two dates, only one Sultan, Sikander Lodhi (reigned 1489-1517), displayed some of the vigour, ability, and love for and patronage of the arts and learning expected of the Sultans.

VI

The Great Mughals

It has already been noted that Zahiruddin Babur, King of Kabul, founded the Mughal Empire of India in 1526 by defeating Sultan Ibrahim Lodhi, son and successor of Sikander Lodhi in the First Battle of Panipat. Babur was descended on his father's side from Amir Timur and on his mother's side from Genghis Khan, and like them he was a great leader of men, and a great general and conqueror, but there the resemblances ended; unlike them he was no destroyer and no sacker of cities. He was indeed high-minded by nature and imbued with artistic sensibilities. In the words of Vincent Smith, "Babur emerges as immensely likable, very vigourous, artistic personality, as able to 'rough it' over the Hindu Kush in winter as to write most excellent Turki verses. His zest was an inspiration to his followers, with whom he shared both hardships and a convivial appreciation of fine gardens or of wine."[1] He then quotes from Babur's memoirs, "They very recently brought me a single muskmelon. While cutting it up I felt myself affected with a strong sense of loneliness, and a sense of my exile from my native country; and I could not help shedding tears while I was eating it."

Babur had inherited, as a child, the small kingdom of Farghana in the upper reaches of Syr Darya, and before he died in 1530 when he was only forty-eight

---

[1] *The Oxford History of India* (Oxford: 1981), pg. 323.

he had built up an empire that extended from Badakhshan and Afghanistan in the west to Patna and Bihar in the east, with Agra and Delhi in the heart and centre, and Ranthambore and Chanderi in the south. Life, however, did not give him time to consolidate the administration and empire; that had to wait till Akbar's reign.

On his death in 1530, Emperor Babur was succeeded by his eldest son, twenty-three years old Prince Humayun, a man of culture, ability, and valour. His reign was marked by the treachery of his three brothers whom he had appointed provincial governors, and the recalcitrance of the Afghan chiefs. Although he started off with some very significant victories against the Afghans, in 1540 he ultimately lost the empire to the then dominant power in Bihar, Sher Shah Suri, his betrayal by his brothers playing no small role in his discomfiture and defeat.

Emperor Sher Shah who came to the throne in 1540 was not only a brilliant strategist and general, he also proved himself a great administrator, as well as a man of fine taste in architecture. He established an efficient civil government, improving and building on Sultan Allauddin Khilji's administrative structure, introduced the system of assessment and collection of land revenue on the basis of measurement of land, anticipating Emperor Akbar, and built a new Delhi at Purana Qila near India Gate of the present day New Delhi, and constructed the Grand Trunk Road from Bengal to Indus. "Sher Shah, like Asoka and Harsha," writes Vincent Smith, "accepted the maxim that 'it behoves the great to be always active.'"[1] He died suddenly in 1545 and thus came to an end his memorable reign.

Humayun, who though lost the empire and had to endure much, never forsook his high-mindedness and never gave up hope; in July 1555 he regained what in May 1540 he had lost; Delhi and Agra and the Indian empire were again his to reign. But unfortunately within seven months of his victory there happened a tragedy; he fell from the staircase of his library and died. He was then about forty-nine.

---

[1] *The Oxford History of India* (Oxford: 1981), pg. 325.

At the time of his death in 1556, the elder of his two sons, Akbar, was only thirteen years old but the emperor had left in the person of Bairam Khan a most responsible guardian of the prince, and a very good general; he was now the regent, too. What would have been the history of the Mughal dynasty and of India had there been no Bairam Khan at this critical juncture is hard to imagine. There had arisen two serious contenders to the throne of Delhi, both nephews of Emperor Sher Shah Suri. Hemu, a baniya by birth, who was the chief minister of one of these nephews, King Adil Shah, occupied Agra and Delhi on behalf of his sovereign, but then treachery entered his heart, and he decided to have himself crowned as king, assuming the honorific title of Raja Vikramajita. Bairam Khan, in the meantime, was marching at the head of his army towards Panipat,[1] taking his ward, Akbar, with him. Hemu, on hearing of it, advanced in the same direction with his army which in numbers far exceeded Bairam's. The two forces met on the plain of Panipat on 5th November, 1556, and a pitched battle was fought; Hemu was killed, his army dispersed, and the prize of the throne of Delhi taken by the victor. From then on, for the next one hundred fifty years, the Mughal Empire did not face any serious challenge to its authority; and when the challenge did come, it came from a Western colonial power, not from inside India.

In 1560 when Akbar was about eighteen years of age, he decided to end Bairam Khan's tutelage and sent him to Mecca for Hajj. This was done partly of his own accord and partly on the urgings of his mother, Empress Hamida Bano, his foster-mother Maham Anga and her son, Adham Khan, all of whom wielded great influence with him at this stage and had their own personal reasons for their dislike of Bairam Khan. But it did not take long for Akbar to free himself from the undesirable influences of these personages and be his own man; this happened in 1562, but even before that he had set about expanding the Empire, always believing that conquest was the preferred way of life for a monarch so no rival or neighbour would dare take up arms against

---

[1]This is known in history as the Second Battle of Panipat; the first was fought between Babur and Ibrahim Lodhi in 1526.

him. He started off by securing the politically important fortresses of Gwalior, Chunar, Mirtha, Chitor, and Ranthambhor, reducing the respective rajas to submission. In time, the Mughal Empire under Akbar extended from the present day Bangladesh in the east to Herat in Afghanistan in the west, and from the foothills of the Himalayas in the north and the Hindu Kush in the northwest to Khandesh, Berar, and parts of Ahmadnagar in the Deccan, and all the lands within these boundaries, including Bengal, Bihar, Orissa, Oudh, Kashmir, the Punjab, Rajputana (Rajasthan), Gujrat, Sindh, and Baluchistan. But Akbar was not just a conqueror, he was essentially an empire-builder; he knew that for the Empire to be stable and to endure, conquest had to be bolstered up with diplomacy and sweetened by blandishments, and a sound administrative structure had to be developed; he did all this. Conciliation with Hindus who constituted a vast majority of the population, respect for their religion and culture, and special consideration for the Hindu Rajput chiefs became the dominant themes of his policy of consolidation of the Empire; he inducted Rajputs and other Hindus in high positions in the army and the imperial civil service, and, in 1562 and 1570, married the Rajput princesses, one of whom became the mother of his son and successor, Emperor Jahangir. Akbar's policy in this respect represented a marked advance on that of the Sultans of Delhi and was immensely successful. However, "his conception of sovereignty was autocratic and this led him to crush the ulema, a religious body of Muslim scholars which constituted a check upon his powers."[1]

Administration was the other crucial area that received his especial attention and his genius in this field showed in the way he organized the central government and the army and instituted the system of checks on the power of the provincial governors. "His system of provincial administration, still discernible in modern India and Pakistan, and drawn in its details from the experience of nearly four hundred years of Muslim rule was based on the subah, sircar, or sarkar (administrative district), pargana and mahal (revenue division), the principal executive officers (whether financial or military) being

---

[1] *Encyclopædia Britannica*, Vol. 12 (1973), pg. 141.

appointed and transferred frequently from the centre."[1] All in all, he was a great success as a ruler and a sovereign, and an atmosphere of peace, prosperity, and hope came to pervade Indian society during his reign which set the stage for the development of art, architecture, and literature. Akbar himself was a great lover of art and had excellent taste in architecture. He obtained the services of Tansen, the best known Indian singer to this day; had the statues of Jaimal and Patta, the heroes of the conquest of the fort of Chitor, carved and mounted on stone elephants at the gate of the Agra fort; built a new capital city comprising a grand mosque and a royal palace at Sikri (Fatahpur-Sikri), twenty three miles to the west of Agra, where the Muslim saint, Sheikh Salim Chishti, lived. Akbar was also a patron of painting, poetry and literature; Faizi was his court poet; Faizi's brother, Abul Fazal, compiled *Ain-i-Akbari* (Institutes of Akbar); Tulsi Das, the author of the Hindi *Ramayana*, flourished in his time. He encouraged Hindu painters to learn the Persio-Islamic techniques that gradually led to the development of the Mughal school of painting. His buildings, too, were marked by a similar fine blending of Hindu and Muslim styles. In time, this synthesis extended to every aspect of Indian life from the arts and architecture to cuisine, gastronomy, dress and pastimes, giving birth to what is best known as the Mughal culture, much of which has survived the ravages of time to this day both in India and Pakistan.

VII

India and the Europeans

But while the processes of integration were at work under Akbar's policies that came to characterize the Mughal rule as such, the European Christian settlers and their ships with mounted arms had started making waves at the Indian seaports which indeed were comparatively recent developments. Since

---

[1] *Encyclopædia Britannica*, Vol. 1 (1973), pg. 477.

the time of the Muslim conquest of Egypt and Persia in the seventh century, the trade between Europe and the East had been under their control. This continued to be the position until the sixteenth century. In 1498, Vasco da Gama, the Portuguese navigator, discovered the sea route around Africa to India and cast the anchor at Calicut before returning to Lisbon in 1499. Soon after, in 1509, the Portuguese king sent out Alfonso de Albuquarque, another Portuguese navigator, to the south Asian seas. His ambition was to found a Portuguese empire in the East; his hope was to ruin Cairo and Mecca by taking away sea commerce from Muslim hands; and "his zeal to injure Islam was so great that he planned to dig a canal from the Upper Nile to the Red Sea to ruin Egypt by the diversion of the river."[1] He had a tremendous advantage over his Muslim rivals inasmuch as his ships were indisputably superior to theirs in size and strength, and his guns more powerful; Albuquarque, consequently, was able to secure for Portugal its strategic position in the power game of the south Asian seas and occupy the Indian island of Goa before he died in 1515. Fifty-seven years hence, by 1572—the year Akbar conquered Gujarat—the Portuguese were virtually ruling the south Asian seas and had extended their control to all the Indian ports from which originated or passed the highly lucrative international trade in spices, cotton piece-goods, calicoes, yarn, silk, indigo, sugar and saltpeter. The annexation of Gujarat in 1572 gave the Empire free access to the sea, and this brought Akbar in direct contact with the Portuguese with whom the terms of peace were negotiated the next year, in 1573, at Surat. Among the notable features of the Portuguese policy in India were also its religious imperialism and its proselytizing spirit: the introduction of the Inquisition in Goa after 1560 was an instance of the first, and the effort of the Jesuit Fathers and other religious orders to convert the local population to Christianity of the latter. Being fully aware of, and encouraged by, Akbar's attitude towards Islam and his deep interest in the study of comparative religion, Goa entertained great hopes of converting no less a personage than the Emperor himself. Accordingly, Jesuit missionaries started arriving at

---

[1] *India: A Modern History*, by Percival Spear (Ann Arbor: The University of Michigan, 1972), pg. 163.

Akbar's court, beginning with Father Julian Pereria in 1576, followed by Fathers Rudolfo Aquaviva and Antonio Monserrata in 1579, and Fathers Jerome Xavier and Emanuel Pinherio in 1595. The missionaries, however, had no success with the Emperor or with the nobles. Nevertheless they did succeed in obtaining from Akbar the right to make converts through their missionary work.

But more than anything else, the Portuguese presence in India signified the emerging dominant role of naval strength in deciding the fates of the existing, evolving, or would-be empires. India with its large peninsula between the Arabian Sea and the Bay of Bengal was peculiarly exposed to the threat that could come from any ambitious and strong naval power. Strangely enough, a sagacious empire builder, statesman and conqueror like Akbar failed to realize the significance of this development and take measures to build a strong Indian navy to meet such situations and extend his own empire beyond the seas. This had grievous consequences for India in the long run. Similarly, when during the siege of the fort of Asirgarh in 1601 he discovered that to breach its wall he needed more powerful guns which he did not have and the Portuguese did but they would not lend those to him, he apparently did nothing to improve his artillery and better the Europeans in this respect. This, too, was to have grave political consequences for India in the long term. However, on balance, Emperor Akbar's place in history as one of the greatest rulers of India is assured; historians as well as the populace call him Akbar the Great to this day.

Akbar's memorable reign of forty-nine years came to an end on his death in 1605. His son, Prince Salim, succeeded him, adopting the style of Nuruddin Jahangir. He continued with his father's policy of conciliation with the Hindus; married Hindu princesses; honoured the Rajput ruler of Mewar and his son by having their statues be carved in marble and erected in the garden of the Agra Fort. He was famed for his love of justice and this reputation of his continues in India till today. He possessed considerable ability in literature, art and architecture and was a bountiful patron of artists; his autobiography (*Tuzuk-e-Jahangiri*) which covers nineteen years of his reign, makes a fascinating reading; a highly useful Persian dictionary, *Farhang-i-Jahangiri*, was compiled under his patronage; he honoured the two most outstanding painters of his reign, Abul Hasan and Ustad Mansur, by conferring on them the title of Nadir-uz-Zaman ("Wonder of the Age"); and he conceived the ideas that got translated into the unique architecture of Akbar's mausoleum at Sikandara.

Politically, the most significant development in Jahangir's reign was the appearance of the Dutch and the English on the Indian scene. The Portuguese who had dominated the south Asian seas for a century and had monopolized Oriental commerce were driven out by the Dutch East India Company from their strategic and prized possessions of Malacca in Malaysia, from Colombo in Ceylon, and from most of the Indian seaports where they had their settlements and trading posts. But the Dutch interest was mainly centered on securing the monopoly of the highly profitable spice trade and had accordingly established their base at Batavia (present-day Jakarta). Given this situation, and particularly after the Massacre of Amboyna in 1623, the English who had followed the Dutch in the East thought better of concentrating on India, and this, in time, changed the course of Indian history.

Queen Elizabeth I of England granted the charter of exclusive rights to trade in the East Indies to the English East India Company in December 1600. The Company's first ship 'Hector' arrived at Surat on the west coast of India in 1608. The captain of the ship, William Hawkins, went to the court of Emperor Jahangir for whom he had brought gifts and a letter from King James I of England requesting trade facilities in India. He was well received at the court and the English were granted certain privileges which the Portuguese considered as threats to their monopolistic interests. Captain Hawkins left for his home in 1611 after three years in India. The following year, in 1612, arrived another English ship 'Dragon' under the command of Captain Best; he had an encounter with a Portuguese fleet and defeated it—an indication that the balance of power on the sea had started shifting—but the Portuguese failed to read the sign, and their navy continued with acts of piracy apparently to retain the monopoly of trade, and, in 1613, had the temerity to seize four of the imperial ships, thus bringing upon itself the Emperor's wrath and consequential disgrace. Paradoxically, the Portuguese at the same time had been hoping and trying to convert Jahangir and the royal family to Christianity. Anyway, two years later, in 1615, arrived Sir Thomas Roe at Emperor Jahangir's court as an accredited envoy of King James I of England, and before he returned to his country in 1619 he was successful in obtaining from the Emperor substantial concessions for the English East India Company which provided it with a solid base for trade in India.

Jahangir died in 1627 when travelling from Kashmir to Lahore; his son Prince Khurram born to him by his Hindu Rajput empress, succeeded him; he had received the title of Shah Jahan in 1616 for conquering Ahmadnagar, a Muslim kingdom south of the Narbada and it is by this name that he is known to history. His reign was marked by the extension of the empire in the Deccan; Ahmadnagar was formally annexed, and Bijapur and Golconda were made tributaries by 1636. But more than anything else Shah Jahan is famed for the magnificent buildings he raised. We have already noted that he built Shahjahanabad, a new city of Delhi, complete with its Red Fort and Jama Masjid, and, at Agra the Taj of unrivalled beauty; he also constructed Diwan-e-Am ("The Hall of Public Audience"), Diwan-e-Khas ("The Hall of Private Audience") and the exquisitely designed Moti Masjid ("The Pearl Mosque") within the Agra Fort, to name just a few more. (The construction of the Agra Fort was started by Akbar in 1565, and in his time it was primarily a military structure; with Shah Jahan's additions it also became an imperial palace.) As in architecture so in other forms of art, works of great merit and charm were produced in his reign, portrait-painting reaching its highest degree of perfection.

In Shah Jahan's reign, in 1639, the English East India Company was granted a piece of land on the Coromandel Coast by the local chief of Chandragiri, the vestige of the old and once powerful kingdom of Vijayanagar, which became one of its earliest settlements in India. This small English trading site and settlement was to develop into the big city and Presidency of Madras under the Company's rule and later the Crown's. But that lay far in the future which probably nobody would then have thought of and imagined. (The city of Madras is now Chennai.)

Since the arrival of the Dutch and the English on the Indian scene, the Portuguese had been in retreat, territorially and politically. They had also aroused people's hostility by consistently engaging in slave trade, seizing Hindu and Muslim children and converting them to Christianity, and committing other acts of lawlessness and cruelty. Shah Jahan, in 1632, directed Qasim Khan, the governor of Bengal, to extirpate them from Hooghly, their centre of activities where they had erected buildings and established a thriving trading post, besides the customhouse. The directive was carried out; however, a few years later they were allowed to return, but they were not able to regain their earlier position. The Dutch had their interest centred on the Spice Islands.

In a word, Shah Jahans' reign (1628-1658) was marked by the Mughals' glory at its best, the English gain, and the Portuguese loss.

In September 1657 Shah Jahan fell seriously ill and the war of succession ensued between his four sons, Dara Shikoh, Shuja, Aurangzeb, and Murad Baksh from which Aurangzeb emerged the final winner, which should not come as a surprise if it is remembered that Dara Shikoh, a man of great natural abilities, had made many enemies because of his violent temper and inordinately overbearing manners; Shuja was too much fond of pleasure and could not rise to the occasion when a decisive action was called for; and Murad, perhaps, the bravest of them was debauched and hare-brained. And as for Aurangzeb, "In courage, long-suffering and sound judgement he was unrivalled."[1]

Aurangzeb's reign (1658-1707) is most remarkable for its conquests and the expansion of the empire. In the east, Assam was conquered (1662), the Portuguese pirates were flushed out from the waterways of the Brahamputra Delta, and the district of Chitagong was annexed (1666). In the south, the Muslim kingdoms of Bijapur and Golconda were incorporated into the empire

---

[1]See *The Oxford History of India*, by Vincent A. Smith (1981), pg. 425, for quotation from historian Khafi Khan.

in 1686 and 1687, respectively. Aurangzeb thus came to rule over an empire which for the first time in history extended to almost the whole of India, besides the territories that lay outside its boundaries. He was also probably the first Mughal Emperor, and the first emperor in history, whose mother tongue was Urdu[1]; he spoke other languages, too, including Turki and Persian; in fact he was very learned in Arabic and Persian, and was thoroughly familiar with the works of Imam Muhammad al-Ghazzali (1058-1111), a highly renowned and respected philosopher, mathematician, and astronomer.

In Aurangzeb's reign, the Portuguese hardly mattered anymore, and French, Dutch and Danish settlements were of little account yet. Sir Josiah Child of the English East India Company got overly ambitious and dreamed of laying the foundation of English rule in India. He succeeded in obtaining from King James II of England the sanction for ten to twelve English warships to sail to India and seize Chitagong, but the expedition ended in disaster, and, in 1688, the English had to withdraw from the province of Bengal, not just from Chitagong. Sir John Child (no relation of Sir Josiah Child) who was heading the Company at Surat, acting under instructions from London, defied Emperor Aurangzeb with the result that the factory at Surat was ordered to be seized and the English to be expelled from the Empire. However, in 1690, the Company was allowed to return, and the English settled on the banks of the river Hooghly. It was this trading port which much later in time developed into the city of Calcutta. But these mindless, failed adventures had one long-term effect: The English eschewed politics and warlike policy in India for the next almost half a century.

---

[1]*Encyclopædia Britannica*, Vol. 2 (1973), pg. 765.

VIII

The Later Mughals

Aurangzeb, the last of the Great Mughals, died in 1707 after an eventful reign of forty-nine years; he was then 89 years of age. His successors generally lacked the energy, the determination, and the statesmanship of their predecessors. Some of them were given to a life of pleasure or were plain profligates, some involved themselves in the palace intrigues instead of providing leadership, and none seemed to possess a commanding personality. For the Mughal Empire, which was an absolute, hereditary monarchy like most others of its time, any of these could prove to be a tragic flaw, particularly in the highly complex political situation that then prevailed in India. The first sign of something not being quite right about the Delhi Empire showed itself when two of the emperors were murdered within six years of each other twelve years after Aurangzeb's death—Jahandar Shah was murdered by his minister Zulfiqar Khan in 1713 and Farrukhsiyar became a victim of court intrigue in 1719. It was in Emperor Farrukhsiyar's reign, however, that two representatives of the English East India Company went to Delhi in 1715, remained there for two years, and succeeded in obtaining valuable trade concessions from the Emperor, including exemptions from customs duties. In 1717, Farrukhsiyar also issued a royal edict granting to the Company possession of five villages around Madras.

With the growing weakness of the government at Delhi, the process of disintegration of the empire set in during Muhammad Shah's reign (1719-1748), with the provinces virtually becoming independent of the centre, one after the other, as if trying to confirm the validity of Thomas Hobbes' political philosophy. Asaf Jah Nizam-ul-Mulk, the Governor of the province of the

Deccan, "a nobleman of the Aurangzeb school of duty and integrity,"[1] when he became the Vizier or First Minister in 1722 tried to strengthen the Delhi government by bringing order, but his advice and services were rejected by Emperor Muhammad Shah, a weak character whose favorite tactic was to set one faction against the other. Seeing no possibility of reform Asaf Jah returned to the province of the Deccan as its Governor, became independent in 1724 and founded the dynasty of Nizam. Saaddat Khan in Oudh (present-day Uttar Pradesh) became independent in the same year and Ali Vardi Khan, the Governor of Bengal some years hence. Also, in Muhammad Shah's reign, the Rohillas, an Afghan clan, carved out an autonomous principality to the north of the Ganges which later came to be known as Rohilkhand. In the meantime, Marathas were emerging as a new force on the political scene of India, challenging the empire. In 1737 they suddenly appeared in the vicinity of Delhi but left without trying to occupy the city. Two years later, in 1739, Nadir Shah, the king of Iran, invaded India, met the imperial army at Karnal not very far from Panipat in a battle that did not last for more than two hours. He entered Delhi and stayed for about two months; when he left he carried with him the city's accumulated wealth of almost three centuries including Shah Jahan's world-renowned Peacock Throne and the Kohinoor diamond, and annexed territories to the west of Indus under a treaty signed by Muhammad Shah. In 1748 Muhammad Shah died and was succeeded by his son Ahmad Shah. Nadir Shah, the king of Iran, was assassinated in 1747 and Ahmad Shah Abdali, the Afghan chief who had become the ruler of the eastern part of his kingdom, invaded India and forced Ahmad Shah in 1748 to cede the territory of the Punjab. In 1754 Ahmad Shah was deposed. He was succeeded by Alamgir II who was murdered in 1759 and succeeded by his son Shan Alam II whose rule lasted till his death in 1806. It was in the reign Alamgir II, in 1757, when Ahmad Shah Abdali again invaded India and seized and sacked Delhi. In 1758 the Marathas occupied the Punjab which was an invitation to Abdali for

---

[1] *India: A Modern History*, by Percival Spear (Ann Arbor: The University of Michigan Press, 1972), pg. 175

invasion which was not late in coming. In 1759 he reentered India and took back the Punjab. Next year, in 1760, the Maratha Confederates comprising the Peshwa at Poona, Gaekwar at Baroda, Bhonsla at Nagpur, Sindia at Gawaliar and Holkar at Indore occupied Delhi, and in January 1761 was fought the Third Battle of Panipat between Abdali and the Confederates in which the latter were overwhelmingly defeated from which they could not recover for the next ten years. But Abdali did not seize the opportunity to occupy Delhi and claim the empire; he returned to Afghanistan.

IX

The Rise of the British

These developments were to the advantage of the British; serious challenges in their path to power were eliminating themselves. In fact while these momentous events were taking place in the west and the northwest of India, the British were making significant gains in the east, in Bengal and Bihar. Ali Vardi Khan had died in April, 1756, and was succeeded by his grandson Siraj-ud-Daula who was only twenty then, but a victim he became not of his inexperience because of his age but of the conspiracy in which the English played the central role, and the treachery of Mir Jafar, brother-in-law of Ali Vardi Khan and the commander of Siraj's forces who acted like an onlooker while the opposing British forces were firing artillery: this was the famous Battle of Plassey (1757) that gave the British the control of Bengal and Bihar, the two provinces that were not only commercially very profitable but also provided them the political foothold from where they extended their authority virtually to the whole of India in less than fifty years. Mir Jafar was rewarded for his services by Lord Clive with the throne of Murshidabad, and four days later Siraj-ud-Daula was executed.

In 1717 Emperor Farrukhsiyar, by an imperial edict, had granted the East India Company exemption from the customs duties, but the private trade of the Company's employees was subject to the usual internal tolls; after Plassey, Clive obtained from Mir Jafar exemption from tolls on the trade carried on by the Company's servants which could not but adversely affect the provincial treasury and ruin the Indian traders' business. In 1760 Clive left Calcutta and Mir Jafar was replaced by his son-in-law, Mir Qasim, as the governor of Bengal and Bihar, and Mir Qasim was no Mir Jafar: he was ambitious, determined and capable. He moved systematically: obtained formal approval of his appointment as governor from Emperor Shah Alam II, removed Clive's appointee from Patna that gave him direct access to Bihar's treasure and resources, started organizing a disciplined fighting force, and transferred his capital from Murshidabad in Bengal to Monghyr in Bihar to avoid British interference. But all this done, he was still short of much needed financial resources, so he tried to negotiate with the Company the payment of tolls by its employees on their private trade, and this not succeeding he abolished the duties altogether to provide a level playing field to both the English and Indian traders. This fair deal was in direct conflict with British commercialism; it clashed with their mercantilist interest and the issue was going to be decided not by negotiation but on the battlefield. At this time Emperor Shah Alam II was trying to recover Bengal with the help of the ruler of Oudh, Shuja-ud-Daula, whose support Mir Qasim obtained; the battle was fought at Buxar in October 1764, and the British were the winners. This outcome virtually sealed the fate of not only Mir Qasim and Shuja-ud-Daula but also of the Mughal Empire. Shah Alam II henceforth became a British ally, and, in 1765, granted them the divan (revenue collection) of Bengal, Bihar and Orissa.

In 1759 when Shah Alam II had succeeded to the throne of Delhi he was a fugitive in Bihar and for twelve years he remained a wandering emperor. On his return to Delhi in 1772 his chief minister, Mirza Najaf Khan, recaptured Agra, and held at bay the Sikhs in the Punjab, and Jats in the south of Delhi, and the Marathas in the west. Najaf Khan died in 1782 and the same year a devastating famine visited Delhi district in which thirty percent of the people are said to have died. In 1785 Shah Alam II made the Maratha chief, Mahadji Sindia of Gwaliar, the Regent of the empire. In 1787 Sindia was defeated in a battle at Lalsont in Rajputana, and, in 1788 Ghulam Qadir Rohilla, entered Delhi, seized the Imperial Palace, and in a fit of frustration and anger at not finding the expected amount of loot, blinded Shah Alam II. Later Sindia retook Delhi, defeated and executed Ghulam Qadir, and resumed the role of a Regent. In the Maratha war of 1803-1806, the British forces under Lord Lake took Agra and Delhi in 1803, and made Shah Alam II a pensioner. In 1806 he died, having endured much in one life. However, besides being an emperor, he had another vocation, too—of writing poetry—which might have sustained him in his darkest hours and given him a pride of a different nature. He took his poetry seriously; adopted the penname of Aftab ("Sun") in his Persian and Urdu poetry, and "Shah Alam" ("Ruler of the World") in Braj Bhasha. He is also said to have been familiar with Arabic, Sanskrit and Turkish languages, and was fond of reading and had an inquiring mind.

After 1803, the Mughal emperors were no more in the imperial game; the French with their trading post at Chandernagar, the Dutch at Chinsura and Negapatam, and the Danes at Tranquebar, too, were not any more major players. It was now between the British and the Marathas; and, finally, at the end of the Maratha wars in 1818, the British emerged as the victors and Lord Hastings went on to proclaim the British East India Company as the supreme political authority in India, which, for Indians, was going to be a totally new experience in more than one way. In the first place, it was a new phenomenon in historical time that the people of an European land had become the effective sovereign power in India. Alexander the Great of Macedonia, after defeating Poros in the battle of the Hydespas (Jhelum) advanced up to the Hyphasis (Beas) and from there went back. Interestingly, his Indian expedition of 326 B.C. to 323 B.C. hardly finds a mention in any Hindu writing of that time, which goes to suggest that it did not make much of an impact. The other strange aspect of significance was that the English came to India as traders and ended up as a colonial power. Earlier, the Arabs, the Turks, the Mughals and the Afghans, all of them belonged to Asia and they all made India their home, whether they came as adventurers, immigrants, or conquerors and empire-builders. As against this the English remained strangers and single-mindedly pursued their economic interests, although in the process they did things that were highly beneficial to the people of India (e.g., construction of railways, canals, etc.), but essentially and in most cases incidental to their overriding mercantilist considerations. However, on the side and in great earnest, they also pursued another concern of theirs—evangelizing the natives—and for this they had at hand the missionaries. Unlike the Jesuit Fathers who in 1595, as we have noted, waited on Emperor Akbar for the grant of right to make converts, the British missionaries under British dispensation were not only free but from 1813 onwards, emboldened to engage in proselytizing Indians, both Hindus and Muslims. Later, in 1818, was founded the Baptist Missionary Society and the British were joined by the Americans. In the words Professor Percival Spear, "The missionary with his black cloth and hat, his church and his band of converts became a familiar sight in many an up-country station."[1]

X

Ghalib and Urdu Culture

In 1818 Ghalib was twenty years old and had lived in Delhi, the political and cultural capital of India, for about four years when these momentous events of incalculable and far-reaching consequences were taking place, and, in a way of speaking, he was a witness to them. The political power that had been lost to the British could be regained at some future undetermined time but if culture and civilization were once destroyed they could not be reconstructed

---

[1] *The Oxford History of India*, by Vincent A. Smith, edited by Percival Spear, the entire Part III on "India in the British Period," written by him (Oxford: 1981), pg. 649.

and the very fabric of that entire culture had come under threat—the culture that was built so assiduously and with such loving care over the centuries and to which had contributed, as it would be evident from the foregoing historical account, the kings, emperors, saints, Sufis, savants, poets, literati, artists, architects and artisans in their own days and distinct ways, with people as participants, and which blossomed during the Mughal period and was in its glory in Ghalib's time notwithstanding the demise of Mughal political power. We may call it Indo-Persian or Indo-Muslim or simply Hindustani or Urdu culture which survives in all its essentials and vigour in Hindustan and Pakistan to this day, assimilating eclectically elements from various sources and enriching itself in progression through time, while the English political power is history now; and of this vibrant culture Urdu language and literature are the vehicle and the hallmark, the greatest and the most precious of all the gifts that the Mughals, the last of the dynasties of the Indian monarchs, gave to India, and Ghalib was heir to this whole culture, and the history of many centuries behind it, and it found expression in his verses, mediated by his poetic genius.

Ghalib started writing poetry in Urdu when he was only ten or eleven years old. It is conjectured from his creative construction of Persian expressions in his earliest Urdu poems that he might occasionally have been writing Persian poetry from the beginning. The first manuscript of his Urdu *Divan* which has come to be known as *Nuskha-e-Hamidiya* was completed in 1821 when Ghalib was in his twenty-fourth year of age. In 1969, the year of Ghalib's death centennial, was discovered and published *Beyaz-e-Ghalib ba Khatt-e-Ghalib* ("Ghalib's Notebook of Poetry in Ghalib's Hand"). Ghalib scholars differ on its date of completion: it could be any date between 1816 and 1819, and many poems are found in both of the collections, viz., *Nuskha-e-Hamidiya* and *Beyaz-e-Ghalib ba Khatt-e-Ghalib*. Apparently, after 1822, when he was past his twenty-fifth year, Ghalib mostly wrote Persian poetry and prose. However, the first edition of his Urdu *Divan* was published in October 1841 and the second with a few additions in 1847. We do not know if there were reprints of these editions. In 1845 had come out the first edition of his Persian *Divan*. In 1850 when contact with the Mughal court of Bahadur Shah II was established, he again started writing mostly in Urdu, and in 1861 was published the third edition of his Urdu *Divan*. How many reprints by how many publishers has his Urdu *Divan* gone through nobody knows, which situation continues to this day. Besides his Urdu and Persian *Divans*, Ghalib also authored about thirty books in prose. But the centerpieces are his Urdu and Persian *Divans*, and it is the Urdu *Divan* with which we are mainly concerned here.

XI

Ghalib the Poet, and the Ghazal

Although Ghalib wrote in different genres, it is the ghazal that is the preferred form in which blossomed Ghalib's genius. But the ghazal genre does not exist in English poetry, which fact calls for a few words of explication.

Ghazal is a genre of lyric poetry in Urdu as in Persian, Arabic, Turkish and some other languages. It is a poem consisting of at least five couplets, there being no consensus on the maximum length, but generally it does not exceed seventeen or eighteen couplets. And every couplet in a ghazal, while a part of it, is also an independent unit complete in meaning.[1] What makes the couplets the part of a particular ghazal is the pattern (*tarah* or *zamin*), the metre and the rhyming scheme consisting of the *qafiyah*, the rhyming syllable at the end of the second line of every couplet, and followed by the *radif* (refrain), if it has one— the identically repeated word or words at the end of the second line: the *qafiyah* is compulsory, the *radif* is not but extremely common. The distinctiveness of the couplet in a ghazal calls for the quality of *rabt* (connection) between its two lines—getting them intimately and mutually involved—achieved by the creative choice of words that enhance both the meaning and the delight of it: the greater

---

[1]This is why ghazals, unlike English poems and other genres of Urdu poetry, are not given titles or headings. They are, instead, given serial numbers, but *not* in the chronological order in which they were composed.

the *rabt* the more charged with meaning and energy is the couplet. "In the hands of a poet like Ghalib," says Frances W. Pritchett, "the verse can become packed, crammed, so charged that it leaps off the page. So much is going on in the same space at the same time that some of his *shi'rs* are like atomic particles—they seem to be held together by their own intense and perfectly balanced energies."[1] Some of the techniques to reinforce *rabt* between the two lines are to make a *dava* (claim or general statement) in the first line and *javab-e-dava* (response), *dalil* (supporting argument) or *tamsil* (example or illustration) in the second line. Another effective way, known as *husn-e-talil*, with an element of surprise in it is to state an effect in the first line and to attribute it to an unexpected cause in the second. Sometimes the thought expressed in the first line of the couplet runs into the second line, binding the two lines into one unit. However, in spite of the couplet being independent and self-contained, it inhabits the ghazal universe and it is in this context that it is read, understood, enjoyed and interpreted, adding to its significations. At the centre of the ghazal world is the lover, pining for his beloved, from whose perspective is viewed this whole world where he has to contend with the *raqib* (rival), with the sheikh and the zealot and other characters, besides facing the society at large. But he as well moves in and enjoys the company of friends and fellow drinkers, the *saqi* (cupbearer) filling and serving the cup of wine. Then is the ghazal landscape: the garden, the social gatherings, the tavern, the desert, the prison cell, the grave and beyond.

In ghazal poetry *istiarah* (metaphor) and *tashbih* (simile) play a central role in creating, enhancing and extending meaning. Other devices used to enrich and extend meaning include *kinaya* (implication), *talmih* (allusion), and the *inshaiyah* modes of expression such as exclamatory, interrogative, imperative, vocative and subjunctive which, not being informative, cannot be falsified.

But ghazal poetry doesn't speak via the mind only, it speaks straight to the heart as well, and as effectively. It possesses that indefinable quality called

---

[1] *Nets of Awareness*, by Frances W. Pritchett, first published by the University of California Press (Berkeley and Los Angeles, California: 1994), pg. 86.

beauty that charms and captivates both the mind and the heart, making the experience at once memorable and highly pleasurable. But the ghazal may also possess another quality, called *shorish*, which literally means commotion, confusion, tumult, disturbance, insurrection, etc., but when speaking in the context of ghazal poetry—*shor angez* being another term for it—it refers to a powerful expression of the lover's experience of life that is unsentimental yet charged with a powerful emotion. Ghazal poetry can have another indescribable quality, *kaifiyat*, the quality of evoking the mood of exquisite, delicious enjoyment in the reader or the hearer even if the meaning is not clear or does not register.

It is with these and other techniques and poetic resources, and the available supply of words that a ghazal poet works to create poetry, and Ghalib was a born poet. In his own words, "I had not the means to ride to war like my ancestors...I said to myself, 'Be a dervish and live a life of freedom.' But the love of poetry which I had brought with me from eternity assailed me and won my soul, saying, 'To polish the mirror and show in it the face of meaning—this, too, is a mighty work... Give up the thought of being a dervish and set your face in the path of poetry. Willy-nilly I did so...My pen became a banner.'"[1] So Ghalib took up this "mighty work," created powerful poetry, extended the possibilities of the ghazal genre, made it a true mirror of life and the universe in all their varied aspects and glories and vicissitudes, and thus fulfilled his destiny.

Ghalib's voice in Urdu poetry is unique, the like of which had not been heard before and has not been since. This may be because of the unusual times he lived in, his personality, his characteristic poetic sensibility, his insight into human psychology, his keen personal observations and his experiences, all of which found expression in his poetry, making it at once distinctive in content and inimitable in style and diction. Love is the predominant, but by no means the only, motif in ghazal poetry, and Mir Taqi Mir (1721-1810) is considered the greatest love poet in Urdu literature. But in Ghalib who is perhaps the greatest

---

[1] *Ghalib, Life and Letters*, by Ralph Russell and Khurshidul Islam (George Allen and Unwin: London, 1969), pg. 28.

Urdu poet, the theme of love finds expression at different levels, in diverse moods, and in varied colours, unlike Mir's or any other Urdu poet's. In Mir love is *the* grand passion, in Ghalib it is one of the powerful passions—the passion that demands of the lover courage, fortitude and sacrifice of every kind, including that of life itself, and at the minimum braving grief, pain and anguish. Ghalib finds in love the joy of living and the elixir for pain, as well as pain for which there is no remedy. This because a human being is possessed of a heart—the source or centre of feelings and emotions, the inmost thoughts, and conscience or consciousness. So there is no escape from grief and pain. If one had not fallen in love the worldly concerns and woes and sorrows would still afflict him. Addressing God Ghalib says if so much sorrow were fated for him, He should also have given him more than one heart: after all there is a limit up to which a heart can stand sorrows. He asks with a touch of dramatic irony, whose playful work it could be that everybody here in this world is complaining? The reasons for complaint can be diverse and many, depending on one's situation in the place and time in which he finds himself, and his sensitivity. In the context of love, however, the reason would be separation from the beloved.

Cognizant of the vicissitudes of life, Ghalib counsels his heart to take even pain and grief as prizes, for, at last there will neither be the morning cries nor the midnight sighs, that even the songs of sorrow be taken as blessings, for one day this, too, will fall silent. Life in this world being what it is—nasty, brutish and short?—the scope for joy, whether pure and simple or involving trials and tribulations, is very limited. So whatever life brings and the universe offers, it should be enjoyed to the last drop and every moment should be lived to the full. Ghalib, a great lover of beauty, delights in it in all its manifestations in nature, thought and emotion, and in form and colour, finding expression in his inimitable, poetic diction. There are hundreds of splendours here to see, says Ghalib, but only if one raises his eyes. He invites us to enjoy the glory of springtime of which the sun and the moon have become the spectators, and which, in beauty and adornment, has put to shame the sphere of the heavens.

Speaking of his beloved's beauty, Ghalib says seeing her is wine[1], desire the cupbearer, and drunk remain the eyes. And as for the assembly of thoughts, it is a tavern without tumult and noise.

Love, as we have already noted, is a predominant theme of ghazal poetry and Ghalib takes it to a different level when he says that a step on the path of love-madness[2] reveals the secrets of the book of the world, and it is a path that is the binding string of both the desolate worlds. The passion of love is the pride of the powerless: it endows a particle with the power of the desert and a drop of water with the ocean's. It becomes a driving force in life and with a new consciousness one is led to seek to understand the mysteries of the universe so he can determine his place in it. The universe or the world like a musical instrument is playing a whole range of music revealing the truth behind the mystery, which can only be appreciated by those who have made themselves familiar with it through close study and experience. Then comes a stage when this world seems like a child's play, a tamasha going on night and day, and Ghalib wishes that he had his abode beyond the empyrean so a viewing platform on a higher plane he could make. The search to understand the universe, the meaning and purpose of life and how man and God relate to each other continues.

The above are just broad indications of but a few aspects of Ghalib's poetry—the poetry which, in Ghalib's own imagery, is a mirror that shows the meaning of life and of the universe in their entire range as experienced by the poet, felt by his heart, and mediated by his mind. There is hardly a situation in the life of a man that matters on which Ghalib has not something very significant to say that is not only fresh and modern, but in fact is timeless and universally relevant. To these characteristics has contributed in no small measure Ghalib's deep insight, like Shakespeare's, into human psychology. And

---

[1]The term "wine" is used more often than not, as here, in a figurative sense rather than literally, signifying the source or object of pleasure and joy, or state of ecstasy, or an antidote to grief and pain.
[2]"Love-madness" signifies the passion of love at its most intense.

all of this is at once brightened up and made poignant by Ghalib's great sense of wit and humour.

XII

Ghalib as a Man

Ghalib, however, besides being a great poet was also "a remarkable man in many ways—remarkable for his personal appearance, for his frankness, for his friendliness, for his originality,"[1] for his individuality and his deep sense of honour and self-respect. But let us pick up the thread of the story of Ghalib's life from where we left. We have seen that on the death of Ghalib's uncle and guardian, Nasrullah Baig Khan, in 1806 (Ghalib's father had died in 1802), under an official letter issued by Lord Lake on May 4 of the same year and approved by the Governor-General in Council, Ghalib would have received a pension of rupees 208 and paisas 33 per month from Ahmad Bakhsh Khan who was excused the payment of the quitrent of rupees 10,000 to the British East India Company and which was to be applied by him towards the payment of pensions to the dependents of Nasrullah Baig Khan. Ahmad Bakhsh Khan, however, claimed that he had received another letter from Lord Lake, dated June 7, 1806, by which the total amount of pension was reduced from rupees 10,000 to rupees 5,000 per year out of which rupees 2,000 were to be paid to one, Khwaja Haji, commander of the contingent of fifty cavalry, who, as far as was known, was no relative of Nasrullah and definitely not one of his dependents. From the remaining rupees 3,000, Ghalib was to receive rupees 62 and paisas 50 per month and not rupees 208 and paisas 33 as he would have under the arrangement that was spelled out in the letter dated May 4, 1806.

---

[1]"Ghalib: A Self-Portrait," by Ralph Russell, in *Ghalib: The Poet and His Age*, edited by Ralph Russell, (Oxford University Press: Delhi, 1997), pg. 12.

There are two significant points about the letter of June 7 which are of particular note: first, it was only Ahmad Bakhsh Khan who knew about it and was in possession of it and it was he alone who benefited from it monetarily at the cost of Nasrullah Baig Khan's dependents; secondly, for reasons not stated but which can be guessed, the said letter was not approved by or sent for approval to the Governor-General in Council at Calcutta as required, rendering it, if it was genuine, a document of doubtful legality. However, the dependents of Nasrullah Baig Khan—the recipients of the pension—and Ahmad Bakhsh Khan being related to each other and the latter being an old grandee, they, perhaps out of courtesy, did not join issue. Ghalib, anyhow, was only nine then and too young for that.

The matters stood thus till 1824 the year Khwaja Haji, one of the beneficiaries of Lord Lake's letter of June 7, 1806, died, but, to add insult to injury, the payment of rupees 2,000 was continued to be made to his two sons notwithstanding the fact that the contingent of fifty horses was disbanded, which, too, under the official letter of May 4, 1806, should have been paid from the part of the quitrent of rupees 15,000 from the very beginning, and not from rupees 10,000 earmarked for the payment of pensions to the dependents of Nasrullah Baig Khan. Ghalib's first response was to go personally to Firozpur and meet Ahmad Bakhsh Khan, which he did, but what he received from him was a promise that he would give Ghalib a deed over his signature and seal providing for payment of rupees 2,000 per year after his own death. Ahmad Bakhsh Khan was very ill at that time. However, he did nothing at all even after he recovered from illness.

Ghalib decided to take up the matter with the British East India Company at Calcutta and set off on his journey via Kanpur, Lucknow, Banda, Allahabad, Patna, and other cities on the way. Ahmad Bakhsh Khan died in October, 1827, and the news reached Ghalib when he was travelling; he arrived in Calcutta after an arduous journey in February, 1828.

Ghalib's was a well-founded and well-argued case—factually incontrovertible and legally indisputable. But, as is evident from the way the decision was made by the British, the same was based on whims rather than facts, laws, rules, and accepted legal procedures—the whims born of the utilitarian and colonial attitudes, and from these considerations Ghalib's case was of little interest, if any, and was accordingly disposed of. Ghalib, for good reasons, having no doubt about his claim being just and rightful, fought for it for twenty years at every level of the British authority, starting from the Resident at Delhi to the Lieutenant Governor at Agra, the Governor-General in Council at Calcutta, the Court of Directors of the East India Company at London, and, finally, appealing to Queen Victoria. But, for the reasons stated above, it was foredoomed from the very beginning. Of all the officers and official bodies through which Ghalib's pension case passed, it was perhaps only George Swinton, Chief Secretary to the Government, who read his memorial and took it seriously, and wrote a highly favourable note. However, when in Calcutta, Ghalib pursued his purpose for which he had taken so much trouble in greatest earnest, called on Andrew Sterling, the then Chief Secretary, and Simon Fraser, Assistant Secretary, and the matter was finally taken up by the Governor-General in Council. Nevertheless, unfortunately for Ghalib, all of it turned out to be an exercise in futility.

But, culturally and socially, he found Calcutta quite enlivening and he enjoyed it. *Mushairah*—a gathering of lovers, connoisseurs, and makers of poetry, before whom poets read their verses, a feature of Urdu culture—was held regularly on the first Sunday of every month, to which Ghalib was naturally invited. Fort William College, which was recently established with the prime objective of teaching Urdu to the East India Company's new recruits arriving from England, had also got translated some English classics into Urdu which Ghalib might have seen during his stay in Calcutta. Printing presses had come there and several daily newspapers were being published, and Ghalib got into a lifelong habit of reading them regularly. On the whole, Ghalib came off with a very high opinion of the material progress the British had brought about in Calcutta, as well as their administrative system, but an equally poor impression of their system of justice which he expressed in a Persian poem in a dialogue form, the last couplet of which, in English translation, reads thus:

> I said, I came here to obtain justice. He said be off with you and
> do not strike your head against a stone.[1]

Ghalib left Calcutta without waiting for the decision of the Governor-General in Council, reaching Delhi in November, 1829. When he had left Delhi he was in debt; when he returned to Delhi, having incurred additional expenditure on the journey to and back from Calcutta and his stay there, if anything, it only went up. And the hope of increase in the pension remained only that—a hope—and Ghalib would not give up hope; he kept up the fight for justice. In January, 1831, the Governor-General in Council decided against Ghalib. The same year, in December, 1831, during the levee in Delhi which he attended as a prominent member of the nobility, Ghalib personally presented a fresh petition to Lord William Bentinck, the Governor-General, for reexamination of his case. In April, 1832, he reminded him through a letter. The Governor-General, in a typically bureaucratic manner, decided that the case should first be examined by the Lieutenant Governor in Agra. Ghalib corresponded with the latter and sent him a list of seven queries which, he said, needed to be answered to meet the requirement of justice. The Lieutenant Governor decided against him without touching any of those points; it was endorsed by the Governor-General in Council and communicated to Ghalib on October 17, 1836. Ghalib for whom honour and dignity came before anything else was not a supplicant for favour; he was seeking justice which was being denied to him for no good reason. So he challenged Lord Auckland, the then Governor-General, in no uncertain terms, to justify his decision on the basis of law and established procedures. In a letter he wrote to him he raised, inter alia, the following points: (1) Whether the Lieutenant Governor's replies to his

---

[1]"Ghalib and the British," by P. Hardy, in *Ghalib: The Poet and His Age*, edited by Ralph Russell (Oxford University Press: Delhi, 1997), pg. 61.

seven queries were obtained, and if so, they received his due consideration? (2) If the Lieutenant Governor's replies to his seven queries were obtained, a copy of the same should have been provided to him along with the grounds on which they were admitted by the Governor-General. And if the Lieutenant Governor was not asked to answer his queries he should have been told why not. (3) That the case should now be transferred with all the related papers to the High Court of Justice in Calcutta for investigation under regular procedure and that the case should be decided on the basis of its findings. (4) If it is not agreed to send the case to the High Court it should be forwarded with all the connected papers to be tried before the King in Council in London.[1] The British in Calcutta followed the easy course and referred it to the Court of Directors of the East India Company in London, which slept over it for six years in spite of the repeated reminders; at last it sent a one-sentence negative decision in February, 1842, without dealing with any of the issues Ghalib had raised. Ultimately, he appealed directly to Queen Victoria in London. In the culture Ghalib knew and represented it was not at all unusual to appeal directly to the sovereign, but to the British it was unknown and unthinkable. They did not know what to do with it and sent it to the Court of Directors which, as would have been expected, repeated itself by refusing it in 1844. With this the door to justice, in the pension case, closed on Ghalib forever.

In 1842 when the pension case was as good as lost and Ghalib wanted badly an additional source of regular income, there came up an opportunity. A post of professor in Persian was created by the newly reorganized Delhi College on the recommendation of James Thomson, the then Secretary to the Government of India who was in Delhi on an inspection of the College. Somebody suggested him three names for this post: Ghalib, Momin Khan Momin and Imam Bakhsh Sahbai. Thomson already knew Ghalib who was on visiting terms with him and it was, naturally, he whom he first asked to see him. Ghalib called upon him and, as usual, waited in his palanquin at the gate to be received

---

[1]*Ghalib: The Man, The Times*, by Pavan K. Varma (Penguin Books: New Delhi, 1989), pg. 23-24, quoted from Foreign Political Consultations, 5 December, 1836, National Archives of India. Mine is a summarized version of the quotation on pg. 23-24 of the book referred to above.

by Thomson. When Thomson's servant informed him of this, he came out of the house and told Ghalib that on formal occasions such as levees, etc., he would do that, but it was a different situation when he had come to enter a government job. Ghalib's response was prompt, plain and simple, that his idea of entering the government service was too enhance honour not to bring it down. He politely excused himself and then left. This episode in Ghalib's life, like some others, shows in sharp relief how he lived by his ideals of life. He turned down the prospective job of a professor in a government college that promised what he had been seeking in great earnest and the absence of which he had keenly felt for long—a secure and regular income—because it clashed with his ideals of life. Call it his mental attitude or philosophy of life, or whatever, he believed in and lived by it and for its sake he was ready to make any sacrifice. This found expression in his poetry, too—the beloved often symbolizing the high ideal of life, as Ralph Russell has made a point of in his several writings on Ghalib. For Ghalib, preserving honour and dignity was one of the ideals of life.

But fate played a cruel joke with him. Ghalib played chess and chauser (a game like backgammon), with small stakes at his home where his friends used to gather and there is even an interesting story about it. It was summer and the month of Ramadan when Muslims fast from sunrise to sunset that Mufti Sadruddin Azurda, a close friend of Ghalib, a poet and a scholar of Islamic laws, visited and saw him playing chauser whereupon he remarked that now he very much doubted what the Books said about Satan being confined in prison during the month of fasting. Pat came Ghalib's reply that the Books were absolutely right and the place Azurda was seeing was the very place where Satan was imprisoned. But what happened in 1847 was, for Ghalib, nothing less than a nightmare, centering, though, around playing chauser. The Police Inspector of Delhi, for some unknown reason, bore hostility towards Ghalib and, one day, he and his men entered his house in ladies' garb and arrested Ghalib and his friends, who as they often did, were playing chauser with stakes. Ghalib was charged with keeping a gambling establishment at his house, was tried by the

Magistrate who sentenced him to six months in prison and a fine of rupees 200. As Ghalib put it in a Persian letter to one of his friends, though the Magistrate was the judicial authority, superior to the Police Inspector, in his case he became the Inspector's subordinate and delivered the judgement he sought. The period of imprisonment, however, was later reduced to three months on the advice of Dr. Ross, the Civil Surgeon.

It can be well imagined how Ghalib's sensibilities, both as a poet and as a man, would have been cut to the quick by this terrible incident. But overwhelmed as he was by this unexpected happening, even stranger and more painful to him was the attitude of his friends and kinsmen, all of whom, except Mustafa Khan Shefta, deserted him at this critical hour. Once he had said, ironically, "Like me, I reasoned, would be the people of the world." Now, from his experience he knew the truth that even honourable people did not live by the high principles of conduct that society proclaimed and they themselves professed if they feared it might in some way hurt them. He also now learned that those who, like him, practiced those principles were going to suffer for that, and suffer severely. But despite these fresh revelations, he continued to live by those principles.

However, after all these buffetings of fate and circumstances things started looking up and, in 1850, Emperor Bahadur Shah, on the suggestion of Maulana Nasiruddin alias Mian Kale Sahib, the Emperor's religious mentor, and Ahsanullah Khan, his Minister and "Court Physician"—both of them Ghalib's friends—commissioned Ghalib to write the history of the house of Timur in Persian for which he was to be paid rupees 600 per year. Ahsanullah Khan was to provide the basic historical material. In the same year, 1850, Ghalib was also conferred the titles of *Najmud Daula* ("The Star of the Empire"), *Dabirul Mulk* ("The Poet of the State") and *Nizam Jang* ("Commander of War"). The first volume of the history covering the period from Amir Timur to Emperor Humayun was published in 1854 under the title *Mihr-e-Nimroze* ("The Midday Sun") by the Royal Press in the Red Fort. No further progress was made after this, though the project was not formally closed. In any case, Ghalib was not too happy about the assignment, for, as he put it—indirectly addressing the Emperor—he was the mirror of secrets and should be made to shine; he was the creator of poetry and should be cherished for this. However, in the same year, Sheikh Muhammad Ibrahim Zauq died at the age of sixty-five. He was one of the major poets of the nineteenth century and had been the mentor in poetry to Emperor Bahadur Shah since the time he was Prince Sirajuddin before coming to the throne. After Zauq's death, Ghalib succeeded him in that position. In the same year, the Emperor's son and heir apparent, Mirza Fakhruddin Ramz, became his pupil in poetry and paid him rupees 400 per annum. About the same time, Nawwab Wajid Ali Shah, the ruler of Oudh, granted him a stipend of rupees 500 per year. With these welcome additions to his income he was able to pay off all his debts and live a comparatively easy life.

As Percival Spear aptly put it, "Long after Delhi had ceased to be the Paris of power it continued as the Versailles of good manners."[1] And Bahadur Shah's court was at its heart and centre, the Emperor himself being the epitome of polish and refinement. Ghalib the poet and the man of elegant manners was known for his ready wit, and his quips became the conversation pieces of the city. He was quite free with the Emperor and in the course of discussions on poetry or some other serious matter he often made witty remarks or comments which must have regaled Bahadur Shah.

It was the end of Ramadan; Bahadur Shah asked Ghalib how many days of fast he had kept. Ghalib replied he failed to keep one, and thus left the Emperor guessing whether he had failed to keep only one or did not keep even one. On another occasion, Sheikh Nizamuddin Aulia (1239-1325), Sufi and saint, and Amir Khusrao (1253-1325), Persian poet, were being discussed in the court in the presence of Bahadur Shah when, Ghalib on the spur of the moment composed and recited a verse:

---

[1] "Ghalib's Delhi" by Percival Spear, in *Ghalib: The Poet and His Age*, Ralph Russell (ed.), (Oxford University Press: Delhi, 1997), pg. 49-50.

Two spiritual guides and two seekers of truth!
By God's grace Nizamuddin got Khusrao, and Sirajuddin, Ghalib.[1]

Indirectly and in a very subtle way he was suggesting that the Emperor should be grateful to God for His kindness that he had Ghalib.

Even in everyday life he consistently and without fail surprised and delighted people by his sparkling repartees. One day, somebody spoke vehemently against wine drinking in his presence and said that God never granted the prayers of a wine-drinker. Ghalib's cool response was that if a man had wine what else did he need to pray for? According to Altaf Hussein Hali (1836-1914), a poet, writer, scholar, literary critic and Ghalib's first and most authentic biographer who had known Ghalib personally—there never was a thing that Ghalib said which was not full of wit and highly enjoyable, and that if all his utterances were collected in a book it would make great reading.[2]

He was a man of great personal charm—warm-hearted, friendly and loving. Anybody who once met him wanted to see him again. His circle of friends was not limited to Delhi but extended to the whole of India and included people of every faith and creed—Hindus, Muslims and Christians—, many of the British senior officials being among them. His letters to his friends show how he shared with them their grief and happiness.

In a letter to one of his friends he regretted that he did not have the means to be the host to the whole world. However, if that was not possible, he wrote, he wished at least he should not see anybody hungry and naked in the city where he lived. It was not just a wish; he tried to do whatever he could within his limited income to help the poor, the disabled and the deprived.

We have seen that his financial fortunes took a turn for the better in 1850 when he was commissioned to write the history of the house of Timur's. That trend continued till 1854. However, two years later, in 1856, Mirza Fakhruddin Ramz died and the same year the British deposed Nawwab Wajid Ali Shah and

---

[1]Translation mine. (Sirajuddin was the first name of Emperor Bahadur Shah.)
[2]*Yiadgar-e-Ghalib* ("Remembering Ghalib"), by Altaf Hussein Hali (Nami Press: Kanpur, 1897), (photo-offset printing by Idara-e-Yiadgar-e-Ghalib: Karachi, 1997), pg. 68

annexed Oudh, and thus came to an end, forever, two sources of his income. But that was nothing, not of the least significance, compared to what was yet to come—the earthshaking event of the year that followed.

XIII

Revolt of 1857, and After

In 1857 the world around him, as he knew it, came crashing down. It all started when the native troops of the three regiments of the British army stationed at Meerut revolted against the British rule in India, shot all British officers in spite of over 2,000 Europeans troops being there, marched to Delhi, and seized the city on the morning of May 11, 1857. It soon became the peoples' movement, spreading through central and northern India. At that time, the British military comprised 200,000 Indians and 38,000 Europeans; roughly 13,000 of the latter were in the Punjab beyond the Sutlej River, and, except for Dinapur, near Patna, there were hardly any European troops between Delhi and Bengal. So when it started, which, to South Asian historians, was the first war of national independence, it must have seemed that it was going to succeed. But it did not because, besides other important factors, it lacked strategic planning, coordination and strong leadership. Bahadur Shah was a reluctant leader, and, at 82 years of age he could not provide the kind of leadership that was called for. The British collected their troops and transport at Ambala in the Punjab, made the assault upon Delhi, and retook the city on September 19, 1857, after fighting a desperate battle for six days in the city streets. With the recapture of Delhi by the British descended a great calamity on its people and a virtual reign of terror started compared to which it was a passing pain what they had suffered for four months when the Indian troops held the city. The way they treated Bahadur Shah Zafar, the poet-emperor, the dejure sovereign, was less than civilized. After a farce of a trial he was exiled for life to Rangoon in Burma. Twenty-one princes of the royal family were sentenced and hanged in one day; some more of them were just shot in cold blood and their dead bodies were displayed in loincloth in Chandni Chauk, the main square of the city, near Ballimaran Street where Ghalib lived. An ad hoc commission with summary powers sent 372 residents of Delhi to the gallows. The number of people killed irregularly by the officers on the prowl, or just for sport was far greater. The whole lot of people, most of whom were Muslims, were driven out of the city and left to face the approaching cold weather without any proper shelter. Ghalib, in 1858, in a letter to Alauddin Ahmad Khan Alai, wrote a poem, the first, third and fourth couplets of which are:

A potentate doing what he wills
Every armed English soldier is.

The Chandni Chauk is an execution ground
And homes feel like prison-cells.

Every particle of Delhi's dust
Thirsting for Muslims' blood is.[1]

Physical destruction followed human misery, grief and death; as Muslims' lives were devalued so were desecrated their mosques. The palaces and buildings inside the Red Fort were almost totally demolished; the space so created was used for English soldiers' barracks; and the famous *Diwan-e-Khas* ("Hall of Private Audience") was converted into an officers' mess. In the Jama Masjid, although not razed to the ground as many among the British had demanded, were quartered Sikh troops and it was not vacated until 1862. The Zinat-ul Masjid was turned into a bakery, which it remained until Lord

---

[1] *Khutut-e-Ghalib* ("Ghalib's Letters"), compiled by Ghulam Rasul Mihr (Sheikh Ghulam Ali and Sons: Lahore, 1993), pg. 48-49. Translation mine.

Curzon's time (Viceroy of India, 1899-1905). The Sunahri Masjid, outside the Red Fort's Delhi's Gate, was not restored until 1913. The Fatahpuri Masjid which was sold to Lala Chunna Mal remained his private property until 1877. The gold plates on the Moti Masjid's domes were removed and sold. The entire built-up area from the Red Fort to the Jama Masjid was demolished to give the Fort a field of fire.

Ghalib remained in Delhi, confined in his home, when this cataclysm was happening. To him it was as much a political, social and cultural tragedy as it was the cause of personal loss, suffering and sorrow. His younger brother, Mirza Yousuf, who had been suffering from mental illness since long and had been living a harmless life in a kind of state of oblivion was shot dead by a British soldier on October 19, 1857. One of his closest friends—perhaps *the* closest—Fazl-e-Haq, a great scholar, was sentenced to transportation for life to the Andamen Islands where he died. A very close and longtime friend, Nawwab Mustafa Khan Shefta (1806-1869), an Urdu and Persian poet of great merit who used to consult Ghalib on poetry, was sentenced to seven years in prison. Countless other friends were either executed or fled the city to escape British excesses. He himself was not obliged to leave Delhi because the houses on the street he lived in were owned by the courtiers of the Maharaja of Patiala, the British loyalist, who had his special guards posted there to protect the vicinity, and had obtained from the British the guarantee that it would not be the target of its troops. Some of the themes in Ghalib's letters of the time were: But where is the Royal Court of Emperor Bahadur Shah? Where the *mushairas*? Where the daily gathering of friends? Where the engaging conversations? Where those serious discussions on poetry and fine points of philosophy? Where the games of chess and chausar? All was gone. Delhi was now a military camp lying prostrate from the impact of doomsday-like catastrophe.

Confined in his house, he began writing history as it was happening, in ancient Persian under the title of *Dastanbu*.[1] A primary purpose was also to

---

[1]A rare word that perhaps means a flower with a stock which is held in the hand for its fragrance. The great Persian panegyrist Afzaluddin Khaqani (1126-1198) used this word in an ode to Princess Ismatuddin.

justify himself to the British. He had remained closely associated with Emperor Bahadur Shah since 1850 and had been attending the Royal Court since then almost daily. He was therefore a suspect in the eyes of the British and high on their list. On October 5, 1857 some British soldiers entered Ghalib's house and took him to a Colonel Burn for questioning. The colonel asked him, among other things, whether he was a Muslim. Ghalib told him he was a half-Muslim. The colonel was surprised and asked what did he mean? Ghalib's reply was: "I drink wine but do not eat pork." The colonel was obviously amused and after a few more questions told him he could go.

But life had to be lived, these tragedies and pains and shocks and sufferings notwithstanding. And living needed means, and means had disappeared. The stipend from the Emperor and the pension from the British had stopped in May 1857. As the Revolt broke out, Umrao Begum, Ghalib's wife, sent all her jewelleries and valuables to the house of Maulana Nasiruddin, alias Mian Kale Sahib, the Emperor's spiritual guide, a friend of Ghalib, and revered of the city, for safe keeping. They were put in a cellar and duly secured. But when the British recaptured Delhi, their soldiers ransacked Kale Sahib's house, taking away all the valuables as booties. Thus was gone the option of raising some money by selling the jewelleries to feed the family of four[1] plus the servants—to look after the latter in those hard times instead of dispensing with them Ghalib considered his duty—a sign of his unfailing sense of obligation towards those less fortunate than he. So he sold his clothes to buy food, or, as he put it sarcastically, while others ate bread, he ate clothes, and if that continued he would die naked and hungry.

He had, however, also kept up his fight for the resumption of his pension by sending panegyrics, celebratory verse, letters and representations to the Commissioner and the Chief Commissioner at Delhi, the Governor-General at Calcutta and Queen Victoria in London. His efforts finally bore fruit: in May

---

[1]I.e., Ghalib, his wife, and two adopted sons, Baqar Ali Khan and Hussein Ali Khan, sons of Zainul Abedin Khan Arif, the nephew of Ghalib's wife, whom Ghalib had earlier adopted as his son and who had died in 1852 at the young age of thirty-five. Ghalib's own seven sons had all died in their infancies.

1860, the pension was restored with retrospective effect and the arrears were paid in full from the date it was stopped. Sometime earlier, the ruler of Rampur, Nawwab Yousuf Ali Khan, his pupil in poetry, had granted rupees one hundred as stipend to be paid from the Rampur treasury every month. In fact, in response to the Nawwab's repeated invitations, he had visited Rampur in January 1860, and had stayed there for about two months. These developments brought him some financial relief. Later, in February of 1863 his rightful place in the Governor-General's durbar was restored as well as the robe of honour. Thus his official position with the British was back to normal. But Delhi had yet to recover.

It is remarkable that despite everything, despite the pain and grief and anguish and anxiety he suffered, he could yet retain his wit and sense of humour and remain deeply engaged in literary and intellectual pursuits. After the completion of *Dastanbu*, he began writing a critical commentary on *Burhan-e-Qate*, a Persian dictionary by Maulvi Muhammad Hussein Tabrizi of the Deccan which was published under the title of *Qate-e-Burhan* in 1859 and raised a literary storm. In 1865 it was followed by an enlarged edition with a new title of *Dirafsh-e-Kaviani*. The collection of his works which his friends had kept in two distinguished private libraries was recklessly destroyed by British troops after they retook Delhi. Ghalib himself never kept copies of his own works. His Urdu poetry was last published in 1847 and a copy of verse written between then and 1857 was now available only with Nawwab Yousuf Ali Khan of Rampur. When Ghalib paid a visit to the Nawwab in 1860, he brought a copy of it with him, and in 1861 it was published. Around 1848 Ghalib began writing letters in Urdu; earlier he used to correspond in Persian. His letters are of inimitable style and beauty and abiding charm beyond compare. The friends and pupils and scholars and litterateurs to whom he wrote would preserve them. Two volumes of his letters were compiled, one of which was published in October 1865, under the title of *Ood-e-Hindi*; the second volume, *Urdu-e-Mualla*, was under print when Ghalib died.

The year 1858 marked the end of the rule of East India Company. By Queen Victoria's proclamation of November 1, the power was transferred to the Crown. Delhi lost its semiautonomous position and became a part of the Punjab. In the words of Percival Spear, "Delhi was a depressed provincial city still numb with communal shock. Only the merchants and those linked with the British prospered."[1] And the English in their zeal to transform the Delhi of Mughal Emperor Shah Jahan into the city of Queen Victoria, built a Town Hall, erected a Clock Tower, constructed Queen's Road and Hamilton Road, a railway station, and a post and telegraph office, and extensively demolished the existing buildings and houses, giving the city the look of a desert, as Ghalib wrote in one of his letters. In their ardour they forgot or ignored the city's infrastructure with serious consequences for its inhabitants. The neglect of wells, for example, led to contamination of potable water, causing infectious diseases like undiagnosed fever, sores and cholera—the last named had hitherto been unknown in Delhi. As if these were not enough calamities famine visited the city taking a heavy toll of lives. There can be no better and clearer picture in a snapshot of the period from 1857 to 1860 than the following description by Ghalib, "Five invading armies have fallen upon this city one after another: the first was that of the rebel soldiers, which robbed the city of its good name. The second was that of the British, when life and property and honour and dwellings and those who dwelt in them and heaven and earth and all the visible signs of existence were stripped from it. The third was that of famine, when thousands of people died of hunger. The fourth was that of cholera, in which many whose bellies were full lost their lives. The fifth was the fever, which took general plunder of men's strength and powers of resistance. There were not many deaths, but a man who has had fever feels that all the strength has been drained from his limbs. And this invading army has not yet left the city."[2]

---

[1]"Ghalib's Delhi" by Percival Spear, in *Ghalib: The Poet and His Age*, Ralph Russell (ed.), (Oxford University Press: Delhi, 1997), pg. 53.
[2]*Ghalib, Life and Letters*, by Ralph Russell and Khurshidul Islam (George Allen and Unwin: London, 1969), pg. 243.

Ghalib's own health had not been in a good shape for some time. He had suffered from chronic constipation for long, but, in 1862 and 1863, he was plagued by sores, the disease that was raging through Delhi at that time as noted above. The sores affected both his hands and right leg. When these got better, he suffered from a very painful swelling in his foot; it took about a year to be cured of the infection. He had as a consequence grown very weak, making bodily movements very slow and difficult. As he put one aspect of it, as if a scene in a slow-motion picture, it took him as much time to stand up as it would to raise a wall up to a man's height. And the recovery was rather slow.

In mid-October 1865 Nawwab Yousuf Ali Khan, the ruler of Rampur, died and was succeeded by his eldest son, Kalb Ali Khan. Ghalib went to Rampur to offer his condolences to the new Nawwab and the bereaved family and stayed there for about two and a half months. On his journey back to Delhi at the end of December, he met with a serious accident. He was travelling in a palanquin and his baggage and bedding were on a bullock cart. He had to cross a bridge on the Ramaganga River which was in flood, and just as he crossed it, the bridge was swept away by a powerful current. He had a lucky escape. But his bedding was in the cart and the cart remained stranded on the other side of the river, and it was an extremely cold winter night, made worse by strong wind and rain. He somehow located a caravanserai where he passed the night in great discomfort. In the morning when the sub-judge of the place who knew Ghalib learned of it, he brought him to his residence, arranged medical aid and looked after him for five days. When Ghalib felt he could travel he left for Delhi. The whole incident, however, particularly the long exposure to the bitter cold when he was not in the best of health and resistance was at its very low because of his earlier extended illnesses, had a very adverse effect on his health from which he never recovered fully, although he improved temporarily after his return to Delhi. He had been experiencing gradual loss of hearing for some time and in the last years of his life he had lost it almost completely, and, from general weakness, also became all but bedridden.

But his intellect never lost its keenness and vigour, not even when he was almost bedridden, nor his wit ever deserted him. He continued to receive poetry written by friends and peoples from the four corners of Hindustan for correction which he would do and return them with the utmost promptness even when bedridden, or would be reading some books. Khawja Azizuddin Aziz of Lucknow visited him in those days and found him lying in his bed with a book on his chest which he was reading. A few days before he died a new symptom developed: he would become unconscious and remain in that condition for hours. It was perhaps a day before he died, writes Altaf Hussein Hali in his *Yiadgar-e-Ghalib*, that he went to see Ghalib. He had come to after being unconscious for many hours, and was dictating a reply to a letter from Nawwab Alauddin Ahmad Khan Alai who had written from Loharu and had asked how he was. Ghalib's reply was, "Why ask me how I am? After a day or two inquire from my neighbours." On February 15, 1869, he breathed his last. The same day, at about noontime, he was laid to rest, close to his father-in-law's grave, in the latter's family graveyard, in Sultanji near Nizamuddin Auliya's mausoleum. Almost all of the eminent people in the city including Nawwab Mustafa Khan Shefta, Hakim Ahsanullah Khan and Nawwab Ziauddin Ahmad Khan Nayyar, besides a large number of Delhi residents, attended his funeral.

Ghalib is dead but Urdu culture survives in spite of everything, marching ahead, unstoppably, in time and space, meeting all kinds of challenges, and absorbing selectively the best in the milieu on the way. And because Urdu culture abides, Ghalib, the writer of immortal Urdu verse, cannot die.

XIV

The Curtain Rises on Ghalib's Divan

Creative literature of any language, besides being other things, is a mirror of its culture in which one can see its characteristic features, its thoughts and feelings, its hopes and dreams and fears, its present and its past, and the sources of its inspiration; and all of these differ from age to age, and, more importantly, from culture to culture, and hence the difficulty of understanding and enjoying the poetry of another language in translation. Keeping this in mind and setting as his aim to make the English version of Ghalib's Urdu poetry speak to the English readers more or less the way it speaks to Urdu speakers, the translator has done a few things in the Introduction above. He has provided an outline history of India (present-day Bangladesh, Bharat aka Republic of India, and Pakistan) from ancient times to Ghalib's day, which gives the reader a view of the complex interactions of various factors and forces that prepared the ground, sowed the seed, and nourished the development of an enduring Urdu language and culture. He has also introduced the readers to the ghazal universe and some of its distinctive features. Coming to the translation part, effort has been directed to make it literal, as far as possible, and at the same time to retain in English the flavour of the original; and commentaries have been provided when needed. And now, with these observations the translator makes his exit and invites the readers to experience and enjoy Ghalib's poetry.

GHAZALS

Divan of Ghalib

[1]

Of whose mischievousness of drawing is the picture complaining?
Every figure in the picture, without exception, is dressed in paper!

What is it to endure the agony of a lonely life, don't ask me;
Passing the nights is digging the mountain to bring the river of milk.

My irrepressible passion of love is a thing to be seen:
From its breast to its edge the scimitar's breath has come.

Let awareness spread its net howsoever it may:
The meaning is the anqa nestled in my world of expression.

Under my feet is fire, Ghalib, though in the prison;
Like hairs touched with flame are the links of my chain.

Commentary:

Couplet 1: The "picture" is of human beings all of whom are complaining. The poet, however, does not say explicitly what is it that they are complaining of, which is typically Ghalibian. He leaves it to the reader, whose sensitivity, situation in life and society, his experience of the world as well as how he relates to God or how he thinks God relates to him and the world, will determine how he handles this question. Nonetheless, the poet's choice of words does provide some unmistakable clues. Thus the word "picture" suggests the insubstantiality of human existence, and the term "dressed in paper," being an allusion to an ancient Persian (Iranian) custom of the plaintiff appearing before the king in the mantle of paper seeking justice (something similar to the ancient Roman custom of *candidatus*, the seekers of office or justice appearing in white gowns), leads the reader to think of the injustices of his own society and of the world. We can thus say that the tenuousness of our life and the injustices in our societies and world are the sources of our grief and hence the causes of our complaints. The other key term is "whose" (in Urdu *kiski*) instead of "His" (in Urdu, *uski*, which scans as does *kiski*). Had Ghalib used the word *uski* it would have more or less definitely referred to God as the Maker of the "picture" to Whom it was complaining because it was grieved and unhappy. By using the term "whose" Ghalib is leaving the question open whether it is God who is the cause of man's grief and pain in this world, or whether the fault, wholly or partly, lies in human beings themselves. What is certain is grief, and Ghalib is leading and urging the reader to look for its real cause, to look for it in ourselves and in society. If we could find the cause we might find the remedy: the search and inquiry have anyway to continue, which may be a never-ending process, suggested by the interrogatory form of the first line of the couplet. However, reading it as a verse about love—the predominant theme of ghazal poetry—the cause of pain and suffering would be the separation from the beloved, whether earthly or divine. Or one can have a passion for a high ideal in life which if not attained can bring great pain and sorrow. So even if read as a verse about love or lofty ideal at a deeper level it remains a human record of the condition of life here on this earth, and Ghalib seems to suggest indirectly to seek a human resolution of a human predicament.

Couplet 2: The reference is to the famed Persian lover Farhad, who, as the tradition goes, in order to win his beloved Shireen, had to dig through a huge mountain to bring a "river of milk" to her palace. These two personages, Farhad and Shireen, are very often alluded to in Urdu and Persian poetry. [The "mountain" here is also a metaphor for endurance, "digging the mountain" for hard work and suffering, and "the river of milk" for the morning following the night of separation from the beloved (lonely life)].

Couplet 3: The lover is so possessed by his powerful passion that he is ready even to sacrifice his life for the love of his beloved, and remains undaunted when the sword is raised to strike him down. There is a play on the words "scimitar" and "breath": the scimitar is also a metaphor for the beloved of overpowering, even fatal, beauty, and the Urdu word *dam*, means both the breath as well as the sharp edge of the scimitar—the scimitar is breathing death and is ready to strike. The wit of this couplet also lies in Ghalib's poetic interpretation of the curved edge of the scimitar as being the effect produced by the passion of his love.

Couplet 4: The "anqa" is an imaginary bird (the phoenix of the Egyptian mythology, the beautiful bird symbolizing immortality) and, by amplification, it means something that is rare, scarce, hard to get or find, something unusual and wonderful. Ghalib seems to say that to discover the rare and unusually wonderful thoughts and ideas in his poetry one has to delve deep into it and remain mentally alert lest the "anqa" of meaning escapes the net of awareness. He also seems to suggest that such "anqas" can only be found in his poetry.

Couplet 5: The "prison" is a metaphor for this world. "Fire under feet" (in Urdu *atish-e-zer-e-pa*) has been used in its idiomatic sense of being restless in the first line of the couplet while its literal meaning has been exploited in the second line—a literary technique often used by Ghalib. The "chain" stands for the constraints of all kinds man has to face in this world in his journey of love. "Hairs touched with flame" suggests that the man truly in love makes nothing of the "chain."

[2]

The battlefield of love nobody else entered but Qais:
The desert, it seems, narrow like a jealous eye was.

The distress of love corrected the colouring of the heart's black spot:
Evident it became that smoke of sighs the resource of the spot was.

3

In my dream, the imagination with you was making deals;
When I woke up, neither a loss nor gain there was.

I still take lesson in the school of grief over the lost heart
Which is this: "What is gone is gone and what was, was."

The shroud covered the nakedness of my moral blemishes,
Otherwise, in every guise, a disgrace for existence I was.

The mountain-digger didn't die but by an axe, Asad:
From the intoxication of custom and tradition befuddled he was!

Commentary:

An ironic look at love, its conventions, and its challenges and predicaments. Overarchingly, the ghazal compares Qais (the celebrated Arab lover also known as Majnoon (one madly in love); he was born in the Aamir tribe in Najd; his beloved is known as Laila, and he is reputed to have spent his entire life wandering in the desert, looking for Laila in case she happened to cross it, and thus to catch a glimpse of her) favourably to the more convention-bound Farhad, who, the poet says in the last couplet, killed himself, but from the sense of the conventions of love (he ended his own life with an axe upon hearing the false report that Shireen, his beloved, was dead). He was not like Qais, who never gave up and, the poet implies, may have been the only person to be so in love that the desert in which he wandered, in spite of its vastness, proved narrow like the eyes of a jealous person inasmuch no one else than Qais could get admittance there. This may be looked at as a Ghalibian tribute to love, as it often is, with Qais as the symbol of the life of love, or it may be looked at ironically, as expressing that no one except this famed lover has ever been so madly in love. This first couplet, incidentally, plays off a similar image regarding Qais in Rumi's *Mathnawi*.

The second couplet, in many ways a bit complex and the central one in this ghazal, can be interpreted to mean that the distress of love expressing in laments and sighs has corrected (deepened) the mark of love in the heart (the black spot of the heart). It can as well be read to mean that the distress of true love has corrected (erased) the more conventional anguish of love, and it has thus become evident that the sigh (the outward and conventional expression of the lover's misery) was nothing more than smoke and the dark spot caused by it was not a permanent thing. Ghalib here seems to be making fun of love, as Rosalind does in *As You Like It*, as being in most people a matter of convention.

Asad, in the last couplet, is the penname Ghalib first adopted at the beginning of his poetic career. Later he used Ghalib as his pseudonym. Asad means "lion" and Ghalib, "victorious," "overpowering," "surpassing." It is a convention of Urdu and Persian ghazals to end them with the poet commenting on himself or addressing himself. It may also be noted that the ghazals in a collection, a divan, are arranged not chronologically, but alphabetically according to the last letter of the second line of the couplets in a ghazal.

[3]

You say you wouldn't give it back if my heart lying somewhere you found;
When was my heart with me that I would lose! My desire fulfilled I found.

In love the joy of living I found;
Discovered the elixir for pain, the pain without remedy I found.

5

The friend of my enemy[1] is it; how can I trust my heart?
The sighs inefficacious, the laments ineffective I found.

Naïvete and artfulness, insensibility and alertness!
The beauty's feigned heedlessness, challenging I found.

The buds are again blossoming and today I see my bloodied heart;
What I had lost now I have found!

The condition of my heart I don't know save this,
That I often looked for it and you always found.

The noise of the moralizer's admonition on my wounds sprinkled salt;
Someone should ask him what pleasure in it he found?

Commentary:

Further meditations on love. The wit is what has to be noted here, as Ghalib works with old conventions of the eternally cruel beloved, full of guiles, whom the poet persists in loving in spite of everything. The first couplet is in a rather playful mode: the beloved, while suggesting, that the lover's heart is of little or no worth, almost showing her disdain for it ("lying somewhere"), still wants to possess it ("won't give it back"): in fact, she already possesses it, thus fulfilling the lover's desire, but she does not want him to have the pleasure of knowing it and tries to keep him guessing. The lover anyway sees through her game. The second line of the second couplet is perhaps where the sharp wit is most poignant: in love the poet has found the elixir for life's pains, but in it he has also found the pain that has no remedy. He wittily berates his heart in the

---

[1]"Enemy" is here used ironically, and means the beloved.

third couplet, and the fourth is a subtly delicate evocation of the guiles of the beloved which though present a challenge yet at the same time both bewitch and bewilder the lover. In the fifth couplet, the poet creates an imagery satirical of the way the beloved treats the lover's heart. The sixth couplet is about the lover's constancy and the lurking hope, the latter suggested by the beloved continuing to possess his heart, signifying her liking. Or is the lover being just too optimistic in spite of the hurt (as expressed in the immediately preceding couplet)? The "moralizer" is a staid traditionalist opposed to love and the joy of life here and now, the exact contrast to the lover, appears in the seventh and last couplet. The sarcasm in the second line of the couplet is obvious.

[4]

My heart from hidden passion without ceremonies burnt up;
Like smouldering fire, so to speak, it burnt up.

In my heart even the joy of union and the beloved's memory are no more;
Such fire took hold of this house that whatever was, burnt up.

Much beyond non-existence am I; otherwise, O heedless one,
By my fire-raining sighs the wings of anqa often burnt up.

Where to express the true substance of my thought's fervour!
Just some notion of wildness had come that the desert burnt up.

Heart is no more, otherwise its blooming wounds I would have shown;
What to do of this illumination when the ruler burnt up?

Here am I expecting only sadness, Ghalib;
Seeing the sham ardour of people, my heart burnt up.

7

Commentary:

This ghazal is centered around the imagery of fire representing the intensity of the fervour of life, love, and thought. The human heart in Urdu and Persian, as in English, is considered as the seat or source of love and passion as well as of inmost thought and consciousness. Each couplet of this ghazal represents a different aspect of the working of this fire. The terms "house" (second couplet) and "ruler" (fifth couplet) are metaphors for the heart. In Ghalib, as pointed out earlier in the note to the first ghazal, the "beloved" who inflames the heart can be an earthly beloved, God as the Beloved or a high ideal in life—all of them or one or two of them, depending on the context of each verse.

The first couplet is about the silent sufferings of a life of love. The second couplet can be interpreted to mean either (1) complete hopelessness because of the beloved's indifference or (2) purified and illumined love, free from any consideration of success or failure in achieving union with the beloved and the consequent pleasure: everything is burnt out, only love remains. In the third couplet, the poet suggests that he has reached such a highly removed mystical state ("much beyond non-existence") that had it not been for this fact his sighs would have burned up the wings of anqa: a delicately imaged state of mind hovering between such authentic mystical experience and his very real "fire-raining sighs" caused by the thought of the heedless beloved. "Non-existence" (Urdu/Arabic *adam*) may be read in a mystical sense suggesting non-existence in some sense and existence is some other, for example, existing as spirit or essence but not as form or body. "Much beyond non-existence" may then be taken to suggest the empyrean (Urdu/Arabic *Arsh*), the Throne of God, thus implying nearness to God. If, however, the "heedless one" is taken to refer to the poet himself ("I" in the same line), instead of the beloved, the couplet would mean that it is his own neglect of his inherent ability that he has been ineffective in achieving his purpose which has so completely devastated him that he is, as if, in a state "much beyond non-existence." (But irrespective of the one or the other interpretation of the state of "much beyond non-existence," the reference to the burning of the wings of the anqa before reaching this state seems to recall with pride the working of the all-consuming passion of love.) In the fourth couplet, "the desert burnt up" suggests that its vastness notwithstanding, it could not contain the fervour of the poet's idea of wildness. The Urdu word *jauhar* (rendered as "true substance") in the original also means "atom" of modern physics, hence its appropriateness in the context of this verse, although in Ghalib's time the power of the atom as discovered by modern physics was not yet known.

(It may be noted that "house" and "ruler" in the second line of the two couplets, viz., second and fifth, respectively, refer to "heart" in the first line of both the couplets.)

[5]

Love in every situation the enemy of necessaries is;
Qais, even on the picture canvas, is naked turned out.

The wound didn't do justice to the constriction of heart, O God:
The arrow itself that entered the heart feather-scattered came out!

The flower's fragrance, the heart's sighs, the smoke of the lamp,
Any that came out from your party, perturbed came out.

My grief-stricken heart is a table set with the delicacies of pain;
My friends partake of it, each according to his ability and his taste.

My difficulty-cherishing ambition the lesson in death had newly learnt;
The hard part is that this task, too, easy turned out.

In my heart, the urge to cry again raised a tumult, Ghalib;
Ah! What had not felt like a drop even, a torrent turned out.

Commentary:

Ghalib is describing the working of love at the deeper level of life. In the first couplet, he says that love is destructive of the necessaries of life and, as a proof, he cites the example of Qais, who even in a picture (where ideal accoutrements and staged appearance would be expected) is shown naked. In the second couplet he talks of the constriction of the heart caused by unrequited love, which is not relieved by the incision made by an arrow. It is Ghalib's way of describing some feelings by creating an imagery of something physical. Scattering of feathers has double signification in the original Urdu: first, it brings an image of the extent of the heart's constriction, which causes the scattering of the feathers stuck at the end of the arrow so it goes straight to the target without swerving, and, secondly, that the arrow itself, because of the constriction, shed its feather and came out perturbed instead of doing "justice" by removing the tightness (the arrow, figuratively the arrow of love, has failed to work which could be because it was wanting in dedication or was not passionate and powerful enough, or because the world's woes, the cause of constriction, were excessive or both).

In the third couplet Ghalib chooses the fragrance of a flower, the heart's sighs, and the smoke of a lamp as some of the representative concomitants of the beloved's assembly, all marked by motion, symbolizing emotional disturbance and perturbation of the lover when leaving her party, so painful is the parting from her seductive company. We can also read into it that such is the magic of her personality that even the fragrance of the flower, etc., in attendance at her party are affected by it.

In the fourth couplet the poet is making the point that his grieved heart has a story to tell, which he tells in his poetry ("a table set with the delicacies of pain"), and which can be understood by anyone who has taste and ability, the corollary being that those who don't, lack one or both.

In the fifth couplet the poet says that at the very beginning of his love-career, so to speak, he realized that as an ultimate price of love he might have to pay with his life. This was welcome, and any hardship on the way was grateful. It is a measure of his courage and ambition that even death proved easy for him. But the wit of the verse lies in the vision of the poet-lover being at once dead and alive and the complete composure of voice in which he speaks of his experience. His comment that he found death easy is also a reflection of the depth of the passion for which he died. There is even a sense of triumph in death. But, coming back to this world there are tears and lamentations, the imagery of the sixth and the last couplet.

[6]

Threat killed him who battle-class was not;
Love's battle-business for a man of valour sought.

All my life, by the fear of death I was haunted;
Even before I took wing my colour had faded.

Compiling the recipes of fidelity I was
When my sum of thoughts still scattered was.

From my heart to liver, which is a bank of the river of blood now,
On this pathway, aforetime the splendour of flowers a mere trifle was.

Do they ever go away, the jostlings of the grief of love?
When the heart was lost, that itself became the pain of heart.

My friends the remedy for my wildness could not find:
Confined in prison, my thoughts across the desert wandered.

This dead body without shroud is of the heartbroken Asad;
May God forgive his sins! What an independent man he was!

Commentary:

In this ghazal Ghalib speaks of the qualities that love demands of a man and the challenges he has to face. This theme is developed in a dramatic manner in each verse.

In the first couplet he sets down the maxim that love is a life-long battle against odds which calls for courage and fortitude. One who does not have these will die at the first thought of the hardships through which the lover has to go. In the second couplet he identifies the first and greatest impediment to a life of love, which is the fear of death. (It may be noted here that in a ghazal even when the poet uses the first person nominative case singular pronoun 'I', the possessive "my" or "mine" or objective "me," the statement would apply, more often than not, to human beings in general as in the case of this couplet.) One afflicted with this fear will go pale before he takes the first step on the path of love, before he takes wing impelled by the passion of love. This is love's second challenge: fear of death. In the third couplet he says that fidelity is the absolute prerequisite of love. He became conscious of this fact when he was still very young (his thoughts were still scattered), but even then he had started compiling the recipes of fidelity.

But love's fidelity does not protect him from the heart's desolation, which is the work of love. However, this was not always so. There was a time when flowers blossomed in the lover's heart which he took for granted and did not give much for it. But then the heart bled. This is the fourth distich and another challenge. The lover has to accept the vagaries of love that are the vagaries of life. But even then, even when it was lost to the beloved, there was no peace, no relief. This is the fifth couplet and the fifth challenge the lover has to face.

In the sixth couplet the poet says that physical restraint is no remedy for the passion of love: it won't know rest till the objective is obtained ("thoughts across the desert wandered"). In the seventh and the last distich an image is created of Asad's dead body without shroud signifying his freedom from wants after death as he was uniquely free from worldly interests while alive. It also suggests that the lover faces the challenges and demands of love all his life until he is dead. But what is of particular note is its irony.

[7]

Counting the rosary beads the difficulty-cherishing idol likes;
The sport of carrying in one hand a hundred hearts she likes.

By the bounty of disappointment, eternal hopelessness has become easy;
This difficult knot has come to be liked by the untying ability.

The desire for a walk in the rose-garden shows the beloved's cruelty;
The way her wounded ones toss and turn in blood she likes to see.

Commentary:

The poet sees the beloved with a rosary (which traditionally has a hundred beads) and immediately the idea flashes through his mind that it is not from a sense of religious piety that she is carrying the rosary — far from it—but from a desire to hold in her hand a hundred hearts (each bead symbolizing a heart), which pleases her because it satisfies her sense of possession and control of a multitude of supplicants for her favour (couplet 1). The moment the poet discovers this trait in his beloved, he naturally feels disappointed and dejected, which sentiments in their turn prepare and harden him to meet headlong the unending discomfiture and hopelessness which is the fate of any mortal, even the best among them. This also leads the poet to think that the most difficult questions of life remain unresolved which he puts in a playful and ironic way that the unraveling quality of mind has come to like the problem as it is (couplet 2).

It may be added here that the second couplet of this ghazal expresses the essence of Ghalib's aesthetic and spiritual attitude towards his art and life, respectively. It may be compared to the penultimate couplet of the fifth ghazal above, where the poet, having newly learnt death, finds that the severe difficulty is that even this easy turned out. Ghalib, both as a poet and as a man, prefers difficulties, knots, the gravest problems of life, to ease and contentment: this is a comic view of tragic human inevitabilities—Ghalib's forte. What would life be without such difficulties? And to see the comedy in the human situation is Ghalib's achievement.

Then the poet notices (in the last couplet) another desire in the beloved: she wants to have a walk in the rose-garden. (It may be noted that in Urdu and Persian poetry although *gul* is a generic term for flower, it almost always means a red rose). The poet immediately knows why she wants this: in the garden the roses in bloom are tossed about in different directions by the wind. This is also the scene presented by the lovers when wounded by the sword of the beloved's beauty or her coquetry, or her feigned disdain, and, as if, the roses were red because they were similarly affected. This shows the narcissism and the vanity of the beloved in contrast with the purity of the poet's love. The interesting thing is that the poet knows the ways of the beloved as she relates to her lover and still he loves her with a passionate heart.

[8]

The injury a gift, the diamond a present, the heart's wound an offering!
Congratulations, Asad! All these has brought your commiserating friend.

14

Commentary:

The poet is saying that he has received as his rewards for love, the injury, a diamond (thought to increase and perpetuate wounds), and the heart's wound. In a playful or sarcastic way the poet welcomes the gifts of injury and wounds brought by love.

[9]

The charm-word of fidelity the cause of comfort couldn't be;
It is just a word that invested with meaning couldn't be.

By the green of down your defiant locks couldn't be tamed;
The emerald, too, a rival of the hissing black serpents couldn't be.

I had wished that from the tribulation of loyalty I would be free,
But my oppressor even to my death wouldn't agree.

Let the heart the passage of the thought of wine and goblet be,
If the breath the pathway to the destination of piety couldn't be.

Your not making any promise, even that is agreeable to me;
My ears beholden to your sweet words doesn't have to be.

To whom to complain of the wretchedness of fate?
I wanted to die, but that even couldn't be.

From the shock of the movement of the lips, Ghalib died:
So weak he had grown, Jesus' breath he couldn't withstand.

Commentary:

In the first couplet Ghalib says that there is no faithfulness in the world, no sincerity in human relations. Fidelity is just a charm-word without charm.

Regarding the second couplet, it should be noted that in the Persian literary tradition, which Urdu poetry follows, the beloved is male. Ghalib we know had no homosexual tendency. He merely uses the old tradition to make a brilliant conceit. The down on a white face appears to be green, and an emerald is also green. According to folklore if an emerald is placed in front of a black venomous viper it renders it blind. In the couplet the poet uses the emerald as a metaphor for the green of down, and the hissing black serpent for the locks of hair; through these metaphors, he creates an image of the beloved who cannot be tamed and who, like the serpent, will continue to tempt. Ghalib overturns the folk legend even as he uses the generic convention of the male beloved, all to suggest the unique power of love.

The third couplet is self-explanatory. In the fourth, the poet says that if there is no escape from the sorrows of life, let him have the pleasure of *thinking* of pleasant thoughts. He concedes without regret that piety is not for him. Even if he has no wine, he likes at least to think of it, as he thinks of the beloved when she is not with him.

The beloved does not, in the fifth couplet, make any promise that could lighten the poet's grief. But he is not bothered by her coldness for he knows that she would never fulfill her promise. In a way, he is better off, as his ears don't have to be grateful to her for her sweet words.

Couplets six and seven go together. Of his own will the poet cannot and does not die. But when death came, it came in a very strange way: Jesus, the Saviour, when he breathed the inspired words, it instead of working the miracle caused his death; he had grown so weak he could not withstand the movement of the lips Jesus made to breathe the words upon him. It should be noted that Jesus in the Islamic faith is regarded as a prophet who, by God's leave, could heal the sick and raise the dead.

[10]

The Garden of Rizwan of which the devotee is getting so rhapsodic
Is but a bouquet in the niche of forgetfulness for us in ecstasy.

How to describe the oppression of her piercing eyelashes?
Every single drop of my blood the bead of a coral rosary is.

Even the killer's awe couldn't stop me from making complaints;
The twig I took between my teeth became the reed-bed's root-tissue.

A spectacle I will reveal if some respite the world gives;
Every scar on my heart the seed of a cypress of lights is.

Your splendour has so transformed the prospect of the hall of mirrors,
As the light of sun shining on the dewdrops in the garden does.

In our very constitution lies hidden an element of destruction:
The farmer's warm blood in the lightning mode destroys the harvest.

All around my house weeds have grown: look at the desolation!
Removing these weeds is now the only use of the doorkeeper.

Hundreds of thousands of desires bloodied my silence hides;
A burnt out lamp in a cemetery for strangers am I!

Still the light of the beloved's imagery lingers on:
My sad heart, so to speak, is Joseph's cell in the prison.

In the arms of my rival you seem to have slept tonight,
Why else did you appear in my dream with mysterious smiles?

Who can say to how many it might have caused deep distress?
What a calamity it is to see tears on your eyelashes!

Of the ultimate path that ends in death I am not forgetful, Ghalib:
It is the string that binds together the scattered elements of this world.

Commentary:

"Rizwan" in the first couplet, literally means "good pleasure" and according to Islamic tradition it is the name of the guardian of Paradise, which can be imagined by the human mind as a garden that is pleasing to the senses. In the first couplet the poet says the Paradise which the pious one is so highly praising is of no significance to those in a state of ecstasy, intoxicated as they are with the love of the Being—it is nothing more than a "bouquet in the niche of forgetfulness"—a typically Ghalibian imagery. But there can be another interpretation, too, which is that the Paradise of which the devotee is so full of praises is to those besides themselves with the delights or griefs of this world a thing totally forgotten; and a thing forgotten virtually does not exist for those who have forgotten it.

The second couplet is about the beloved's sharp eyelashes which, as if, piercing through the lover's heart make it bleed from his eyes in drops as tears, giving them the appearance of a rosary of read coral beads.

In the second line of the third couplet there is a reference to the Indo-Persian custom of old times (now only used as an idiom, but Ghalib also uses it in its literal sense) that when a person took a twig between his teeth it was a sign of submission and humility. The lover, submitting to the authority of the beloved (the killer), put a twig between his teeth but it turned into a root-tissue of the reed that grew into a reed-bed and gave out a plaintive music. In a word, the plaints could not be suppressed; in fact, the effort to suppress had a contrary effect. The plaintive note from a reed is also a convention in Persian literature, the most famous instance of its use being in the opening verse of Rumi's *Mathnawi*.

The "cypress of lights" in couplet four is the display of a distinctive type of fireworks, so called because the lights and sparks they emit appear like cypress in form. Couplet five is self-explanatory. The sixth couplet is about the tragic paradox of human existence: the first line is a general statement of the truth as observed, and the second line an example in support of it. Reading both lines together they seem to suggest as if, unawares, we live and work for the sake of dying—a rather disturbing thought. (In the second line "the farmer's warm blood," while one of the vital signs and essential for life, is, at the same time a factor in wear and tear leading to death inasmuch as it is involved in the physical and chemical process whereby the body cells and tissues are broken down to produce energy needed to live and work. And, also, the heat in the form of lightning (discharge of electricity) destroys the crop, the yield of human efforts.)

Couplet seven needs no explanation. In the eighth couplet, the "burnt out lamp" in the second line is a metaphor for "silence" in which are hidden hundreds of thousands "bloodied" (i.e., killed, wasted, frustrated) desires, and this burnt out lamp is in a graveyard, which adds to the sombreness of the imagery; and it is not just any graveyard but for the strangers which adds another dimension and creates an atmosphere of pervading forlornness, desolation and oppressiveness—all of this lying hidden or revealing the piercing silence. One may see in this picture the poet's perception of the political and social situation which, perhaps, is true of all times.

In the second line of couplet nine, the prison cell is a metaphor for the stricken heart, which lights up from the reflection of the beloved's imagery as did the prison cell from Joseph's presence. (Joseph is the celebrated Joseph of the Bible and the Quran, son of Jacob.)

11

However much it may tire me, my pleasure it won't diminish:
My footprints are the bubbles on the waves of my desert wanderings!

I used to love gardens, but now so out of humour am I
That by the waves of fragrance of flowers harassed feel I.

Commentary:

In the first couplet the poet says that no amount of fatigue or weariness is going to lessen the great pleasure and delight that wanderings through the desert gives him. Wanderings through the desert is a metaphor for hardships that one has to go through in this world, particularly in a life of love, and the allusion is to the desert wanderings of Qais. In the second line of the first couplet, bubbles are used as a metaphor for footprints, and waves as a metaphor for movement; his restless movements are so unceasing that they transform even such a stationary thing as the footprints (symbolizing tiredness) into bubbles which keep moving with the waves.

The second couplet needs no explanation except that in the second line the Urdu phrase, *nak main ata hai dum maira,* literally means "into the nostrils comes my breath," which is an idiom for "greatly harassing and/or making very unhappy". In Urdu, the use of this idiom is highly apt as this condition in the poet is produced by the scent of flowers that goes up his nostrils.

12

Wholly pledged to love, and love of life is inevitable;
The lightning I worship and the consequences I regret!

Like your generosity, O cupbearer, is my thirst for wine:
If you are a river of wine, its stretching shore am I.

[13]

So it is that with the music of Mystery you are not conversant,
Otherwise, what veils the world is but the screen of the instrument.

My faded colour presents the view of the dawn of spring;
Now the flowers of her coquetry are going to bloom.

You there, casting towards the stranger repeated sharp looks,
And here am I, feeling the pain of your long eyelashes.

It is to my advantage, suppressing my sighs—otherwise
It would of me make a morsel, just one life-destroying sigh.

From the fervour of wine the goblets are jumping in such a manner
That every spot of the party floor looks like the head of a dancer.

The heart is demanding from the fingernail more effort,
For still it owes the debt of fully untying the half-open knot.

By the intensity of grief of separation it was devastated, Asad—
The breast in which the treasure of pearls of secrets lay buried.

Commentary:

In the first couplet, the "instrument" symbolizes the world, and its "screen"
the disconnection between the music and the people of the world. A musical

21

instrument, such as a drum, a sitar, a piano, or a violin has some kind of "screen" (e.g., the drum has a drumhead) that gives out a whole range of music. The Mystery is truth that the music reveals only to those who make themselves conversant with it through close study and experience. For others it remains a Mystery hidden behind the "screen" of the musical instrument.

The remaining couplets require no explication, except for the penultimate one. In it, the "knot" symbolizes the pains and sorrows that the heart suffers caused by perplexing problems and felt as tightness in the chest, and the "fingernail" is the means by which a problem is resolved (untying the knot). The poet says that the knot is still only half-undone, and therefore the effort needs to continue. This, so to speak, is the debt owed by the fingernail (it has not been diligent enough) to the knot, which the latter is demanding to be paid up. The heart wants the effort to relieve the pain to succeed. The debt can only be paid when this work is done and the knot has been untied. The concept of debt and its settlement has been brought into play to stress the point that the need is urgent and necessary and just. It also suggests that though the "knot" is half-undone, still the pain remains unbearable and hence the urgency. The idea that the knot has been half undone suggests both that (1) the effort already made has worked, thus encouraging more of it to achieve complete success, as well as that (2) the pain will endure because the cause is going to persist. But who has tied this "knot?" It can be the vicissitudes of life and the universe but if we carry the ghazal world in our heads, the "beloved."

[14]

In the Emperor's assembly the books of poetry have opened:
Keep, O Lord, the door of this treasure of gems always open!

It is night and again the bright shining stars' view has opened
With such adornment as if the door of the idol-temple has opened.

22

Though mad am I, but why get deceived by the friend's guiles?
In the sleeve is the dagger hidden, in the hand the lancet open.

Though comprehend not her speech, though I can't solve this riddle,
But is it a small thing that she, the fairy-like, has opened up with me?

Thinking of beauty is like doing good deeds:
Inside my grave has opened a door to Paradise.

Though the face not unveiled, yet such a beauty never seen before!
More than her tresses, the veil is showing to advantage her face.

At the door I was told I could stay, but then how fast she reneged—
In the time my rolled-up bedding I spread out!

Why is grief's night so dark? Because the calamities are descending!
Turned up and away, in that direction will remain the stars' eyes tonight.

How can I be happy in a foreign land when such be the misfortune?
The letters the messenger brings from my native land are often open!

Of his people am I, how can my purpose remain unfulfilled?
The King for whom, Ghalib, the dome without door was opened.

Commentary:

I have not come across any external evidence, but the first two couplets of
the ghazal indicate that it was perhaps written for some poetry reading session
organized within the Court (which was not unusual) by the last Mughal
Emperor, Bahadur Shah Zafar, who himself was a poet of no mean merit. After

the Revolt of 1857 he was dethroned by the British and sent to a prison in Burma where he died.

The first couplet is self-explanatory. In the second couplet the poet presents a beautiful image of the poetry reading session that was then and even now, always held in the evening and continues till late into the night. In the first line of the couplet the poet speaks of the beauty and the charm of the starlit night and in the second line he compares it with the brightly lighted temple adorned with idols that people worship. This is quite an imaginative picture created by the poet and a little complex. In many cases the idols in a temple represent some well-known stars which the devotees worship. The idols can be compared to the poets and their poetry, and the lovers of poetry to the devotees.

Couplet three and four need no explanation. The fifth one expresses a witty, charming idea. Muslims generally believe (though this is not in the Quran) that once one is dead and buried, two angels, Munkar and Nakir appear in one's grave and ask the dead about his past life; if he gives a satisfactory account, a door in his grave is opened to Paradise and he starts sharing some of the bliss of the heavenly life. The poet says that the thought of the beauty, his beloved, has changed the aspect of his grave which is similarly blissful and a door to Paradise has opened. In other words, the thought of beauty has the same effect as that of good deeds.

The opened letters that the poet mentions in the ninth couplet refer to the sub-continental practice of sending a letter partly torn or open if it carried bad news.

In the last couplet the reference is to Prophet Muhammad's spiritual experience of the "Night Journey" and the "Ascension" to heaven as mentioned in the Quran. The tradition resulting from this may have been, when introduced into Western culture, the germ of Dante's poem. The dome without door is the sky, which opened up for the "king," Muhammad. In Muslim poetry, he is often referred to as "the spiritual king."

At night by lightning of my heart's ardour the cloud's gall to water turned
And every eddy of the flood to a whirling flame turned.

There, for her graciousness the rain was an excuse for not coming to me;
Here, from torrent of tears my pillow's cotton wool into froths became.

There, contemplating stringing pearls on her hair for self-adornment:
Here, in the profusion of teardrops my line of sight was lost.

There, the roses' reflection illuminated the water-stream;
Here, from my weeping eyes pure blood streamed.

Here, my head, tumultuous from sleeplessness, was seeking for a wall;
There, the head of that playful one, deep in sleep, on a silken pillow was.

Here, my breath was lighting the candle of the assembly of sighs;
There amidst splendour of flowers, she was enjoying the company of friends.

There, from earth to empyrean was a flood of waves of colours;
Here, the entire extent was on fire from earth to the heavens.

Thus all at once it started dripping tears of blood—
My heart that had tasted the pleasure of pain.

Commentary:

If it is kept in mind that "there" in this ghazal refers to where the beloved
is, and "here" to where the lover is, the poem becomes lucid. However, in the

first and the last couplets the poet only speaks of what is happening in the lover's heart.

In the first couplet the poet presents a composite picture that has three parts, three pictures, each one of which has to be viewed in sequence to comprehend the overall image. First, there is the picture of the poet whose heart is burning with great ferocity from the sorrows of life, particularly from discomfiture in love. The intensity of the heat of the burning heart sparks lightning that causes terror or great distress to the cloud [in Urdu the phrase "*pitta pani hono or zahra aab hona*" ("the gall to turn to water") means to be terrified or greatly distressed] which yields its entire charge of water. This is the second picture. The third picture is of the eddies of flood turning to whirling flames. Normally, the floodwater should have extinguished the fire in the poet's heart but, instead, by the overpowering heat of the fire in the poet's heart, it itself got transformed into whirling flame. So the overall picture is that of the elements moved by the poet's all-consuming passion.

The other couplets are self-explanatory.

[16]

The night was lonely and effectiveness was wanting in my heart's laments;
For her merrymaking strangers' party the wild rue's burning seed it was!

With the coming of the flood how the heart started playing joyous melodies,
As if the lover's house, the musical instrument of water was.

The pride of the days of sitting on the dust, what to say of that!
All of my apprehensions lay in peace on the bed of ermine.

It was deficiency in my love that nothing it could achieve,
Otherwise, every particle here rivalled the world-illumining sun.

Why is it that for your captives you don't care anymore?
Till yesterday your heart, too, a chapter of love and loyalty was.

Remember the day when every single loop of your net,
Like a sleepless eye remained open for the prey.

Last night I stopped Ghalib, otherwise you would have seen
That the heavens were the froth of the flood of his tears.

Commentary:

The first line of the first couplet is about the lonely night of separation, that is, when the lover is not with his beloved and, therefore, the night of grief, finding expression in wailing and moaning (the heart's laments) which would normally be expected to evoke a favourable response from the beloved. But this is not what happened. Instead, it had quite a contrary effect of "the burning seed of wild rue" (the second line of the couplet), protecting from harm the beloved's merrymaking assembly of strangers (to the lover, but friends of the beloved). The wild rue seed when burnt gives out a distinctive crackling sound, and, according to the folklore of Indo-Pakistan sub-continent, it is supposed to avert the mischievous effect of the evil eye. (The similarity between the heart making lament when grieved and the rue seed making a distinctive sound when burning is obvious.) The couplet is in a satirical mode.

The musical instrument of the water in the second couplet is the musical instrument *jaltarang* (literally, the wave of water or water in a state of rapture) of Indo-Pakistan sub-continent, consisting of seven bowl-shaped cups, all of the same size but each filled with a different amount of water. When their edges are struck with two sticks by a master player they produce a whole range of tunes.

The phrase "sitting on the dust" (*khakaster nishin* in the original) in the third couplet means humility and contentment.

27

For every drop of blood with tears of blood a full account I rendered:
The blood in my heart in trust I held for the eyelashes of my beloved.

Now it is I and my mourning for my myriad desires unfulfilled;
The mirror[1] you broke their images it held.

Drag my dead body through her alleys, for,
All my life I pined for the streets she trod.

About the waves of mirage in the desert of loyalty, don't ask me;
Every particle of this desert like a flash of a sharp scimitar was.

I, too, didn't make much of the grief of love, but now I know
That if they become less, the worldly sorrows take their place.

Commentary:

This ghazal is self-explanatory. Perhaps the only couplet that calls for comment is the fourth one. In it the poet is saying that this is a faithless world where love is never returned. Loyalty is like a mirage in a desert that appears like waves of water, but in effect its every wave is like a flash of a scimitar. By using the metaphor of a sharp scimitar the poet heightens the feeling of pain caused by disappointment in love. In a word, the life of love is a life full of tribulations—not everybody's cup.

---

[1] I.e., the heart

[18]

Hard indeed it is for any task to be rendered easy;
For human beings to attain humaneness is not easy!

My weeping, it seems, is intent on destroying my dwelling;
Its doors and walls are showing that to wilderness it is turning.

O my! the intoxication of love compulsively takes me there,
But with bewilderment I am struck just when there!

The manifestation of the beloved's beauty demands it be seen:
Even the mirror's polishing streaks want to become its eyelashes!

How to describe the lovers' joy at the execution ground?
To them it is a delightful sight[1] to see the scimitar bared!

To the grave I carried the scar of my desire for pleasure:
May you enjoy yourself in a hundred ways forever!

For a broken heart, to suffer the wounds of desire is a pleasure;
For the wounds of the liver, it is a joy to remain immersed in the salt-cellar.

After killing me, cruelty and injustice she renounced;
Ah! How quickly she repented, the fast-repentant one!

Woe to the fate of that quarter yard of cloth's, Ghalib,
To whose lot it fell to be the lover's shirt's breast!

---

[1] An allusion to Eid-crescent (see the commentary on the is couplet).

Commentary:

Most of the couplets in this ghazal are self-explanatory.

The construction of couplet three may cause some difficulty. The central idea is that a person in love is so absorbed in the beloved that he can think of nothing else, can cherish nothing else; every breath, every moment compulsively drives him towards the beloved, but then he is struck with bewilderment. Why? Because the beloved (earthly or Divine) remains inaccessible or the vision cannot withstand the glory

The fifth couplet can be read in the Sufi tradition of Islamic mysticism. For one in love with the Being there is no greater joy than death that brings him in direct contact with Him. The term coined by Ghalib, *Eid-e-nazzarah*, in the second line of this verse means a "delightful sight" and is also an allusion to Eid-crescent. Eid is the Islamic holiday celebration marking the end of the fasting month of Ramadan. Since the Islamic calendar is lunar, the day of Eid is determined each year by the appearance of the moon. The poet has used the metaphor of the Eid-crescent (which has been alluded to, though not specifically mentioned) for the scimitar, both being curved and shining. The Eid-crescent brings happiness to Muslims, coming as it does after a month of dawn to dusk fasting, just as death brings happiness to the mystic after a long span of hungering and thirsting for the Beloved. The brilliance of this couplet lies in Ghalib's injecting into the commonplaces of mysticism a bold system of imagery. At the "execution ground," the poet says, seeing the scimitar "bared"—drawn from its sheath—is like sighting the Eid-crescent, a moment of great delight for those in love of the Being. The construction of this imagery is important here, not the conventional longing of a conventional mystic, which merely forms a backdrop for Ghalib's great stroke of originality. Interpreted in a general way, the verse would mean that the one fired by the passion of love for his ideal is happy to offer the ultimate price of his life; in fact, he triumphs in death as it may help keep the ideal alive, which his death has brought into a sharp focus and may inspire others.

In the seventh couplet, the poet is saying that love so completely changes a man that he accepts its pain with pleasure. The discomfiture in love breaks his heart (*dil*), but it does not in any way dampen his desire; it rather sharpens it. The same happens in the case of the liver (*jigar*) which, according to Persian and Urdu poetic convention, is also the seat of love as is the heart. But the liver is also considered to be the seat of patience and fortitude, and this latter sense, too, is useful in interpreting this couplet. (See also the commentary on couplet 2, ghazal 31.)

[19]

At night the languor was as on Judgement Day, longing for the cupbearer,
Till the wine in the goblets, decanters and flagons pictures of yawning were.

One step on love-madness' path revealed the book of the cosmos' secrets;
This path is the binding string of the elements of both the desolate worlds.

Whatever prevented Laila from walking into the desert?
The desert-wandering Majnoon's house had no barriers!

Don't ask how the beauty's claim of freedom from want has been shamed:
The hands to henna and the cheeks to rouge are indebted.

My laments blew the pieces of my heart like leaves in the air:
The memories of these laments is my divan without a binding string.

Commentary:

One of the pictures commonly drawn of the Judgement Day is that when the dead will be raised, they will be in a state of extreme languor, stretching and yawning as if awoken from a deep sleep. The poet says that the condition of a person is similar when the effect of wine is wearing off. While in this state, he is in the tavern; the cask, the decanter, the cup—in short, all the vessels—are full of wine, but the cupbearer is not there. And the tradition is that nobody can drink unless served by the cupbearer. So, there is languor and extreme longing for the cupbearer, so much so that it influences the wine in the containers until the entire tavern becomes a picture-gallery of yawning and stretching. In this first couplet, Ghalib manages a very artistic comparison of the sensation of waking from death and the longing for wine.

In the second line of the next couplet, the poet has used the binding string (which keeps the pages of a book together) as a metaphor for the path of love-madness, which keeps the elements of both the worlds in harmony. Without love-madness this world as well as the next one would be desolate. This couplet may usefully be compared to the concluding couplet of the tenth ghazal, where death is seen as the string that binds the scattered elements of *this* world.

[20]

What helpful measures can they take, my friends who feel my pain!
Before the wounds are healed, won't the nails grow long again?

Your indifference has crossed all limits, but O gracious one for how long this
That I tell you what my heart is suffering and you ask me, "What?"

If the good counselor comes, my eyes and heart will be a welcome-mat;
But will someone tell me, he is going to tell me what?

Today I go there carrying sword and shroud;
For not killing me what excuse will now she find?

If the good counselor has me in the prison, so be it;
But will the ways of the madness of love go away like this?

A born slave of your curling locks, why should I flee the chains?
I am a captive of fidelity, how could prison scare me away?

Now in this populous city love and sorrows of love are scarce, Asad;
So if in Delhi I continue to live, where will I sustenance find?

Commentary:

Most of the couplets are self-explanatory.

Regarding the third couplet, it may be noted that in the ghazal world the lover and the beloved are the central characters. The "good counselor" is also a denizen of this world. Love is the all-consuming passion of a lover that appears destructive to the friendly counselor, who would like to counsel the lover to change his ways. In colloquial Urdu and Persian as well as in their literary traditions, "spreading one's eyes and heart in the way" (translated above as "my eyes and heart will be a welcome-mat") is to respectfully welcome somebody. The poet is ready to respectfully welcome the good counselor but he knows what his advice is going to be, which can have no effect on him, and thus his exclamatory question almost showing annoyance.

In the fourth couplet, the poet expresses his resolve and readiness to sacrifice his life. Working within the ghazal tradition, he says that grief has driven him to such desperation that he wants to die, but only at his beloved's hands. He reasons that she will not do that as she wants him to continue to suffer, but what excuse would she have now that the sword is there to kill him and the shroud for the funeral rites?

Delhi, which is referred to in the final couplet, was the political capital of India and a great cultural center, but it was in decline when Ghalib lived there. (In fact, it ceased to be the political capital in 1857 when the British captured Delhi and the last Mughal Emperor Bahadur Shah was dethroned and exiled.

The British later moved their capital from Calcutta to Delhi in 1910-11.) The poet in this couplet laments this political decay and extols its past glory.

[21]

It wasn't destined union with the beloved I would have had;
Had I lived longer this very agony of waiting I would have suffered.

If you think I survived on your promise you got it wrong, my love;
Wouldn't have I died of happiness had I believed your word?

Your delicacy told me your promise was lightly made;
Never could you break it if it were firmly made.

My heart alone knows what it is—the pleasure of your half-drawn arrow!
Had it gone through and out of my heart, when this pricking I would've had!

What kind of friendship is this that friends have become sermonizers!
Some should have found some remedy, others assuaged my grief.

Its veins would emit blood, not sparks, that wouldn't stop
If what you call grief had but struck a stone.

Though grief is life-destroying, but whenever can the heart escape it?
If the sorrows of love it weren't suffering, worldly woes would afflict it.

To whom may I tell what is it? The night of grief is a vicious calamity!
If death were a one-time experience, why should I mind it?

If after death I were to be disgraced, why didn't I drown in a river?
Then there would have been no funeral and no grave either.

He is One and Unique, who could see Him?
Had there been even a hint of duality, one might have seen Him.

Such subtleties of mysticism and your beautiful expositions, Ghalib!
For a saint we'd have taken you if a wine-drinker you were not.

Commentary:

It is a part of the ghazal tradition that the beloved's beauty is a deadly weapon, of which her eyebrows, eyelashes, eyes and glances are the special aspects. The eyebrows are the bows and the glances are the arrows and the beloved is the archer. It is this theme that the poet has developed in the fourth couplet. A half-drawn arrow is Ghalib's imaginative creation of a novel metaphor. If the beloved had cast a fully-drawn arrow—ogled boldly at the poet showing her desire—it would either have caused his death from joy, which would have been his fulfillment, or it would have caused a wound which would have healed in time. But it is the half-pulled arrow—a glance or a side-glance—that has lodged in his heart which is going to cause him lasting pricking sensation, thus always reminding him of his beloved and her near fatal glance.

The imagery of the sixth couplet is a bit intricate. Stones have veins, and so do human beings. But stones are devoid of feelings of any kind whereas humans are all feelings and sensations. If a stone is struck with another stone or an iron hammer, it gives out sparks. But if a human being is stricken with grief his heart bleeds, he sheds tears of blood. From these simple observations the poet has developed the idea that the grief humans are made to suffer is of such power and intensity that if it had struck a stone—hard, insensate—even the stone would have bled ceaselessly instead of just giving out sparks. This is the poet's reading of the human situation as he saw it to which he has given expression by creating a striking imagery. We should not, however, miss the point that the poet, in fact, is paying tribute to human courage, endurance, and determination.

The penultimate couplet alludes to the Islamic belief in the absolute uniqueness and oneness of God, who has no duality or plurality. God cannot be seen, and here Ghalib is saying that had there been any duality, any non-oneness in God, then along with His transcendent side there would have been something else, so that it would have become possible to see him. Ghalib here has used the concept of Oneness of Being (*Wahdat al-Wujud*) of Islamic mysticism to create yet another original web of thought. But notwithstanding these ideas about religion and mysticism, his irrepressible wit comes into play in the final couplet of this great ghazal.

[22]

What lively delight our desires find in all kinds of endeavours!
If there were no death, when would our life have zest and flavour?

Your feigned ignorance, what do you mean by that?
For how long, O true coquette, this what, what!

I see you bestowing on others unmerited favours;
To my loving grievances why do you take exception?

A bold look from you is what I yearn for;
Your patience-testing indifference—what for?

The light of trash's flame lasts but for a moment:
What respect for fidelity's honour can have lust?

My every breath a wave of the ocean of intoxication is!
Why then complain of the indifference of the cupbearer?

It is not just the fragrance of her dress that I desire;
For the wayward breeze wafting it what do I care?

From the heart of every drop rises the music: "I am the ocean."
I am of Him; who can tell who am I!

Why this hesitation? I take the responsibility; look towards me:
For the martyrs of a glance, how can there be blood money?

Hear me, O ravager of precious fidelity, hear me!
How can it make any sound, the crash in the value of heart[1]?

Whoever claimed courage and fortitude?
Whenever has patience the lover's heart!

O killer, why these patience-trying promises?
O infidel[2], why these endurance-testing mischiefs?

Everything about her is a wondrous calamity, Ghalib:
What of her expression, what of her glance, what of her grace!

[23]

When worthy of your wrath and punishment there is none like me,
How then is it wrong to say that none was ever born like me?

I am the one who keeps his independence and pride even in devotion:
From the Kaba I would come back if its door I didn't find open!

---

[1]Heart considered as the seat and source of "fidelity" (line one).
[2]Infidel, i.e., the beloved, because she is supposed not to believe in true love, loyalty and constancy.

The claim of your uniqueness everybody accepts.
O beloved with mirror-like face! Nobody can see you face to face.

It is no small pride to be the namesake of the beloved's eyes,
So how is it bad that your lovesick lover has not recovered?

Lament that does not come up to the lips becomes a blemish for the heart;
The drop of water that doesn't reach the river becomes a morsel for dust.

The pain and grief that no one suffered were fated for me;
The calamities that never happened before were meant for me.

If from each hair-root pure blood doesn't drip when the story is told,
It is Hamza's tale then, not the story of love.

If in a drop one doesn't see the Tigris, and in the part the whole,
He is like a child watching sport, not a sage with discerning eyes.

The latest news was about making mincemeat of Ghalib;
I, too, went to see, but no such spectacle happened.

Commentary:

Couplet 3: Because the beloved's face is like a mirror (second line of this couplet) whoever wants to see that face only sees the reflection of his own face not the beloved. This simile has been brought into play to prove the point made in the first line that the beloved is unique, of whom there cannot be an image even. A similar thought has been expressed in a different way in couplet 10 of ghazal 21.

Couplet 4: In Urdu as well as in Persian *chasm-e-bimar* ("sick eyes") and *nargis-e-bimar* ("sick narcissus") are metaphors for the half-opened, coquettish, intoxicated eyes of the beloved. The term "sick" is shared by both—the "sick narcissus" and the "lovesick."

Couplet 7: *Dastan-e-Amir Hamza* (*The Tale of Amir Hamza*) is a long Urdu fiction consisting of many parts, of which "*Tilism-e-Hoshruba*" ("The Enchanting Story") is the most popular. Hamza, Umru-Aiyar, and Laqa, etc., are its famous characters. It is read and its stories are told for pure entertainment.

Couplet 8: The Tigris, a river in Iraq, is here used as a generic term for river.

[24]

A mendicant without means running madly in the desert am I, Asad;
For me the gazelle's eyelashes are the back-scratching instrument's fingers.

Commentary:

In the life of the lover, as in that of the mendicant, things of comfort have no place. But while the mendicant at least carries with him a back-scratching instrument (shaped like a hand with fingers, and a handle), the lover doesn't have that even, and the gazelle's eyelashes do this job for him, which, by implication, brings in another comparison: such is the frenzy of the lover that he is running faster than the fast-running gazelle, which is left behind and its eyelashes do the back-scratching. Running in the desert also brings to mind the story of Majnoon, the celebrated lover of Arabic, Persian, and Urdu literature. "Desert" may symbolize the dreariness of the world without the beloved, "running" the struggle to meet and be one with the beloved, as well as the impatience and restlessness pushing the lover ever to increase and accelerate his efforts. (The beloved may be a human person, God, or a lofty purpose in life.)

[25]

To the Merciful One I bring the offering of shame of unworthiness—
All my claims of piety discomfited[1] in a hundred ways!

May not the beauty's love for self-display be blamed for faithlessness!
A hundred eyes are setting their seals to her claim of blamelessness!

Give me the charity of your beauty, O light of my eyes, so that, like the sun,
The begging-bowl becomes the lamp of this dervish's house.

Knowing me for my innocence, you killed me not, but, O killer,
You now have the blood of the right of friendship on your hand.

The desire for a tongue is lost in thanking speechlessness,
The thing that removed the need for complaining of helplessness.

It is one and the same; what is breath here is fragrance of flower there:
That which brings on splendour in the garden inspires my colourful songs.

The mouth of every beauty taunting you is a link in a chain of infamy;
Up to non-existence, O faithless one, the popular topic is your inconstancy.

Don't make your letter a long story, Ghalib; just say this:
"To tell you in person of the tyranny of separation I am longing."

Commentary:

Couplet 2: The beauty (=beloved) protests that her love for self-display is not a sign of faithlessness. The poet says: Yes, no disgrace may attach to you

---

[1] Literally, stained with blood, bloodied.

for this, and then adds sarcastically that all the eyes that are gazing at you are setting their seal to your claim of blamelessness.

Couplet 3: The begging-bowl is a metaphor for the eyes (the ones used by the mendicants in India were shaped liked that), which light up on seeing the beloved's beauty and fill the heart with light. House here is a metaphor for heart. "*Zakat*," the word used by Ghalib in the original, is generally rendered as "charity, purifying dues or poor-rate." It literally means receiving increase and blessing from God. According to the Quranic injunction, every Muslim is required to pay a certain percentage of his wealth to a fund to be used mainly to provide for the needs of the poor. The payment of *Zakat* is believed to both purify and increase the wealth. The aptness of the term *Zakat* as used in the original is obvious.

Couplet 7: All beauties are unfaithful, the poet says, but his beloved excels them all, so much so that other beauties, too, now talk of it, their mouths as if forming the links of the chain of infamy around the poet's beloved. Amongst those now dead, this remains a popular topic in the other world (non-existence).

[26]

If to the agony of the night of separation I don't give expression,
Frankly, then, the moon would be a dark spot sealing off my mouth.

If this is how, in the evening of separation, the gall into water turns,
The moonlight, too, will change into a torrent, destroying my house.

I very much want to kiss her feet while she is asleep,
But such a circumstance will make the infidel[1] suspicious.

---

[1]Infidel, i.e., the beloved because she is not supposed to believe in true love, loyalty and constancy.

My heart, I thought, I would enduringly use to serve fidelity;
How could I know at the very first test it would be a casualty?

You are in everybody's heart; if you be pleased with me,
The whole world would be gracious towards me.

If her furious looks continue to teach me lessons in restraint,
Like blood in the arteries, the fire will hide in the straw.

To the garden don't take me, for, seeing my condition,
Tears of blood would shed every freshly blossomed rose in the garden.

Ah! If even on Judgement Day justice between you and me isn't done!
As of now I still have hope that on that Day it will be done.

What's the advantage? Think of it! After all, Asad, you too, are a wise man.
Your life it is going to cost you, your friendship with the indifferent one.

Commentary:

Couplet 1: The beauty of the moonlit night makes the agony of separation so unbearable that if it were not given vent to, the moon would seem like a dark spot that sealed the mouth of the lover.

Couplet 2: The lover imagines that the distress of the evening of separation, which has turned his gall into water, may also be affecting the elements. And if it be so then the flood of moonlight may turn into a torrent of water destroying his house. (For "gall turning into water" see the commentary on the first couplet of ghazal 15.)

Couplet 6: The passion, if suppressed, would destroy a man like fire in a straw. Fire is a metaphor for the lover's passion, and straw for his person.

Beholden to the remedy the pain didn't have to be;
That I was not cured was not bad indeed.

Why are you gathering my enemies together
As if not a complaint but an entertainment it were?

Where should I go to try my luck
When on me you even didn't try your dagger?

How sweet are your lips that my rival,
On having a taste of your abuses, felt no unpleasantness!

The latest news is that me she is visiting
And today not a mat even I have in my dwelling.

What to say of Nimrod's claim to godhood?!
My humble submission to God brought me no good!

I gave my life; it was given to me by Him!
The truth is, the obligation was not fulfilled.[1]

If the wound was closed, the bleeding didn't stop;
It didn't restart when my enterprise came to a halt!

Highway robbery or heart-stealing, what is it?
She just took my heart and walked away with it!

---

[1] I.e., life was not put to its ideal or best use and thus the obligation owed to God, the life-giver, was not fulfilled.

43

Read something, for people say,
Ghalib hasn't recited a ghazal today.

Commentary:

Couplet 6: Nimrod, according to tradition, was a king in Abraham's time who claimed godhood. In the Bible he is referred to as a mighty hunter whose kingdom extended from Babel to Calneh, in the land of Shinar (Genesis 10: 8-9). Shinar probably was Sumar in Babylonia in the lower valley of the Tigris and Euphrates rivers of the present day Iraq.

[28]

Love is complaining of the heart even as wanting in capacity;
Can in the pearl get absorbed the tumult of the sea?

You and a reply to my letter! I know it isn't going to happen;
But what can I do, obsessed by the desire to keep writing to you!

If indeed there is spring, the henna on the feet of autumn it is:
The short-lived worldly pleasure a perpetual vexation of heart is.

Grieved by separation, for a walk in the garden don't press me;
For the inopportune laughters of flowers I have no fancy.

For familiarity with the Beauty still I am thirsting,
Though every pore of my body is an eye discerning.

I gave my heart even before the pleasure of her coquetry I had;
When did I have the patience to wait for the beauty to make its demand!

Don't tell me that my weeping is in the measure of my grief;
Of the accumulation and outflow of this river who knows better than I?

Seeing the sky, her I remember, Asad;
In its cruelty the style of the ruler of my heart is.

Commentary:

Couplet 1: The word "*dil*" in the original, here rendered as heart, means in Urdu and Persian, heart; mind; soul; spirit or valour; seat or source of emotions. The poet says that even the heart which takes in the whole universe, with all its unsettling turbulence of all kinds, is too narrow to withstand the perturbation of love which is a much mightier force than the agitation in the sea and asks, in exclamation: can the pearl absorb the tumult of the sea? Here, as pointed out by Ghulam Rasul Miher in his *Nava-e-Surosh*, Ghalib is apparently disagreeing with Khwaja Mir Dard (1758-1820), a major Sufi poet who, addressing God, said:

"The earth and the heavens, when do they have the capacity to take You in!
It is my heart alone where You can take up room."

(translation from Urdu. mine)

Couplet 3: The henna is of bright red colour, signifying spring and joy. But the colour of henna lasts but for a very short time, signifying the transience of spring, i.e., the pleasures of this world. The henna on the feet also restrains movement and thus autumn (a metaphor for vexation) remains in place. In a word, spring is short-lived, and the vexation of autumn is an ever-lasting state. In fact, spring only serves to accentuate the pain of autumn, for if one hadn't known spring, the pain of autumn wouldn't hurt so much.

Couplet 4: "Laughter" is the blossoming of flowers in the garden, symbolizing happiness, which, normally would gladden a heart but not if it is suffering the sorrows of separation.

[29]

The drops of wine, from wonderment,[1] self-indulgent became;
The measuring-lines of the wineglass the strings of pearls became.

See what devastation her trust in my love has brought on me!
My rival said "Ah," and angry she became with me.

[30]

When for my beloved's journey the camel was readied,
My ardour of love, on every particle of the way, a heart fastened.

In the wonderland of her playful coquetry saw the discerning eyes that
The mirror's glistening marks were the slaughtered parakeet's flutterings.

The conflict of hope and despair made of the heart a battlefield:
The lack of aspiration cast a spell and made it a supplicant.

For love's insatiable thirst, Ghalib, adequate expression I couldn't find,
Though, giving free rein to my imagination, it a riverbank I called!

Commentary:

   Couplet 2: The imagery is of the beauty sitting in front of the mirror, playfully appreciating her own coquettish airs and styles. This charmed the entire atmosphere of her room into a state of wonder, freezing everything in its place. But the discerning eyes could see that behind the stillness was a great perturbation, and in the wavy, glistening marks on the mirror they saw the images of the slaughtered parakeet (the lover's perturbed heart). (The mirror is

---

[1] I.e., wonderment at the cupbearer's beauty and charm.

46

of tempered, polished steel, the wavy marks on which scintillate in light, suggesting the fluttering of the freshly slaughtered parakeet.)

Couplet 3: The pronoun "it" in the second line refers to "heart" in the first line.

Couplet 4: The riverbank symbolizes the insatiability of the love's longing, while the river itself symbolizes the available source from which satisfaction could be obtained. In spite of the water flowing through the river, its bank always remains dry or it won't be a riverbank anymore. We may also read in it that even if the entire volume of water in the river were soaked up by the riverbank not only will it still remain dry (thirsty), the river itself will dry up and will be like the riverbank itself—dry and thirsty.

[31]

I and coming from the wine party like this—with the palate parched!
Even if abstinence I had vowed, whatever to the cupbearer happened?

Pierced through by one arrow, both are now in the same state;
Those days are gone when from my heart my liver was different.

In the midst of miseries, Ghalib, if one could avail that would be great!
When the thread had no knots, I had the fingernails that could undo the knot.

Commentary:

Couplet 1: Syed Muhammad Ahmad Bekhud Mohani, in his *Sharh-e-Divan-e-Ghalib* (*Interpretation of Ghalib's Divan*), quoted by Maulana Ghulam Rasul Miher in his *Nawa-e Sarosh* (*Voice of Gabriel*), has brought out interesting points about this couplet, some of which are summarized here which the reader may find of interest inasmuch as it gives an idea of how the lovers of Urdu poetry read Ghalib and other great poets. For example, the words "I and", etc., in the first line suggest that "I" is a hard drinker, and so coming back from the drinking party without tasting wine is particularly painful to him, implied by the term "palate parched." But the most devastating and perplexing aspect is the treatment by the cupbearer ("whatever to the cupbearer happened?"). Is it that she, too, has vowed abstinence? Or is it that she is angry with him at his renouncing drinking? Or is it that she just ignored him, showing her general displeasure with him? There are other possibilities, too. Why did she not realize that if she had offered and insisted on a drink it would have given him a good excuse to break his vow, which seems to be his greatest regret. In short, these and a host of other questions can arise, expanding the meaning of the couplet, which are left to the imagination of the reader.

Couplet 2: In Urdu as well as Persian literature *dil* (heart) and *jigar* (liver) are generally used as interchangeable terms, but when a distinction is made, *dil* is considered as the seat of passion and *jigar* of fortitude, patience, and courage. There was a time, the poet says, when the liver displayed these characteristics, but now both are in the same state of agitation—both pierced through by the arrow of love.

Couplet 3: The thread is a metaphor for life, knots for the difficulties and trials and tribulations of life, and the fingernails for the ability and the means by which they could be resolved.

[32]

My house, even if I hadn't wept, desolate would have been:
If the ocean weren't an ocean, a desert it would have been.

Why complain of the sadness of heart? That thankless wretch it is
Which if sad it were not, perturbed it would have been.

After a life of abstinence, he would, at last, have granted admittance:
Would that Rizwan guarded the entrance to my beloved's house!

Commentary:

Rizwan, mentioned in the third couplet, is the keeper and guardian of Paradise. In a subtle way Ghalib is suggesting that his beloved's house is a paradise and its guard is equal in honor to Rizwan who could have replaced him. From this it is not difficult to imagine the glory of Ghalib's beloved. There is also another interesting point suggested by the first line of this couplet, particularly by the use of the words "at last." First, that in the case of Rizwan who, though a stickler of principles and rules, at last grants admittance when convinced of the merit of the case. Not so the beloved's gatekeeper, which suggests another point, that the lover has pleaded his case with him, but to no avail, notwithstanding the soundness of the case.

[33]

When nothing was, God was; had nothing been, only God would be:
My being was my undoing; had I not been what would have I been?

When from grief so benumbed it became, why bemoan my smitten head?
If from my body it weren't severed, on my knee it would have lain.

It is a long time since Ghalib died, but is yet remembered for this:
In every situation he would say: "Had it happened thus, what then?!"

Commentary:

Regarding the third couplet of this ghazal: Urdu and Persian poets don't use interrogatory, exclamatory, or punctuation marks, a convention that has the

49

effect of increasing the possibilities of interpretations and hence the pleasure of discovering new meanings. Thus, the second line of the couplet, with a note of interrogation, would mean that Ghalib was in the habit of asking searching questions about possible choices and their anticipated consequences. It also suggests a sense of regret that things could and should have happened differently and better. However, with a note of exclamation, the line would mean that whatever and however differently things would have happened, this would have made no difference. At a deeper level, life's predicaments remain the same.

[34]

Not a particle of the garden's soil is idle or without use;
Even the pathway here like the wick of the tulip's lamp is.

Without wine who can withstand the tumult of awareness?
The failing aspiration has drawn the line on the wineglass.

At the nightingale's ways the flowers are laughing:
What is called love a disorder of mind is!

To the intoxication of poetry not new am I;
An old opium-smoker of this lamp am I.

A hundred times from the bonds of love I became free,
But what can be done when the heart is the enemy of ease!

Without tears of blood in the eyes, like dust are the waves of sight:
This tavern[1] is desolate, not finding any trace of wine[2].

---

[1]"Tavern" is a metaphor for the eyes in the first line.
[2]"Wine" is a metaphor for "tears of blood" in the first line.

Your blooming beauty is the source of my heart's delight;
To whose high spirits is the vernal cloud the tavern of joy?

[35]

From my knitted brow, my hidden grief she knew,
As from an incoherent salutation, the letter's contents one would know.

To the furbishing of the mirror not a line has been added yet,
Though ever since I came of age I have been rending my shirt's breast.

To describe the causes of constriction in my heart, don't ask me:
Just know that so oppressed is it that like a prison cell it feels!

My misgivings didn't like she should be walking:
The sweat on her face looked like astonished eyes.

It was from humility that I thought hot-tempered she was:
By the pulse of grass was judged a blazing fire she was!

Weak and weary from love's journey, for repose I looked:
At every step, my own shadow for a bed I mistook.

The beloved's eyelashes my heart avoided until I died:
Averting the arrowhead of death so easy it thought!

Why you thought she would be faithful and gave your heart, Asad?
An unbeliever[1] you took for a person of faith—a mistake you made.

_____

[1] I.e., one who doesn't believe in true love, an infidel.

51

Commentary:

Regarding the second couplet: Just when the process of furbishing a steel mirror is started first a line is formed on its surface that only disappears at the end of the process when it becomes highly polished. The line so formed is straight like the shirt's breast, and rending the shirt's breast is a sign of passionate love. The mirror is a metaphor for the heart. Polishing the mirror is a metaphor for cleaning the heart of all its murkiness so that nothing remains but the passion of love. The point the poet is making is that it is a life-long process, and the progress is frustratingly slow: begun at an early stage of life, it has to continue to the end.

Couplet 5: "The pulse of grass" in the second line symbolizes "humility" in the first.

[36]

My weeping eyes again I remember;
Again my heart is athirst for lamentation.

The doomsday hardly had a pause yet;
The time I bade adieu to her again I remember.

Look at the naïvete of my desire!
She of magical glances again I remember.

Accept my plea of helplessness, O my heart's regrets!
Laments I was about to make that my liver I remembered.

Life somehow would have passed;
Why did your street I remember?

What an interesting fight with Rizwan[1] I will have
When, in Heaven, your house I will remember!

Ah! When does it have the courage to complain?
Getting weary of the heart, my liver I remember.

Again to your alley goes my thought;
My lost heart it seems to remember.

Ah this desolation! What a desolation it is!
Seeing the desert my house I remember.

In my childhood, to hit Majnoon, O Asad,
Just as I picked up a stone, my head I remembered.

Commentary:

Couplet 2: The poet felt devastated when he had to bid farewell to his beloved; he felt as if the doomsday were here and now. This feeling had hardly abated—there was hardly a let up in the doomsday-like feeling—that he remembered the parting time again, and again he was overwhelmed by the same feeling of wretchedness. This wave of the feeling of misery continued to devastate him. These two lines conjure up the whole scene before the reader's mind's eye. Most people go through such an experience and they would know how true is this imagery.

Couplet 4: If the desires cannot be fulfilled at least the regrets should find expression. But, no, even this is not possible: the liver cannot sustain the effort, so worn out is it by woes and afflictions. The heart and the liver are generally interchangeable terms, but if a distinction is made the heart is considered the

---

[1]For Rizwan see the commentary on couplet 1 of ghazal 10.

seat of passion, and the liver of fortitude, patience, and courage, as noted earlier in the commentary on couplet 2 of ghazal 31, but it is totally exhausted and may even collapse, and, consequently, even though the pain is insufferable, lamentation is not possible: a picture of helplessness. (This distinction between heart and liver has also been used in couplet seven of this ghazal to berate the heart.)

[37]

You are late, but what could be the reason for this?
You were coming but was someone drawing in the reins?

Unfair is my complaint to you for my misery;
Some foul role my fate too played in this!

If you have forgotten me I give you this clue:
Did you ever hang a game from your saddle-strap?

For your mad lover it's the same in the prison, remembering your tresses!
True, some vexation from the weight of chains he also suffers.

A lightning flashed before my eyes, but was that all I wanted?
She should have talked, as for her words too I thirsted.

I called her Joseph and she said nothing; it was just as well.
Had she become angry, I fully deserved her chastisement.

Seeing my rival thus, how wouldn't I feel gratified?
Lamentation he was making but efficacy it lacked!

No disgrace attaches to his profession; don't give Farhad a nickname:
Dying in his prime, one of us mad lovers he, too, was!

I was ready to die and if she didn't come close unto me, so be it;
But, didn't the playful one have an arrow in her quiver to shoot me with?

Unjustly are we faulted on the basis of what the angels write;
At the time of recording was a representative of ours present?

Of Urdu poetry you alone aren't the master, Ghalib;
It is said in the time gone by Mir, too, was another one.

Commentary:

Couplet 3: The hunters used to hang their games by the saddle-strap of their horses. The beloved is the hunter and the poet is the one who was the game. He creates this imagery to convey the sense of the lover's constancy and helplessness and the beloved's cruel indifference.

Couplet 6: As the Prophet Joseph is traditionally considered as beauty incarnate, the poet compared his beloved to him, but soon he realized that he had made a mistake, for his beloved was far more beautiful than Joseph.

Couplet 7: Two things make the poet happy. First, that all the clever maneuverings of his rival have failed and he is now reduced to making lamentation. Second, the sure knowledge of the poet tells him that however much his rival may wish for his laments to have an effect, it will not, for it was not from a heart afflicted with true passion, and, in any case, the efficacy of lamentation is suspect.

Couplet 9: It is an expression of the poet's desire to die for no other cause but love and at the hands of his beloved. So if for some reason she was hesitant to come near unto him she could use her arrow. Here as always in Ghalib, the desire for death symbolizes complete devotion to, and readiness to lay down one's life for, the "beloved." (Keeping the ghazal tradition in our minds, his beloved could have killed the poet with the deadly weapons of her airs and graces, her coquetry and blandishments or just by her sheer beauty if she had come near unto him, and from a distance by casting a full glance at him—the arrow in her quiver. The poet was denied both.)

Couplet 10: It is generally held among Muslims that God appoints two angels for every human being, one to record his good deeds and the other the bad ones. Nothing escapes Ghalib's wit. He raises a question based on human jurisprudence: how can a one-sided testimony without witnesses from the other side form the basis of a just decision? Also, how can a human be judged by the standards of angels?

Couplet 11: While admitting the importance of Mir in Urdu poetry, Ghalib, by a clever choice of words, subtly makes the point that he remains the master. First, "it is said" suggests that it is not an agreed and accepted proposition, Ghalib himself not agreeing or disagreeing. Second, "Mir, too, was another one" has a ring about it of being a rather vague and tentative statement. (Muhammad Taqi Mir (1723-1810), born in Agra, India, lived most of his life in Delhi and in his last days in Lucknow, where he died when Ghalib was thirteen years old. He is considered one of the greatest masters of Urdu poetry. Mir left behind six volumes of the collections of his Urdu poetic works. He also wrote Persian poetry.)

[38]

The parched lips of those who died of thirst am I;
For those grieved in heart the place of pilgrimage am I.

Complete hopelessness and complete distrust!
The heart of the victims of feigned fidelity am I.

56

A friend of nobody you ever became, O oppressor!
But the pains you inflicted on me, others weren't made to suffer.

Like Nakhshab's moon, the hand of destiny left it deficient:
In radiance, the sun had not become her equal yet!

Divine favour in the measure of courage since eternity is:
The drops not content to be pearls, find their place in the eyes.

Till such time I hadn't seen the beauty of the beloved's figure,
In the commotion of the Judgement Day I didn't believe.

I, the simple-hearted, at the beloved's displeasure am happy;
This because it gives the hope that the lessons in love be repeated.

The ocean of sins from the scantiness of water became dry:
Even the hem of my garment's skirt hadn't become wet yet.

My heart's burning spot, Asad, has long been the seed of fire;
The fireplace hadn't yet become the fief of the salamander.

Commentary:

Couplet 2: Nakhshab was a city near Samarqand in Uzbekistan, now known as Qarshi. Hakim bin Ata, aka Muqanna, lived there. He claimed prophethood and, according to the legend, to bolster his claim, among other things, he made something that looked like the moon in shape, but less than a poor comparison to it in brightness and the area over which it was visible. The poet compares the sun to Nakhshab's moon to make the point that his beloved is a perfect, radiant beauty, in contrast to the sun which was left incomplete by the destiny's hand as was Nakshab's moon by its maker.

Couplet 3: To find a place in the eyes is to be held in the greatest honour and adored, an allusion to the teardrops in the eyes.

Couplet 6: The phrase "skirt becoming wet or moist" (in Urdu, *daman tar hona*) means sin or sinning, in which sense it is primarily used here. However, by a witty play on its literal meaning, as Ghalib often does, he uses the imagery of the ocean and the fringe of the garment's skirt to create a vivid sense of the vast possibilities of sins (water in the ocean) as being insufficient for the desire for and the pleasure of sins, the ocean not wetting even the margin of the garment's skirt.

Couplet 7: The fire of love in the human heart has pre-existed the mythological salamander. The salamander thrives in fire, as does the human heart in the fire of love, but then, the myth of the salamander is a much later development.

[40]

The night when the party illumining was sitting coy in her chamber,
Like a thorn in its side was the wick of every candle in the chandelier.

For miles on end from the place of the lover's martyrdom the henna grows;
O Lord, how he yearned to kiss his beloved's feet that its martyr he became!

The outcome of love I haven't seen but in the defeat of desire;
Heart to heart joined, as if they were lips saying: "Ah me!"

How to describe the freedom from want the pining from love brought;
My own life-blood that I consumed without obligation to chyme was!

Commentary:

Couplet 2: The phrase "to kiss (one's) feet" (in Urdu and Persian *pa bose*) means, figuratively, to adore someone, which is the primary sense here. But the poet, at the same time, uses the literal meaning to create dramatic scenes. The lover wanted to kiss his beloved's feet as a mark of adoration. This ardent desire remained unfulfilled, which ultimately killed him. He became a martyr for love. From his blood grew henna. The lover hopes that one day the beloved will use this henna to adorn her feet and thus what he desired in his lifetime would finally be accomplished after his death. (The henna leaves, when ground and applied on palms and feet, dye them red.)

Couplet 3 While uttering "Ah me!" the lips join, but as soon as they join they separate.

Couplet 4: "Consuming one's own life-blood" (vexing or worrying oneself to death, in Urdu, *khun-e-dil* or *khun-e-jigar pina* or *khana*) as a consequence of the pain of love (non-fulfillment of love's desires) brought freedom from the needs of physical nourishment involving chyme and chyle.

[41]

Seeing herself in the mirror she was struck with embarrassment:
That she never lost her heart to anyone, how proud she had felt!

With your own hand don't smite the messenger's neck;
His fault it was not, it was my mistake.

[42]

To make offerings to love I am not able anymore:
The heart I was proud of, it isn't the same anymore.

I go away carrying with me the wounds of the regrets of life:
A candle snuffed out, suitable for the assembly I am not anymore.

For death, O heart, think of some other way;
Worthy of the hand and arm of the killer[1] I am not anymore.

On all the six sides are open the doors of the mirror;
Here no distinction remains between the saint and the sinner.

From the desire for manifestation the Beauty has undone its veil;
Other than the eyes no other barrier remains anymore.

Though pawned to the afflictions of the world I have been,
But remiss in remembering you I have never been.

From my heart gone is the desire to cultivate loyalty;
No other yield than the yield of grief I expect anymore.

Of the oppression of love I am not afraid, but, Asad,
The heart I was proud of, that heart is not the same anymore.

Commentary:

Couplet 4: The mirror is a metaphor for the world; it is also a metaphor for truth, inasmuch as it shows up everyone and everything exactly as they are, and while there may be a distinction, as between the saint and the sinner, the mirror, that is, the world, will give a place to each one of them with complete impartiality. It can also be interpreted to mean that though in this mirror—the world—is reflected the Truth, but both the deficient and the excellent, the sinner and the saint, are so wonder-struck by it that they both fail to see beyond

---

[1]The killer, i.e., the beloved.

the appearances. So, at a deeper level, the distinction between the so-called excellent and the deficient disappears. If, however, the mirror is taken to be a metaphor for the poet's heart then it would mean that he has reached a stage in his spiritual journey where it has received illumination, changing the entire perspective of his perceptions. In this altered state, the mirror of his heart makes no distinction between the sinner and the saint, suggested by the doors of the mirrors being open on all the sides: he is now a universal soul.

[43]

Jealousy tells me that, alas, she is sincere to my rival,
Reason says: "When can the loveless one be in love with anyone?"

Every particle here[1] is in revolution, as a goblet in a tavern:
Majnoon's wanderings in the desert follows Laila's winks!

Love and ardour provide the means of pride to the powerless:
A dust particle has potentials of the desert, a drop of water the ocean's!

It is I and this calamitous piece that my wild heart is—
A friend of wandering and enemy of comfort and ease!

Let us not, from mistrust, complain to each other:
My knee is my solace-giver, and your companion the mirror.

Bound only by the string of wildness are the elements of spring:
The grass an alien, zephyr a wanderer, and flower a stranger!

---

[1] I.e., this world.

61

The mountain-cutter,[1] Asad, was just a sculptor of Shireen's portrait:
If one took enough pains wouldn't one make out of stone a sweetheart?

Commentary:

Couplet 3: The poet here is talking of the possibilities that lie hidden in every human soul, however humble, which can be actualized by the ardour of love as the motive force. The particles of dust carry within them the inherent possibility of becoming a desert and the drops of water an ocean—alluded to here as examples.

Couplet 6: "Wildness" is a metaphor for the apparent freedom of the elements ("bound by the string of wildness" = sharing in common the characteristic of wildness), which nonetheless are bound by an ultimate meaning and purpose ("spring"). The self-growing grass, the zephyr, and the flowers apparently do what is inherent in them, but the total effect is spring, which is the purpose. (It is interesting to note that in the backdrop of chaos and "wildness" ("alien," "wanderer," and "stranger") emerges peace, tranquility, and the beauty of spring ("grass," "zephyr" and "flower").)

[44]

Praise and glorification of the fairy-faced, and that, too, in my words!
He became a rival of mine—he who once my confidant was.

O my Lord! Why did she drink so much wine in the stranger's party?
Had it to be this very night when her threshold she wanted to test?

A viewing-platform on a higher plane I could have made;
Would that beyond the empyrean my abode I had!

---

[1] I.e., Farhad.

However he disgraces me, I will take it lightheartedly:
Her sentinel, it turns out, is an acquaintance of mine.

For how long to keep writing of my heartache! Let me go and show
My fingers wounded, my pen dripping blood.

By constant rubbing your doorsill would have been effaced;
In vain, from shame, you replaced it for I touched it with my forehead.

So that against me backbiting he may not do before my friend[1],
I have made my enemy[2] speak my language when complaining of her.

When in wisdom did I excel! In what art was I unique!
Without cause, O Ghalib, why the heaven became my enemy?

Commentary:

Couplet 6: The lover, in his ardour, bows and touches with his forehead the doorsill of his beloved's house, an act of adoration, *sijda* or *sajda*. The beloved, from contrariness, imagines it would bring her shame and gets the doorsill replaced, as if the lover's *sijda* had left a mark on it. At this the lover tells the beloved that there was no need for her to do that, for his constant *sijda* was in any case going to efface it, thus subtly suggesting that he would continue to do *sijda* at the new doorsill. In a word, love cannot be bent, suppressed or discouraged from pursuing its purpose even by the most unhelpful act or the harshest opposition.

---

[1]Friend = beloved.
[2]Enemy = rival.

I am a free gift of collyrium and my recompense is this:
An abiding benefit for his eyes whosoever avails of it!

Grant me leave to make laments, O tormentor,
Lest your countenance show my hidden sorrows!

Commentary:

Couplet 1: Collyrium (*surma* in Urdu and Persian) is thought to improve the eyesight and make vision clearer. Here it is used metaphorically in the sense that it is an agent for bringing about deeper and clearer insight which Ghalib's poetry would do for the reader. His poetry is available to everybody who takes the trouble of reading it (using this collyrium). Ghalib would be content to know that people are benefiting from his poetry: this would be his recompense. There is also a subtle suggestion that as the eyesight is a free gift of God to man so is Ghalib's poetry a free gift of insight to his readers.

Couplet 2: The poet's beloved—his tormentor—showed her displeasure when he made laments. The poet says that if he is not allowed to give vent to his feelings it would make him sick, which would affect her, too, and which her face would show, her indifference towards him notwithstanding. The poet is making two points: first, that his emotional pain is too great not to be given vent to, so great indeed that it would make him sick if he continued to hold it in—and, secondly, under no circumstance would he like to see his beloved unhappy, which would be the consequence if he continued to keep his sorrows under the lid, making him sick. Or it can be said that the couplet is about extreme sufferings of the lover's heart.

[46]

The thoughtless ones take false pride in their self-adornment;
Here even the crest of grass isn't without the comb of the zephyr!

From the drinking party don't expect pleasure, for
Merriment is the escaped game of this place of snares.[1]

Divine mercy might receive favourably my sense of shame deep—
The shame that keeps me from offering any excuses for my sins.

To the place of execution with what joy I proceed that
The thought of wounds fills with roses the valley of sight!

Asad lives on his desire to die by your ardent look:
The moth is his advocate pleading for justice from you.

Commentary:

Couplet 1: The poet is saying that whatever success man achieves in this world through endeavours is made possible with the help and aid of the Unseen. Thus, man is completely mistaken in giving the entire credit to himself, which makes him self-conceited. The poet adduces the example of grass and its beauty as a proof: even the humble grass, in beautifying itself and adding to its charm, receives a helping hand from the gentle, invisible breeze.

Couplet 5: "The moth" in the second line is, by Urdu and Persian literary convention, an ardent lover of the candlelight, burning in its flame, and thus best fit to represent the poet's case before his beloved about his desire to burn

---

[1]"The place of ensnares" i.e., this world as we know it, and "the drinking party" is one of the esnares.

65

by the heat of her ardent glance. (Also see the commentary on couplet 3 of ghazal 82.)

[47]

Oppression she has renounced, but what a renunciation!
Says she now: "How can I show my face to you, how can?"

Night and day, the seven heavens are in revolution,
So why worry? A change for the good may very well happen!

Had she shown hostility even, that as attention I would have taken;
But when there is neither why be under any illusion!

Why am I going all the way with the messenger?
O my God! Am I going to deliver my letter in person to her?

Even if a river of blood flows rising above my head,[1]
Am I going to move from the door of my beloved?

All my life for death I have been waiting:
Let me see what He shows when I am dead.

How strange that *she* is asking who is Ghalib!
Someone here tell me what's there to tell her!

[48]

The spirit without matter manifest cannot be:
The blooming garden the coating of the mirror of spring breeze is!

---

[1] I.e., even if it brings untold disaster.

A counterpoise to the river in flood the composure of shore cannot be:
When you are the cupbearer vain is the claim of sobriety.

Commentary:

Couplet 1: The Urdu/Persian word *latafat*, used by Ghalib in the first line of the couplet refers to something that is extremely subtle, fine, pure and abstract, and therefore beyond human perception; it has been translated as "spirit" which encompasses all these senses. The other key word is *kasafat*, which means impurity, density, thickness, grossness, which has appropriately been rendered as "matter." In the first line of the couplet the poet postulates the thesis that the spirit can make itself manifest only through something material or physical. In the second line he gives an example as proof: the spring breeze—ethereal, incorporeal, and transparent—makes itself manifest through the medium of garden which is a form of matter. It may as well be put this way, which would be closer to the text, that the spring breeze which is transparent like glass becomes a mirror with the flowering of the garden, as if it were its coating, and thus makes itself manifest, reflecting the spring in its glory. The couplet as a whole can be read to mean that God created the entire material world to make some aspect of Himself manifest, or to hide in or behind it.

[49]

The pleasure for a drop of water is to be absorbed in the sea:
The pain when it exceeds all limits becomes its own remedy!

It was written in my fate that, like a combination lock,
When the thing would work out, separated we would be.

The heart, in the struggle to cure it of its affliction, died:
As constant attempts at undoing the knot wears it off, it died.

O my God! O my God! Oppression even I am now being denied!
How can she become such a great foe of such a loyal friend!

From exhaustion, my weeping has changed into sighs:
Now I know how water into air turns.

From my heart to erase the thought of your hennaed fingers
Is like separating from the flesh the fingernails.

To me it is like the clearing of the vernal cloud after rain—
To die while shedding the tears of grief of separation.

If the scent of the flower doesn't long for you,
Why does it follow the breeze like dust to waft in your alley?

So that the miracle of the desire for polish is to you revealed,
Look at the mirror how in the rainy season it turns green.

The flowers' splendour, Ghalib, creates the taste for nature's wonders;
Let's keep our eyes open and appreciate the changing colours.

Commentary:

Couplet 4: Two words, "even" and "now" in the first line are critical to the understanding of this couplet. They clearly suggest that the nature of the relation between the poet and his beloved has undergone changes in the recent past. Earlier she used to reciprocate his love by showing her pleasure in his company. This changed into annoyance and vexation, which naturally tormented the poet. But with this he could live, for even oppression was a sign that the beloved was still emotionally engaged with him, though negatively. But when she started to totally ignore him as if he did not exist, it completely devastated the poet, who cried out in anguish and surprise: "How can she become such a great foe of such a loyal friend!"

Couplet 8: The beloved is so delightfully fragrant, the poet is suggesting, that the fragrance of flowers is trying to get near her in order to partake of some of its richness: that is why it is floating with the breeze in her alley.

Couplet 9: Every created thing in this world, the poet says, is motivated by a desire to be its best, free from all blemishes, shining with merit that is there in it. This desire works miracles. Look, for instance, at the steel-mirror. In the rainy season it turns green (false verdigris forms on it), making known its desire to be cleaned and polished bright and thus attracting the attention of the polisher. But who is the polisher? The beloved, divine or human. Though the beloved or the polisher is not specifically mentioned as such, nor is the lover, but in the ghazal context and in the context of this couplet it is an obvious and absolutely legitimate assumption. So the mirror here is a metaphor for the lover, and the polisher for the beloved. The mirror desires polish and desires it so intensely that it acquires rust (false verdigris) in the rainy season to get the beloved's attention and thus achieves its purpose. The rust on the steel mirror may as well be taken as a metaphor for the lover's wounds caused by his intense ardour, comparable to stigmata in some devout persons in a state of intense religious fervour, which, too, will attract the beloved's attention. (For the idea of comparison between the lover's wound caused by the intensity of his desire and the stigmata, I am indebted to Shamsur Rehman Faruqi's *Tafheem-e Ghalib*, Ghalib Institute, New Dehli, 2005.) In a word, if the desire is genuine and passionate, its magic is going to work.

Again it is time for the wave of wine to spread its wings,
The time when the wine's wave empowers the wine boat to swim.

About the cause of intoxication of the garden plants, don't ask me!
Passing through the vinery, the breeze becomes the wave of wine.

He who is drowned in wine, he it is who really lucky is;
Passing over the head, the wave of wine becomes Huma's wings.

The rainy season is that season when a strange happening it won't be
If, by the breeze's bounty, the wave of life becomes the wave of wine.

All around, four waves rise from the flood of festivity:
The flower's wave, twilight's wave, zephyr's wave, wave of wine!

To the extent that plant life thirsts for growth and grace and beauty,
With the draughts of the water of life satisfy it the wave of wine.

Turning into lifeblood it courses through the veins of vine:
On the wings of colour is racing the wave of wine.

The wave of flowers has illuminated the pathway of thought:
In the imagination is fully manifested the wave of wine.

In the guise of intoxication it is they lost in watching the mind,
Such great concern for its development has the wave of wine.

In a beautiful state is the rollicking enjoyment of the season,
From the wave of verdure to the wave of wine.

The interpreter of life's tumults is it; how wonderful is springtime!
The drop's guide to the sea, how blessed is the wave of wine!

Seeing the splendour of flowers, my senses are taking leave of me, Asad!
Again it is time for the wave of wine to spread its wings.

Commentary:

This ghazal celebrates the rainy season (from the middle of June to the middle of September), which, according to Ghalib, is springtime in India. The entire ghazal is marked by movements of one kind or the other. The term "wave" has been used also as a visible symbol of inner movements of exhilaration, excitement, and exuberance that pervade the whole atmosphere of this ghazal.

Couplet 1: The rainy season is here again, and it is time for wine parties. The picture presented is of such a party on the poolside. The wine has been poured from the bottles (the wave of wine has spread its wings) into a duck-shaped floating decanter (wine boat), which is swimming in the pool. From this "wine boat" the merry-makers sitting on the poolside will help themselves. [Before the wine boat was filled with wine, it was sitting idle on the poolside. It was set into motion (swimming in the pool) only when it was filled with wine (empowered by wine).]

Couplet 3: Huma is a fabulous bird. In Asia it is generally regarded as a bird of happy omen. It is supposed to fly constantly, never touching the ground. Any head that may come under the shadow of its wings will in time wear a crown. Idiomatically, "drowned in wine" means drinking too much, which is the primary sense here. But its literal meaning is also exploited: one drowned in water would die, but drowned in wine one would be lucky—the wave of wine will become the wings of Huma.

Couplet 6: "The draughts of the water of life," i.e., the rainwater of the rainy season infusing life in plants. And this is also the time of the year for the wine parties, the wave of wine, vide the opening couplet of this ghazal and the commentary thereon.

Couplet 8: The waves of flowers is a metaphor for the wave of wine as well as the illumination. In the poet's imagination is manifested the wave of wine like the rows of flowers, illuminating thought.

[51]

Ah! The heavens made them the food for worms,
Those whose fingers had deserved the strings of pearls.

Enough for me is this memento—your not giving me a ring—
And at the parting time, showing your finger without a ring.

I write powerful poetry, Asad, from a heart full of ardour,
So nobody at a single word of it can point his finger.

[52]

Even if somebody till Day of Judgement lives,
One day he has to die: Long live His Highness!

Love that thrives on my blood greets my liver:
"Long live the lord of bounty!"

A martyr of loyalty am I, my enemy's ill will notwithstanding:
Congratulations for a life of eternal bliss! Congratulations!

If the ability to comprehend Reality one doesn't have, so be it.
Long live the spectacle of changing, miraculous appearances!

[53]

I was trying to keep my eyes open but they closed, Ghalib;
My friends brought her to my bedside, but at what time!

Commentary:

The expressions *to keep the eyes open* and *the eyes closed* when used
metaphorically, as here, mean to live and die, respectively.

[54]

With the appearance of down went down my friend's[1] popularity,
As if an extinguished candle's smoke were the down on my friend's face.

Restrain your desire, O heart, oblivious of the consequence!
Who has ever withstood the glory of the beloved's countenance?

See the spectacle of ruin my state of wonder brought to my home!
Bewitched by the beloved's graceful gait like a footprint I became.

Because of love, by the tyranny of jealousy of my rival I died:
Lovelorn because of the beloved, but because of the enemy I died!

---

[1] Friend is *dost* in Urdu and Persian, which means a friend, one beloved, the beloved, a lover, or a
sweetheart.

73

My eyes have lighted up, seeing my oppressor delighted:
My eyes brimming with blood are wineglasses for my beloved!

While separated from my beloved, my rival inquires after me
As if a frank friend he were, commiserating with his friend.
So that I would know that to her he has access,
He delivers the message that to see me has promised my beloved.

When I complain of the decrepit state of my mind,
He starts the story of the ambergris-scented tresses of my beloved.

Silently and quietly I weep, and if he happens to see me thus,
He laughs and describes the sprightliness of speech of my beloved.

Should I complain of the kindness I receive from my enemy,
Or praise my beloved for the pleasure of pain she causes?

This ghazal of mine I like with all my heart, Ghalib, because
In every couplet is repeated the word "friend" or "beloved"!

Commentary:

Couplet 1: Shamsur Rehman Faruqi has given a very perceptive appreciation of this couplet in his *Tafheem-e Ghalib*. Apparently, the couplet is derogatory of the beloved ("my friend"), but, as Faruqi rightly points out, a closer look will reveal that, in fact, it mocks the false, untrue lovers who gravitate toward the beauty of the face, and, as it starts fading with time, they withdraw and disappear from the scene. But not so the true lover who remains steady in love (suggested by the phrase, "my friend") in whose behalf the poet is speaking. Thus the couplet is satirical of the sham lover, not the beloved. It may be added here that though expressed differently and in a different context its spirit it is like Shakespeare's,

Love's not Time's fool, though rosy lips and cheeks
Within his bending sickle's compass come.
(From his sonnet 116, "Let me not to the marriage of true minds.")

[55]

In the garden, arrangements of a different kind have been made today;
The turtledove has been turned out and the door is locked against it today.

A piece of heart I cough up every time I make laments:
Effectiveness is a prey of the string of breath's nooses today.

O peace and comfort, be to one side! O order of things, be gone!
The flood of tears is after the walls and doors of my house today.

Commentary:

Couplet 1: Very special arrangements have been made in the garden for the poet's beloved's visit to ensure privacy and exclusiveness. Even the turtledove, a bird of the garden known for its plaintive cooing and love for the mate, has been turned out and is not allowed entry: an indirect way of speaking of the grandeur and greatness and indifference of the beloved. Some Ghalib scholars, however, give it a political interpretation. According to them the couplet is about Bahadur Shah Zafar, the last Mughal emperor and a poet, who was confined to Delhi and the Red Fort while arrangements were being made by the British to occupy the garden of India.

Couplet 2: This couplet is in an ironical mode. If somebody had thought that the poet's (the lover's) laments would make of the beloved's heart a prey he was mistaken. Quite the contrary has happened. Imagine the poet's string

75

(series, successions) of breath (laments) as a string with nooses of which the pieces of his own heart are the preys (effectiveness of laments), which he is bringing up with every breath. In short, the poet's laments have indeed proved effective, but in a quite contrary way than expected.

[56]

Lo! I become the attendant on the lovesick one and call in the Messiah,
But if cure he can't work, of his healing power what will be said?

Commentary:

The "Messiah" is Jesus Christ in his aspect of the healer. But for lovesickness there is no cure (the central idea of this couplet), and not even the Messiah will be of any help. So calling on him will only have the consequence of calling into question his healing power.

[57]

Not a single breath outside the company of hope and desire you take;
If wine[1] is presently not there, for a round of drinks you wait.

Of the extent of my fervent efforts to find a perceptive mind don't ask me!
The marks of merits in my mirror[2] be removed as thorns in my sides.

---

[1]"Wine" stands for the object of "hope and desire" (in the first line of this couplet).
[2]"Mirror" is a metaphor for the poet's heart, the source of his poetic genius with all its virtues. The mirror is a steel-mirror and its polishing streaks, "the marks of merits," have been compared to thorns in the poet's side, which are hurting him. Why hurting? Because people are wanting in perception to truly appreciate his poetry. Ghalib, it seems, is indirectly suggesting what Rousseau said in so many words that he did not know the art of making himself intelligible to those who were not attentive. But, then, Ghalib's imagery is very powerful—a telling satire.

For you, waiting is an excuse for ease, O heart!
Whoever guided you to the blandishments of the bed?

Towards you[1] is looking the narcissus with longing;
May the enemy[2] be blind in eyes and heart! Enjoy the drink.

By a glance render me my due for holding your apathy in trust;
From the sheath of my heart's wound withdraw your dagger[3]!

In my goblet[4] is the wine in which is hidden fire[5],
Bring for me for repast the salamander's baked heart.

[58]

Beauties are free from the trouble of coquetry when I am no more;
All at once the tormentors are quiet when I am no more.

Now there is none worthy of the demanding office of a lover;
The amorous ways and graces have been dethroned when I am no more.

When the candle is extinguished, from it rises smoke:
The flame of love is clothed in black when I am no more.

At the circumstance of the beauties my heart bleeds in the grave;
Their fingernails are in want of henna when I am no more.

---

[1] "You" refers to the beloved.
[2] "Enemy" refers to the narcissus, in the first line of this couplet.
[3] "Dagger" refers to "apathy" in the first line.
[4] "Goblet" stands for heart.
[5] "Fire," i.e., fire of love.

To display the art of oppression now there isn't a proper place:
The beauties' eyes have no use for the collyrium when I am no more.

Love's intoxication is bidding farewell to the people in love;
Rending is parting with shirts' breasts when I am no more.

Who wants to drink the wine of love of overwhelming strength?
A second time is this call on the cupbearer's lips when I am no more!

I die of grief that there is none in this world to mourn
The passing away of love and loyalty when I am no more.

At the forlornness of love I cry, Ghalib!
Where is this deluge of calamity to find its home when I am no more?

Commentary:

This whole ghazal is about the poet's unrivalled passion of love and how the entire love-scene has changed when he is dead.

Couplet 4: In the first line of this couplet, the phrase "my heart bleeds" is used in the idiomatic sense of grief, sorrow and suffering. In the second line this term is carried forward in a kind of its literal sense without actually using it. When the poet lived, the beauties painted their fingernails with his heart's blood. Now they have to use henna when he is no more. The second line can also be read to mean that the beauties are mourning the poet's death, suggested by not wearing the henna, a sign of mourning.

Couplet 5: Collyrium (*surma* in Urdu and Persian) is used as mascara (besides its medicinal use to sharpen eyesight) that makes the eyelashes, and thus the glances, strikingly beautiful and attractive. But the fair one's eyes have no use for this when the poet—the great lover—is dead. (It may be added here, though not applicable in the context of this couplet, that collyrium (*surma*) comes in the form of powder and it is reputed that it causes loss of voice if ingested.)

[59]

Never mind if hindering my sight are the doors and walls;
For my viewing ardour, wings and feathers are doors and walls.

The torrent of tears have so changed the aspect of my house
That the walls and doors have become the doors and walls.

They aren't shadows, rather hearing the glad tidings of my beloved's arrival,
A few steps forward have gone to greet her, the doors and walls.

How bountiful has become the wine of your unveiled face,
That on your street are drunk all the doors and walls!

If you want to see the wares of waiting, come out, O beloved!
The shops of the merchandise of gazing are your doors and walls.

Was it ever that I was ready to burst into a torrent of tears
And they did not fall at my feet, the doors and walls?

Now that she has moved to my neighbourhood, my doors and walls,
By their shadows, are showing devotion to her doors and walls.

Without you it hurts, the liveliness of my house;
I always sob and shed tears seeing my doors and walls.

Of the ecstasy of joy on the coming of the flood, don't ask me:
From end to end are dancing the doors and walls.

Don't tell anyone, Ghalib, for in this world there is none
With whom you can share secrets of love but the doors and walls.

[60]

Now that I have installed myself at your abode's threshold,
Even now won't you know where I live unless you are told!

Now she says this, when I am left with no strength to talk even:
"How can I know what in your heart is unless I am told?"

I have to deal with the one whose name, in this whole world,
Nobody mentions without calling her a tormentor in the same breath.

The thing is, no ill will I harbour in my heart, otherwise
Nothing could stop me from speaking out, not even if my head it cost.

Never will I give up worshipping that beloved infidel:
No matter if people won't stop short of calling me an infidel.

The idea is to describe her airs and graces and amorous glances,
But one can't do this faithfully without speaking of dagger and knife.

Even when speaking of the ecstatic experience of the vision of God,
One can't truly convey the sense except in terms of the intoxication of wine.

If I am deaf, as you say, then two-fold attention you need to pay:
If I can't make out what you say, over and again you have to say.

Don't keep repeating your submissions to His Majesty, Ghalib!
Your entire circumstance he knows even without your ever telling him.

[61]

Why didn't I burn up seeing the radiance of the beloved's face?
Now at the endurance of my vision from envy and anger I burn.

The people of the world call me a fire worshipper
Seeing that fire-raining laments I fervently make.

Where is love's honour when so indiscriminate is your oppression?
It gives me pause seeing you cause unmerited affliction.

She comes to kill me, carrying a sword in hand,
But I die of envy, seeing its closeness to her.

On the flagon of wine has been proven the peoples' blood;
Tremble the waves of wine seeing you walking drunk.

What a pity my beloved has stopped oppressing,
Seeing I was greedy for the pleasure of pain she was causing.

Along with the treasure of my poetry I, too, get sold,
But only if the buyer is blessed with the touchstone of taste.

Wear the sacred thread, break the hundred-bead rosary;
The traveller prefers to journey on a level pathway.

These blisters on my feet had made me wearied,
But seeing the way ahead is full of thorns, I am pleased.

What a misconception she has about me! In my mirror she sees
The false verdigris and thinks the reflection of a parakeet it is.

The lightning of Manifestation should have fallen on me, not Sinai:
The wine is poured keeping in view the imbiber's capacity.

That well-known event of love-mad[1] Ghalib breaking his head,
Seeing the wall of your house, instantly I remembered.

Commentary:

Couplet 5: The beloved's figure has an indescribable beauty that kills when she walks drunk. The responsibility for killing would lay with the flagon from which the wine was poured that made her drunk. Now, the flagon and with it the wine are trembling from the fear of blame.

Couplet 8: The word *zunnar* used by Ghalib means both the cord worn round the middle by Eastern Christians and Jews and Persian Magi, as well as the sacred thread worn across the shoulder by the Brahmins of India. In the translation the term "sacred thread" has been adopted, which is not to be taken to limit its meaning. Similarly, the rosary whether with a hundred beads (as in the couplet) used by Muslims, or with fifty-five beads used by Roman Catholics for devotional, meditative exercises, makes no difference to the basic sense of the couplet, which is that the religious rituals and externalities are of no significance. Remove the beads of the rosary and what remains is the thread, the inner core and truth in all religions. The "traveller" is the traveller on the path of truth and the thread of the rosary is the level pathway.

Couplet 10: This couplet is about the jealousy of the beloved. She wants nothing less than complete devotion from her lover. So when she sees the false verdigris in his steel-mirror she mistakes it for the reflection of a parakeet, and becomes suspicious that he has some other interest, too, besides her. Even a very minor thing—a parakeet—makes her jealous.

Couplet 11: Sinai is Mt. Sinai and the reference is to the Quranic version of the Biblical story of the burning bush (Exodus, 3:2). Chapter 7, verse 143 of the

---

[1] I.e., desperately in love.

82

Quran reads as follows: "And when Moses came (to Mt. Sinai) ... he said, 'O my Sustainer! Show (Thyself) unto me, so that I might behold Thee!' God said: 'Never canst thou see Me. However, behold this Mountain: If it remains firm in its place then—only then—wilt thou see Me.' And as soon as his Sustainer revealed His glory to the Mountain, He caused it to crumble to dust; and Moses fell down in a swoon."

There is also an implied reference to chapter 33, verse 72 of the Quran which reads: "Verily, We did offer the trust (of reason and volition) to the heavens, and the earth, and the mountain: but they refused to bear it because they were afraid of it. Yet man took it up ..." The verses of the Quran quoted here are from Muhammad Asad's translation, *The Message of the Quran* (Dar al-Andalus Ltd., Gibraltar, 1980). These references to the Quranic verses provide the conceptual basis and point to man's position in the universe. The poet, speaking for the human race, says that it was he who deserved and could withstand the "lightning of Manifestation," not the mountain, his lack of physical strength compared to the mountain notwithstanding: this because man accepted the challenges and responsibilities of using reason and the freedom of the will which no other creature of God dared. And while they bring with them onerous responsibilities, they also open up the possibilities of higher destiny for man as intended by God.

[62]

My heart trembles at the pains the radiant sun takes;
I am that dewdrop that on a tip of a thorn in a desert is.

Joseph didn't forsake adorning the place there even:
The white of Jacob's eyes moved over the walls of his prison.

I knew self-annihilation through lessons in the ecstasy of love
When Majnoon still wrote on the school-walls letters "N" and "O".

83

How free I would be from the anxiety of finding an ointment
If the pieces of my heart mutually agreed to share the salt!

In the realm of love there isn't one story of beauty's blandishments
Not bearing the seal of turning the eyes away after casting a glance.

Now I remember, seeing the cloud dyed red by the setting sun,
That, during your absence, it rained fire on the rose-garden.

Of the martyrs what will remain except longing for the beloved?
Judgement Day will be but a high wind scattering their grave's dust around.

Don't quarrel with the counselor, Ghalib; what if he caused distress?
After all, we, too, have the power to tear our shirts' breasts.

Commentary:

Couplet 2: The pronoun "his" in the second line refers to Joseph in the first.

Couplet 7: After death, the human body turns into dust, but one thing remains unchanged for the martyrs for love—their longing for the beloved. This will remain unaffected on Judgement Day that, like a high wind, will only help scatter their dust which will be of no consequence.

Couplet 8: The severity and persistence of the counselor's objections causes distress. But anger and argument won't avail against him. The better strategy will be to tear at one's own shirt's breast: it will show defiance and at the same time give release to the pent-up resentment. Essentially, the couplet has the undertone of irony: one pitted against a much superior power is often prone or forced to take actions that are really hurtful to one's own interests.

[63]

Because her every gesture has at once different significations,
Even when she means love I construe it as something else.

O Lord! She doesn't understand and she won't understand what I say;
Give her another heart if to me You don't give another tongue.

With her eyebrows what relation her glance can have!
The arrow is infallible but its bow is something else.

When you are in town what worry should I have?
Another heart, another life from the marketplace I will fetch.

However dexterous in breaking idols we may have become,
As long as we are, a ponderous stone will remain in our way.

Grieved, the blood is in tumult; to my heart's content I would have wept,
If a few blood-raining eyes in addition I had.

So desperately enamored of her voice am I that even if it kills me
I wish she goes on telling the flogger: "Yes, give him more of it."

People are deceived it is the world-illumining sun:
Everyday I bring into view a new hidden wound.

Hadn't I lost my heart to you, some moments of peace I'd have had;
Hadn't I died, laments for some more days I'd have made.

If the river is blocked, its water rises and forces its way out:
If my genius is thwarted, in a more powerful expression it finds its vent.

Indeed there are other fine poets too in this world,
But people say Ghalib's style is in a class by itself.

Commentary:

Couplet 3: Comparing the eyebrow with bow and the glance with arrow is an established convention of Urdu and Persian ghazal poetry. Ghalib is breaking with this convention here. He says that the infallible arrow of glances has nothing to do with the eyebrow; it comes from somewhere else—the total personality of the beloved—as much from the beauty of her soul as from her grace and charm, all of these subtly suggested by the expression "bow is something else."

[64]

The mirror's complacent wonder causes it to rust after all:
The stagnant water is covered with moss after all.

The things of luxury and grandeur couldn't cure me of madness;
The emerald wineglassful seemed like leopard-spots to me after all.

Commentary:

Couplet 1: The state of complacent wonder is a state of complete inaction when all movements stop. This is what happens to the mirror, a metaphor for the heart, in which is reflected the miracles of this world. Because of this state of complacency in wonder it fails in its basic motivational and inspirational functions resulting in inaction—rusting—, just as water if it stagnates instead of flowing gets covered with moss. (The metaphor of mirror is that of a steel-mirror.) It is not enough to experience wonder at the mysteries of the world; one is expected to be inquisitive and make efforts to understand these mysteries. The underlying sense of the couplet is an invitation to thought and action.

Couplet 2: "Madness," by established poetic convention, is to be madly, passionately in love with somebody (the beloved) or something (a high purpose in life). The provisions for a life of luxury and grandeur are not going to satisfy this passion. In the second line, the emerald wineglassful is a symbol of prosperity, pleasure and grandeur. But to the poet it seems as if it were leopard-spots, exciting wildness.

[65]

Who would extend a helping hand to madness except nakedness?
To my tattered shirt's breast I am beholden for its kindness.

Like paper set on fire is my strange agitation:
On every tremor's[1] wings are fastened a thousand heart's[2] mirror!

How stubbornly our lost luxuries we claim from the heavens,
As if the possessions plundered were debts the robbers owed to us.

She and I—she, angry without cause and enemy of friends,
Seeing the sunrays, blames the skylight for peeping eyes!

Annihilate the self if the truth about yourself you want to know;
The glory of its destiny, the trash in the furnace finds!

How strange a martyr Asad is that he prompts his killer:
"Continue your coquetry! For casualties I will answer in both worlds."

---

[1] I.e., tremor of agitation (in line one).
[2] I.e., the heart in agitation, referred to in the first line of this couplet.

[66]

Tyranny I endure as an expediency, for beauty's are in love with you:
Frankly, one of my rivals[1] will eventually be my ally someday.

[67]

You should have waited for my death for some more days;
Alone why did you go? Now stay alone for some more days.

My head will be destroyed if your tombstone won't wear off;
I will be beating my head at your grave for some more days.

Only yesterday you came and today you say you are going;
Well, if not forever, stay at least for some more days.

Departing, you say: "We will meet on Judgement Day."
How well said as if Judgement Day were some other day!

Listen, O old heaven, still young was Arif!
How could it hurt you if he lived for some more days?

You were the full moon of my house:
How come then you didn't show up for some more days.

When were you so prompt in paying your debt?
The angel of death could have dunned for some more days.

_____

[1]"Rivals" = "fair ones" in the first line.

Even if you hated me and with Nayyar you had a quarrel,
You should have seen your children playing for some more days.

After all, your time passed somehow—in happiness and in sorrow;
O you who died so young, you should have lived for some more days!

Ignorant are they who say: "Why is Ghalib still alive?"
It was fated that I keep wishing for my death for some more days.

Commentary:

This ghazal is, in fact, an elegy written on the death of Zainul Abidin Khan Arif (1817-1852), a nephew of Ghalib's wife whom Ghalib had adopted as his son, and who lived with him. He died at the young age of 35. Ziauddin Ahmad Khan Nayyar (mentioned in couplet 8) was a cousin of Ghalib's wife and the younger brother of the Ruler of Loharu, a principality in the province of Uttar Pradesh, India. Both Arif and Nayyar were poets. The mention of Arif's hatred for Ghalib and his quarrel with Nayyar have nothing to do with the facts of their relationships: it is just a fiction created as a background of supposed annoyances against which the pleasure of watching his children playing is to be seen.

[68]

Don't think I am disengaged, for, like the sun at dawn,
The wound of love still adorns the opening of my shroud.

The indigent ones show their pride in the wealth since gone:
I, too, yet display the mark of glory of my old wound of love.

Now in the tavern of my heart nothing is left, not even a drop;
But my beloved, given to oppressing, thirsts yet for the wine of blood.

Commentary:

Couplet 1: The imagery is of the poet speaking from his grave, suggested by "shroud." The sun is a metaphor for the wound of love (warm and bright) and "dawn" for the shroud (both being white). And as the sun is inseparable from dawn so is the wound of love from the shroud, symbolizing the afterlife. In a word, the passion of love is everlasting; it does not die with physical death in this world.

Couplet 3, line 2: Tyranny or oppression is supposed to thrive on the blood of its victim of which the poet (the lover) has none left in his heart (line 1 of the couplet), suggesting that he has for long been the victim of the beloved's oppression. The second line suggests that the beloved is used to and takes pleasure in oppressing her lover (thirsting for his blood/wine) as a drunkard would in drinking wine.

[69]

In achieving a difficult purpose doesn't work the magic of prayer:
May Khizr live a long life! O God, grant this prayer!

Don't wander vainly in the wilderness of conjectures about being;
If you do, still in your thought are the lows and highs.

True, union with the beloved is seeing beauty in splendour,
But who has the patience to keep shining the mirror of waiting?

Every particle of the lover's being is a worshipper of the sun:
Even as dust his passion for the beauty's glory is not gone.

Don't ask how great is the tavern of love-madness, Ghalib,
Compared to which this bowl of heaven is but a dustbin!

Commentary:

Couplet 1: Though Khizr is not mentioned in the Quran, Muslims generally
believe that he was a prophet who discovered and drank of the water of life.
The couplet is in a satirical mode.

[70]

See the extent of exertions to bestow bounties that from end to end
Traverses yet the cloud, its feet covered with blisters, raining pearls.

The entire desert is now like a sheet of paper burning:
In my footprints there yet is the heat of my fervent wandering!

[71]

How can I hold my life dearer than my idol?
Is my faith not dear to me?

Right through my heart it went, but not exactly;[1]
The head of your arrow is too dear to me!

There is no choice but to bear with it, Ghalib;
The calamity is grievous, but then, life is precious!

----

[1] I.e., its memory continues.

I am no sweet melody nor a note of the gamut am I;
The sound of my own breaking am I!

You there, arranging in style the ringlets of your tresses,
And here I, thinking anxious thoughts of things far and beyond.

The boast of self-possession is the deception of a simple heart;
It is I and the unsolved mysteries gnawing my bosom.

A prisoner of love of the fowler am I,
Not that I don't retain the strength to fly.

May that a day also comes when I enjoy
My tormentor's airs and graces rather than pine for them.

In my heart there hasn't been a drop of blood
With which, like a rose, haven't played my eyelashes.

O beloved! Your amorous glances are passion-exciting!
O tyrant! Your tyranny is amorous playfulness!

Welcome! At last you have shown up!
Congratulations to my long drawn out supplication!

If you inquired after me, not an awful thing you did!
You are the one kind to the needy and I the one in need.

Asadullah Khan's time has come to an end:
Ah, alas! What a rake and a lover he was!

Commentary:

Couplet 10: Asadullah Khan, i.e., Mirza Asadullah Khan Ghalib, the poet.

[73]

Glad tidings, O desire for captivity!
An empty snare I see beside the cage of the captive bird.

My heart's thirst for pain was never quenched,
Though at the root of every thorn a river of blood I bled.

Ah, alas! My eyes closed while still trying to open;[1]
What a time to come to your lovelorn one!

I wouldn't have had to suffer the agony of dying haltingly
Had my sympathizer used a sharp dagger instead of his sharp tongue!

Better go and sit in the mouth of a tiger, O heart!
But don't ever get near the heart-tormenting sweetheart.

Seeing you, with such exuberance the garden flourishes
That spontaneously the flower onto your coiffure reaches.

Died by breaking his head, that mad Ghalib; ah, alas!
How he used to come and sit by the wall of your house!

---

[1]See commentary on ghazal 53 which consists of only one couplet.

93

Hadn't the twigs of streaks derived freshness from the down on the face,
The glow of the beauty's face would have set on fire the hall of mirrors!

The beauty's light solves the lover's difficulties:
The candle couldn't get rid of the thorn[1] but for the flame.

Commentary:

Couplet 1: The streaks are the streaks on a highly polished steel-mirror that look like twigs. The glow on the face of the beauty would have set the twigs on fire and with it the hall of mirrors, had the twigs not received freshness from the down on the face of the beauty.

[75]

For the evening sun the rays of its light are its exit path;
By the new moon has heaven opened its arms for the parting embrace.

[76]

The beloved's radiant face makes the candle burn enduringly:
The flame of flower has become the elixir of life for the candle.

In the idiom of the masters of the language, silence is death;
This came to light in the party by the candle's tongue.

---

[1]"Thorn" is a metaphor for the candle's wick inasmuch as it pierces through and is supposed to hurt the candle.

Getting a sign from the flame it brings its life to an end:
Like mystics' self-annihilation is the story of the candle.

It is the grief at the affliction of the moth, O flame!
Your trembling shows that it has rendered the candle frail.

Just thinking of you creates in my soul the stir of mirth,
As a gentle wind makes the candle flame dance.

Of the joy of the blooming wound of love's grief, don't ask me:
With the candle's fall-affected flower desperately in love the spring is!

Seeing me at the bed-head of my beloved, with envy it is burning;
How, then, my heart won't bear the mark of mistrust for the candle?

Commentary:

Couplet 1: "The flame of flower" (*aatish-e gul* in the original) in the second line is a metaphor for the beloved's "radiant face" in the first line. While *gul* generally means flower, specifically it means rose—a red rose. The lighted candle symbolizes life and it is lighted because it is in love with the beloved, the source of its life.

Couplet 2: "Tongue" is a metaphor for the candle's flame which it resembles in shape and movement. Extinguishment of the candle's flame would be its virtual death and would result in the dispersal of the party as well.

Couplet 6: The "candle's fall-affected flowers" is a metaphor for "the wound of love's grief" (both flower, i.e., rose, and wound being red in colour) and it also means snuff, the burnt end of a candlewick. To elaborate, in the first line the poet speaks of the "wound" of love's grief in terms of its being like a damask rose in beauty and charm. In the second line he says that even if one denied or ignored this truth and compared it to the "candle's fall-affected

95

flowers," it won't make any difference, for the spring would still be madly in love with it (flowers bloom in the spring). In a word, the wound of love is a sign of life, and beauty and joy.

[77]

From the fear of the rival, of my senses I can't take leave:
Constrained to such an extent am I! O freedom of choice, what a pity!

My heart is in anguish why I didn't burn up instantly;
O insufficiency of my fire-raining breath, what a pity!

[78]

On my wounds, when the careless children would ever sprinkle salt!
What a pleasure it would be if the stone they hit me with contained salt!

For my heart's wound, the dust of the beloved's lane is a thing of pride,
Otherwise, in this world when is there a dearth of salt.

May it be granted as my portion and you remain ever blessed,
For me the nightingale's piteous trill, for you flowers' laughter!

On the seaside today whose galloping steed created such a tumult
That the seashore's dust, on the sea-waves' wounds, acted like salt?

How great! The wounds of my heart she appreciates
And remembers me wherever salt she sees.

Abandoning the wounded body of the lover! What a pity!
My heart demands more wounds and my injured limbs salt.

I won't have to be beholden to others for the increase in pain:
My wound, like the beloved's smile, is piquant to perfection.

Do you remember, Ghalib, those days when in the ecstasy of joy
With my eyelids I would pick up the salt dropping from my wounds.

[79]

For the sighs to have an effect, a lifetime is required:
Who will live that long that your curling locks are conquered?

A net with a hundred nooses of crocodiles' gullets every wave is;
Let us see what the sea-drop goes through before a pearl it becomes.

Love demands patience and desire is restless;
How to deal with my heart till the liver bleeds to death!

Granted you won't be neglectful of me, but
Before you would realize my condition I would be dust.

For the dewdrop, the light of the sun is a lesson in death:
I, too, exist till towards me a kindly look is cast.

Our time here, O heedless ones, is like a twinkle of the eyes:
The glow of the party lasts only till the dancing spark of fire.

For the sorrows of life who has a remedy, Asad, save death?
The candle, whatever the situation, keeps burning till daybreak!

[80]

If you believe that the prayers are answered, don't pray;
That is, other than for a heart without desire, don't pray.

Of my heart's countless wounds of regrets I am reminded;
O God! To render an account of my sins I better not be asked!

[81]

How madly in love with the illusion of constancy of flowers is it!
Seeing the nightingale's ways, flowers broke into laughter.

Congratulations to the fragrant air on its freedom!
Lying broken are the nooses of the net of desire for flowers.

One and all are completely enamored of the riot of colour;
Ah, alas! The bleeding moans on the roses' lips nobody hears!

How happy is the situation of the one dead-drunk with love,
Who, like a flower's shadow, is lying at the foot of the flower[1]!

For you alone spring creates it;
The scented breath of flowers my rival is.

In the spring season they cause me to feel shame—
My goblet without wine and my heart without desire for flowers!

_____

[1]Flower, ie., the beloved.

98

The majesty and awe of the splendour of your proud beauty
Have rendered vapid in my eyes the blandishments of flowers.

It is the delusion of your presence that to this day
The flowers are blossoming spontaneously one after the other.

O Ghalib! I yearn for her to be in my embrace
Whose thought even is an ornament for flowers.

Commentary:

Couplet 2: The first line of the couplet is in a sarcastic mode; the second is about the coming of autumn: the net of desire for flowers, of which the air has been a captive, has lost its function with the advent of fall (the nooses are lying broken—the flowers have wilted.).

[82]

The independent spirits for more than an instant don't grieve:
By the lightning I light the candle of my house of mourning!

The players of the game of cards of thought keep them shuffling:
In my mind, so many bewitching images I keep revolving.

Though a world of tumult am I but there is no outward sign:
Like the illumination in the chamber of the moth's heart am I!

From weakness, not contentment, is the forsaking of the quest:
For the trustworthiness of manly resolve a bane we are.

Incarcerated for life in it are hundreds of thousands of desires, Asad.
My heart is to me like a prison filled with their blood!

Commentary:

Couplet 3: The heart is the seat of passion and the chamber (i.e., the bedchamber) is a very private place, a recess to which no outsider can have access. So what happens in the bedchamber of the heart nobody can know, illuminated though it is with the passion of love, creating quite a tumult within. It becomes manifest only in action exemplified by the moth when it dies for the light of the candle. The poet says that his own situation is like that of the moth; in his heart, too, is a tumult of passion of which there is no outward sign. The beauty of the couplet is in the imagery created in the second line. (Also see the commentary on couplet 5 of ghazal 46.)

[83]

Making laments is gathering the yield of the bonds of love:
The valuables of the house of chains[1] are nothing but sounds[2]!

[84]

Away from my native country, in a foreign land I died;
God be praised! From the shame of forlornness[3] I was saved.

O my God! Those ringlets of her hair are lying in ambush;
May the honour of my claim of freedom from fetters be saved!

---

[1]"House of chains," i.e., "bonds of love" in the first line of this couplet.
[2]"Sounds," i.e., "laments" in the first line.
[3]I.e., "forlornness" (in the sense of abandoned or deserted) in one's own native country. The couplet is in a satirical mode.

[85]

From my sleeping fortune, sound sleep I would have borrowed
But, Ghalib, the trouble is how will I return the loan.

[86]

Where is now that pain of separation and where the joy of union!
Where are those nights and days and months and years?

Who has now the time for the affairs of heart?
Where is now that longing to catch the beauty's sight?

What to say of the heart, even the mind is not the same as of yore;
Where is now that clamour of desire for the beauty of face and figure?

It was because of somebody who was always in my thoughts;
When do I have that beauty and loveliness of imagination now?

It is not all that easy to weep tears of blood;
Where is the strength in my heart? When is my liver in its proper state?

The gaming-house of love I haunt no more:
If I go there, where is now the hard money to wager?

I now trouble my head only with worldly cares:
Where I and where these vexatious burdens!

My strength and vigour have wasted, Ghalib;
Where is now that balance in the elements!

Commentary:

Couplet 6: "Hard money" is a metaphor for the heart, which, like the mind, is not "the same as of yore" (couplet 3, line one, above).

[87]

When she keeps faith with me, my rivals call it tormenting:[1]
To call good people bad has always been the way of the world.

Today, of the miseries of my heart though I go to tell her,
But who can tell what will be said?

Simple souls of times gone by they are, don't argue with them—
Those who say wine and music steal away grief and anxiety.

It returns to my heart, the moment from swooning I get a respite;
If not this then what else is an efficacious lament!

Beyond the bounds of comprehension is the One I worship;
For the insightful people, the qibla is a compass pointing to Qibla.

Since the time that for my injured foot you felt pity,
The root of mandrake I call the thorns on the way.

There is a spark in my heart, why by it I be scared?
The flame is what I want, so I say air is what I need.

Let us see what troubles the sprightly one's aspiring pride is going to cause;
To whatever she says, I say: "May God preserve you from evil eyes!"

---

[1] I.e., tormenting by tantalizing.

Wahshat and Shefta may now write elegies;
People say that Ghalib of the soulful songs is dead!

Commentary:

Couplet 2: The second line of the couplet suggests the uncertainty of the outcome of the meeting with the beloved. One that could happen is that the lover would be so overwhelmed by the beauty and charm of the beloved and the joy of being face to face with her that he would not be able to say anything. But there is also the possibility that the beloved remains unaffected by whatever the lover says. In any case, there is no way to know how she will respond and what she will say. The word "though" in the first line sets up the mood of the couplet which is of perplexity, anxiety, and uncertainty.

Couplet 5: In the first line of the couplet the poet speaks of the One he worships as the One who is beyond human comprehension. Verse 103 of Chapter 6 of the Quran reads as follows: "No human vision can encompass Him, whereas He encompasses all human vision: for He alone is unfathomable, all-aware." The term "qibla" that occurs in the second line of the couplet is the Kaba in Mecca to which Muslims turn their faces at prayers. The poet says that the qibla is only a compass guiding to the real Qibla, the One he worships. In the words of the Quran (Chapter 2, verse 115), "God's is the east and the west: and wherever you turn there is God's countenance. Behold, God is infinite, all-knowing." (Both the verses of the Quran quoted here are from Muhammad Asad's translation, *The Message of the Quran*, Dar al-Andalus Ltd., Gibraltor, 1980.)

Couplet 9: Syed Ghulam Ali Khan Wahshat was a prominent personality of Delhi, and both he and Nawwab Mustafa Khan Shefta were friends of Ghalib and very good Urdu and Persian poets. Particularly Nawwab Musafa Khan Shefta (1806-1869) was one of Ghalib's closest and dearest friends.

[88]

What honour the flower would have if in the garden it weren't?
The shirt's breast be a disgrace for it if rent to its hem it weren't.

From exhaustion, O weeping, nothing is left in my body;
The blood that soaked through my shirt has also like colour vanished.

The constituents of the sun's sightline have gathered there;
In the skylights of her house, they are not the particles of dust.

How to say how dark the prison of sorrow is;
Not less than daylight would seem the cotton wool in its skylight!

The sparkle in life is from love that destroys homes:
The barn without lightning is a banquet without candlelight!

On getting my wounds stitched I am taunted for seeking remedy;
The rival thinks there is no pleasure in the needle piercing the wounds.

I am a martyr of the beloved's blooming airs and graces,
In my grave is no dust, only the splendour of flowers.

Every drop of my blood is the material for a new runny sore;
How can then I be free from the pleasure of pain![1]

The cupbearer's pride has been humbled by my limitless capacity:
Today the vein of the wave of wine is gone from the decanter's neck![2]

---

[1] Literally, "In my body, the blood even isn't free from the pleasure of pain."
[2] I.e., the decanter is empty (the vein of pride shown by the wave of wine in the decanter's neck, indicating it was full, was gone).

Squeezed from all the sides, how can weakness show itself?
My body doesn't have the ability even to bend itself.

What glory had I in my country, Ghalib, that in a foreign land be honoured?
Frankly, like a handful of straws am I that is not in the furnace.

[89]

Her infinite variety of bewitching ways are all beyond praise;
If it were just one ravishing style, I would call it a decree of death.

The ringlets of her hair are the wide-opened eyes directed at my heart;
Like a line of sight of collyrium-adorned[1] eyes is its every strand.

Here am I making a hundred thousand heartrending laments,
And there you are turning a deaf ear to my cries.

O my cruel love! Let not mistrust shame me that I was wrong;
Ah, alas! God forbid that I will have to call you disloyal!

[90]

Be gracious and ask me over whenever you want;
Time gone by I am not that come again I can't.

So worn out that my rivals' taunts I can't even protest,
But they are mere words, not a burden that I can't tolerate.

Poison I cannot get my hands on, otherwise, O oppressor,
Is it an oath not to meet you that I cannot take?

---

[1]For "collyrium-adorned eyes," see commentary on couplet 5 of ghazal 58.

105

[91]

Shed your reserve with me someday while drinking wine,
Otherwise, making intoxication an excuse, I will tease you one day.

Don't be vain about the rising edifice of this world;
These heights are destined to be humbled one day.

On credit I used to drink wine but I always knew
That being poor and drunk would bring trouble one day.

Even the songs of sorrows, O heart, take for a prize;
It will fall silent one day, this instrument of life!

Airs and graces from head to foot, fighting is not her way;
It was I, Ghalib, who took the initiative one day.

[92]

She oppresses me never doubting loyalty I won't forsake:
It is just to tease me, to test me is not her aim.

When can I find words to thank her for her special favours?
She inquires after me but not a word to that effect she utters.

To me cruelty is dear and to the cruel one I am dear;
Not unkind to me is she if kind to me she is not!

If you don't give me a kiss, don't; call me names!
You do have a tongue if a mouth you don't have.

Although your wrath and reproach are destroying my life,
Although the support of endurance and strength I don't have,

Yet my soul sings the song of "Is there more of it?"
And the chant of "mercy! quarter!" is not on my lips.

If into two the heart is not split, with a dagger slit open the chest;
If from the eyes blood is not dripping, pierce a knife into the heart.

It is a disgrace for the chest if the heart isn't a furnace;
It is a shame for the heart if the breath isn't strewing fire.

There is no loss in madness; what if the home become desolate!
For a hundred yards of land not a bad bargain is the desert.

You ask me: "What is written in your fate?"
As if my forehead bears no marks of prostrating before the idol.

For my poetry, from him I get some appreciation,
Although Gabriel's tongue is not the same as mine.

Life is the price for a kiss but why should she say it yet?
She knows that Ghalib is not half-dead yet.

[93]

Against my desert-wandering no expedient can avail:
These are wheels in motion, not fetters on my feet!

Driven by the passion of love I run in a desert where
There is no path except the sight of the eyes of a picture!

107

Alas! The desire for the pleasure of pain will remain unfulfilled:
The path of fidelity is nothing but a sharp edge of a sword!

May the grief of eternal disappointment remain agreeable to me!
I'm glad my lament hasn't been disgraced by obligation to efficacy.

The head itches as soon as its wound heals;
The pleasure of being hit with stones is beyond words.

When her graciousness allows you to be bold and saucy,
There would be no other fault than the shame of default.

It is my belief, Ghalib, that, in the words of Nasikh,
He is wanting in poetry who doesn't acknowledge Mir.

Commentary:

Couplet 7: Sheikh Imam Bakhsh Nasikh (1775-1838) was born in Faizabad, but lived most of his life in Lucknow. He left behind three volumes of the collections of his Urdu poetry. For Mir, see the commentary on ghazal 37, couplet 11.

[94]

Don't think that the pupils of my eyes are the focuses of sight;
They are my eyes' hearts' cores where have accumulated my sighs!

[95]

It is the rainy season for the lover's eyes, let us see what happens;
In a hundred places like flowers blossoming have opened the garden's walls!

From the love of flowers to claim freedom is an error:
The cypress, despite its freedom, of the garden remains a prisoner.

Commentary:

Couplet 2: By Urdu literary convention, cypress, being evergreen and
unaffected by the cycle of seasons, is considered to be free and independent.
"Garden" in the second line is a metaphor for the world and the "flowers" for
its attractions from whose power the cypress (i.e., anyone who thinks he is an
independent spirit) is not free.

[96]

Love, of its fruitfulness, is not despaired;
Staking one's life is not a barren endeavour.[1]

Kingdom passes from hand to hand;
The goblet of wine is not the signet-ring of Jamshed.

Your Light is the cause of all existence:
Particles come to life only in the sun's rays.

To my beloved's secret notoriety it may bring,
Just this and no other inconvenience in my dying.

---

[1]Literally: Staking life is not like a rattan tree. (Rattan is not supposed to bear fruits.)

An adverse turn in the happy state is what I fear;
Eternal deprivation is no cause for worry!

It is said people live on hope;
I don't have the hope to live even!

Commentary:

Couplet 2: Jamshed is the name of a legendary king of Persia said to have invented wine. The glass of wine like a kingdom passes from hand to hand, unlike the signet-ring, which is a thing personalized, and cannot be handed down from person to person. In his time, Jamshed ruled over the kingdom of wine, but in his own time, the poet implies, he rules over this kingdom.

[97]

Wherever your footprints I see
There the flowerbeds of paradise I see!

Those losing their hearts to the beauty spot on the beloved's lips' side,
They are the ones enjoying the view of non-existence in the black spot.

In the measure of your cypress-like, statuesque figure
I find the calamity of Doomsday less by a human stature.

Lost looking at your image in the mirror, O you!
Look at me, with what longing I am gazing at you!

To trace the steaming lament's source, look for my heart's burn-mark,
As, to track down the thief, for his footprint we look.

I have taken on the guise of a mendicant, Ghalib,
To see what's to be seen about the bounteous ones.

[98]

Similar in nature to my beloved is the flaming hellfire;
An infidel am I if in the torments of hell I don't find pleasure.

Since when am I in this wretched world, how can I say,
If the nights of separation, too, into account I take!

So that, in anxious expectation, all my life I don't sleep again,
A promise she made to come to me when in my dream she came.

By the time the messenger returns, another letter let me write;
For sure I know what in reply she is going to write!

In her party, when was it that my turn came for a glass of wine!
I wonder if in the drink the cupbearer has mixed something!

One who doesn't believe in loyalty, how can guile work on such a one?
Why should then I be suspicious of my friend concerning my enemy?

My rival's fear causing me perturbation amidst joy of union!
What notion is this causing you such agitation!

I and the pleasure of union with you! It was a godsend.
In my excitement, to make the offering of my life I forgot!

There is a frown I guess behind the veil:
A crease I see on the side of the veil.

Her myriad ways of attentions and her casting a furtive glance!
Her infinite styles of adornments, and her reproaching me in ire!

The lament that on her heart hasn't the impact of a straw even
Is the lament that would make cracks in the sun.

The magic that in achieving a purpose is of no avail
Is the magic that in a mirage would make a ship sail!

Ghalib, I have given up wine but even now, once in a while,
I drink on days when the sky is overcast, and on moonlit nights.

[99]

How so! For tomorrow's sake, niggardly don't be in serving wine today;
An unbecoming thought is it concerning Kausar's cupbearer.

Why are we so disgraced today when till yesterday
The Angel's disrespect to our honour was discountenanced?

How is it that life starts leaving the body while listening to music
When it is *His* voice that echoes in the lute and the rebeck!

Life's steed is speeding on; who knows where it stops?
Neither the hands are on the rein nor the feet in the stirrups!

More am I alienated from my own reality
The more I agonize over the notion of other beings.

When seeing, the seer and the One seen are in reality One,
I wonder where then does the experience of seeing come!

The ocean's entity comprises of different visible forms,
But what is there in the waves and the bubbles and drops!

Coyness is a way of the Beloved, be it with Himself:
How unveiled is He, being thus behind the veil!

From adorning the beauty not yet free is He,
Behind the veil the mirror is always in front of Him.

He is an absolute mystery, the One we consider manifest:
We are yet in a dream while dreaming that we are awake!

The Beloved's friend has the fragrance of the Beloved, Ghalib;
I remain dedicated to God while submitting to Abu Turab.

Commentary:

Couplet 1: "Kausar" means "abundance" and it is in this sense that it has been used only once in the Quran. However, some Muslim scholars say and Muslims generally believe that it is a fountain of wine in Paradise. It is also a common belief that those who don't drink wine in this world will be served in the next. The poet says that He who is going to provide wine in the next world will provide in this life too, and to a man's content, so why be niggardly? It will be an unbecoming thought concerning the Provider that he won't.

Couplet 2: The allusion is to the Quranic story of the creation of man when Iblis (literally, one who despaired), refused to prostrate before Adam and thus fell from God's grace, and Man was elevated. The couplet can be read as an expression of surprise at the disgrace mankind has brought on itself by its deeds or at God forsaking mankind, or both.

Couplet 6: In Islamic mysticism (Sufism) two expressions are used: Oneness of Being (*Tauhid-e-wujudi* or *Wahdat-al-wujud*), that is, nothing exists but God, and Oneness as experienced (*Tauhid-e-shuhudi* or *Wahdat- al-shuhud*), that is, a stage in devotional and meditative concentration on God when everything fades and the mystic (Sufi) experiences the vision of God, revealing some aspect of Himself or His divine attributes. Ghalib expresses his wonderment at the authentic mystical experience and examines it dialectically in a poetic mode.

Couplet 11: Abu Turab (literally, father of the earth) is the title of Ali, the son-in-law of Prophet Muhammad.

[100]

I wonder whether to weep for the heart or mourn the liver:
If only I could afford I would keep with me a mourner!

Jealousy won't let me say it is your home I want to go:
In perturbation I ask everyone: "What to do? Where to go?"

A thousand times by my rival's door I had to pass;
I wish the street you live on I hadn't known!

What is there that you say you have girt up your loins?
What do I care! Your waistline don't I know?

Lo and behold! Even she says I am without honour and esteem!
Had I but known, I wouldn't have sacrificed my house and all.

I go some distance with every fast-footed one;
I can't yet tell the true guide from a false one.

My desire for her the fools call worship;
That cruel idol do I really worship?

In ecstasy, I lost myself there and the way to her alley I forgot,
Otherwise, one day, to enquire after me there I might have gone.

Like me, I reasoned, would be the people of the world,
Delighting in the treasures of knowledge, wisdom, and art.

O Ghalib, God grant that I see the high-born Ali Bahadur
Riding the steed of pride and honour!

Commentary:

Couplet 4: For the explanation of "waistline" (waist) see commentary on couplet 3 of the next ghazal. Reading both the lines together, the poet is not only making light of the beloved's threat, he seems to be enjoying it.

Couplet 10: Nawwab Ali Bahadur was the ruler of the principality of Bandah in northern India (1849-1857), and was related to Ghalib on his mother's side. He joined the Rebellion against the British Rule in 1857 and lost his principality. He died in 1872.

[101]

To speak of me, even in derogatory terms, she likes not;
If it spoils my rival's game, unexpected it would be not.

She has promised a stroll in the rose garden; hail lucky desire!
The good news of killing me is implicit which is mentioned not.

The waist of the Beloved, the Absolute Being, is this world:
People say it is, but to me acceptable it is not.

My drop of being, too, is in reality an Ocean, but
The shallowness of Mansoor I will imitate not.

What a pity, O desire for destruction! The strength I had is gone:
Fit for a life of love full of battles my afflicted body is not.

When I tell her: "On Judgement Day you will be mine,"
With what pride she says: "Houri I am not!"

Torment me, yes, torment me if kindness you grudge me;
In being indifferent to me helpless you are not.

Clearly, the imbibers to the dregs from Jamshed's cup we are;
Fie on the wine that pressed from grapes is not!

Compared to Zahoori, I am Khifai, Ghalib;
The argument is that famous I am not.

Commentary:

Couplet 3: The beloved's waist, because of its delicateness and narrowness, is, by poetic convention, regarded as non-existent. The poet uses this convention to make the point that the world has no real existence and creates the imagery of the world as the non-existent waist of the Beloved. Besides, the Beloved being an Absolute Being (*Shahid-e Hasti-e Mutlaq*) is totally independent of and bears no reference to anything else—including the "waist." In a word, whether people are right, or the poet is right, about the existence or non-existence of the world, whatever, the poet seems to suggest, we all agree on this: the existence of the Absolute Being. (Also see commentary on couplet 6 of ghazal 99.)

Couplet 4: Hussain Bin Mansoor Hallaj (858-922), commonly known as Mansoor, was a Sufi. Born in Al-Toor, a small town in the northeast of Persia, he travelled widely and finally settled down in Baghdad where he became a disciple of Junaid Baghdadi, a highly respected Sufi. Mansoor was the author of over 47 books and short treatises on Sufism. In his spiritual journey he reached a stage where he saw naught but the One Real, and called out in exclamation, "I am the One Real." This was considered a blasphemy for which he was tried and finally hanged after spending eight years in prison. Ghalib says that he, too, has reached that stage in his spiritual journey (he sees only the Ocean, not the drop), but he has the capacity to contain that experience, and will not allow his passionate ecstasy to overflow—he is not shallow like Mansoor.

Couplet 8: See commentary on couplet 2 of ghazal 96 above.

Couplet 9: Zahoori was the court poet of Ibrahim Adil Shah II (1571-1627), Sultan of Bijapoor, present day Karnataka in India. Zahoori literally means something visible or prominent. He had earlier adopted the pen name of Khifai, literally, something hidden or unnoticed. However, he is generally known and remembered by his latter name, Zahoori, and very few, if any, would call him Khifai.

[102]

My lament, O inventive oppressor, is nothing but a way of request—
Importunity for more torments, the complaint of cruelty it is not!

Love and manual labour for Khusrau's pleasure palace, how strange!
The good reputation of Farhad I don't acknowledge.

Less in desolation that too is not, but where is this vastness?
In the desert I find such pleasure that my home I don't remember.

117

For the perceptive people the deluge of calamities a school is:
Buffetings of waves are no less than the buffetings of teachers!

Ah, the futility of acquiescence! Alas, the sad plight of fidelity!
She thinks the strength to make complaints I don't have any?

Why is the colour of dignity and grandeur of roses and tulips in ruin
If just a display of lamps in the pathway of the wind they are not?

In the flower-basket confines you the flower-gatherer;
Congratulations, O nightingale! The fowler is not in the garden.

As one would say, from the denial is inferred the affirmation:
At her creation, instead of a mouth the word "no" she was given.

In splendour Paradise is no less than your alley;
It has the same features but is not as populous and lively.

With what face can you complain of the foreign land, Ghalib?
The unkindness of your own countrymen don't you remember?

Commentary:

Couplet 2: Khusrau was the title of the Emperors of Persia, as Caesar and Czar were the titles of the Emperors of Rome and Russia, respectively. The name of the Emperor of the legend of Shirin and Farhad was Pervez (d. 628 A.D.) and Shirin was his queen and Farhad was madly in love with Shirin, the queen. He was told that if he made the river flow into the garden of the pleasure-palace of the Emperor by cutting through a mountain, he would get his Shirin. Farhad undertook this job in full earnest and just when he had completed it, an old woman was sent from the palace to inform him that Shirin was dead. Farhad, on hearing the news, committed suicide, but the news was an invention. The point Ghalib is making in this couplet is that to work for the "pleasure palace" of the one who is a rival in love brings disgrace to love. In Ghalib there is a distinction between the "lover" and the "rival" or "stranger": the lover, by definition, is a true, passionate lover and the rival is a fake one, stranger to love—a pretender. So, as a true lover how could he act on the terms of a pretender?

[103]

Bestowing both the worlds, He thought I would be happy:
On my part, out of modesty, I thought why argue.

Getting too tired, at each halting place a few stayed back,
If they can't find You, what can the helpless ones do?

Of the candle are the people of the assembly not the well-wishers?
But if the sorrow be soul-melting, what can the sympathizers do?

[104]

The sweet talk of the stranger has proved successful with her;
She doesn't even imagine the silent ones passionately love her.

[105]

Terrible! Hearing that Laila went to see Qais in the desert,
Surprised she said: "Something like this, too, happens in this world!"

I feel pity for your beloved's tender heart, Ghalib;
Better not incite that infidel to put your love to test.

106

Having fallen in love, she, too, sits lonely now;
At last my forlornness got justice in this very world.

Tending towards decay and death are all things created:
The sun in the heaven is but a lamp in the path of the wind!

[107]

Being away from the beloved, at the door and the wall I look:
Sometimes for the messenger and sometimes for the breeze I look.

She and visiting me at my abode! It is a godsend!
Sometimes at her and sometimes at my abode in wonderment I look.

May not their evil eyes cast influence on her arm and hand!
Why are these people staring at my heart's deep wound?

What is there in them to see, the jewels in your coiffure?
But I do see how on the rise the stars of rubies and pearls are.

Commentary:

   Couplet 1: By Urdu poetic convention, "breeze" is sometimes used
metaphorically, as here, for a courier, bringing or carrying news and messages.

[108]

Not that in the Judgement Day I don't believe,
But worse than the night of separation Doomsday can't be.

Tell me what is wrong with a moonlit night?
If in the daytime there is no breeze and no clouds, never mind.

When I meet her, "Welcome" she would never say!
And when I leave her, "Farewell" she wouldn't say!

If ever she happens to remember me, this she says:
"In the party, there is no mischief and disorder today."

Besides feast days, on other days, too, wine we are served:
The beggars of the tavern street are never disappointed!

Maybe grief and happiness come together, so what?
God has given me the heart that hasn't known happiness!

Why bring it up with her, Ghalib, what she promised?
Say you remind her and she says: "I don't remember!"

[109]

For your steed we use the metaphor of breeze:
Just to impress we invent these expressions.

Who has ever seen the effect of sighing?
It is no more than our way of romancing.

Compared to your time here, O life!
Of the lightning we say, it wears henna on its feet!

From the bonds of life where is the escape?
The wretched tears are under restraint kept.

121

Intoxicated by their colours, the flowers open up:
When do the drunk ones keep their shirts buttoned up?

Of the fallacies of themes, don't ask me!
People keep saying laments are effective!

Look at the helplessness of the masters of expediency!
To the blisters on their feet henna they apply!

Naïve and full of guiles are the beauties, Ghalib.
The pledge of loyalty my beloved makes to me!

Commentary:

Couplet 7: The blisters on the feet are impediments to movement. Henna is considered to have a cooling effect on blisters, but at the same time it restrains movement. (To apply henna to the feet (*panw mein menhdi lagana*) is also an idiom for being unable to move.)

[110]

I swear by Asad's life! The world is minimally afflictive!
In fact, I for one was expecting much more from it.

[111]

Lying permanently at your door am I not?
Damn such a life! Stone I am not.

How won't the never-ending vicissitudes perturb my heart!
After all, a human I am, a cup or a goblet I am not.

O my Sustainer! Why is time wiping me out?
On the tablet of the world a word redundant I am not.

For correction, to the term of punishment there needs to be a limit:
After all, only a sinner I am, an infidel I am not.

What could be the reason you don't hold me dear?
Ruby or emerald or gold or pearl I am not.

Why do you place your feet away from my eyes?
In status, less than the sun and the moon I am not.

Why don't you let me kiss your feet?
Is it that equal even to the heavens I am not?

You are a stipendiary, Ghalib, and you should pray for the King;
Those days are gone when you used to say: "Servant I am not."

[112]

When did all? Only a few have happened to appear in tulips and roses;
What beauties in what state remain hidden in the earth, who can say?

The colourful parties I used to give and attend I, too, remembered,
But, now, like pictures in the niche of forgetfulness they are.

The seven damsels in the sky in daytime were hidden in their veils;
At night whatever came over them that they uncovered their faces!

123

Though Jacob couldn't take care of Joseph while in jail,
Yet, his eyes the apertures in the walls of his cell became.

Though every lover hates a rival, but with the ladies of Egypt,
Zulaikha was pleased they were enthralled by Canaan's moon.

Let blood stream from my eyes in the night of separation;
For me they are like two candles that have lighted up.

With these fairy-like beauties, in Paradise I will get even
If there, by God's pleasure, houris they become.

Sleep is for him, pride is his, the nights are for him
On whose arms lie disheveled your tresses!

As I entered the garden, as if the school of art came into session:
Hearing my laments the nightingales started singing ghazals.

O God! Why are they penetrating through my heart, those glances
That, because I am short on luck, don't reach beyond her eyelashes?

I kept repressing and they kept rising in my chest:
My sighs became the stitches of my torn shirt's breast!

Though I managed to reach her, but how to respond to her revilement?
All the best wishes I remembered on her gatekeeper I had lavished!

Life-enhancing is wine in whomsoever's hand the goblet comes;
All the lines on the hand as though the arteries of life become.

I believe in the One and Only God; renunciation of rituals is my way:
When the religious groupings are gone, they constitute one true faith.

When humans to pain become accustomed, the pain is no more felt;
Hardships came over me with such persistence that easy they became.

If Ghalib continues to weep like this, O people of the world,
You will see that these inhabited places wastelands become!

Commentary:

Couplet 3: "The seven damsels," so called in Urdu, are the seven stars (Big Dipper) of the constellation Ursa Major. Ghalib has used the expression in both these senses opening a window of new meanings.

Couplet 5: Zulaikha was the name of Potiphar's wife who had a passion for Joseph, "Canaan's moon."

Couplet 11: The "torn shirt's breast" or the torn bosom, is the sign of a strong passion of love—love-madness—and stitching it up symbolizes the return of an apparent and temporary calm ("I kept repressing and they kept rising"), in no way affecting the ardency of love. By these imageries, the poet is suggesting that love is a passion that can't be repressed, as well as that it entails pain and sorrow ("sighs" being their outward expression).

[113]

Not even the sacred thread on my shoulder has my madness left,
That is, of my shirt's breast not even a warp is left.

To fulfill my desire to see her, I offered up my heart:
The next thing I knew, my sight too I had lost!

125

If to meet you isn't easy, it is easy on me,
But the hard part is it's not difficult even!

Life cannot be passed without love, but such is my condition
That I don't have enough strength for the pleasure of pain even.

Ah, my madness! On my shoulder my head is a burden!
O my God! In the desert I don't see a wall even!

The capacity for enmity towards my rival! Leave that alone;
Worn out, my heart can't hold the beloved's desire even!

Fear my piteous laments and have fear of God!
They are not after all the wailings of a captive bird!

To face up to the beloved's eyelashes is my heart's desire
Though even a thorn's prick I haven't the strength to endure.

Who wouldn't offer up his life to such naïveté, O God!
Giving battle but not even a sword in the hand!

I have often seen Asad—in privacy and in company;
If not mad, wise too he is not!

[114]

Not one of my body's wounds is such that it can be stitched up:
The thread in the needle's eye the string of tears of despair is!

Hindering the enjoyment of view is the desolation of the house:
Like cotton wool are stuck in the walls' breaches the flood's froths.

126

I am the treasure house of the tyranny of the piercing eyelashes:
Every drop of my blood is a gem bearing my beloved's signet.

Who can describe the darkness pervading my abode!
A moonlit night it would be if in its skylight cotton wool were placed.

My friends' reproaches kept in check my love-madness:
Their derisive laughs have become the stitches of my shirt's breast.

Seeing the splendour of her sun-like presence, the streaks of the mirror[1],
Like the particles in the sunlit skylight, are in flutter.

I know not whether good or bad am I, but the company is uncongenial:
If a rose, in the furnace I am; and if trash, in the rose garden!

Thousands of hearts the fervour of my love-madness has given me:
Every drop of my blood, turning black, the core of these hearts has become.

I am a captive of the charms of the beauty's intimacy, Asad;
Like yokes around my neck are the curves of their caressing arms!

Commentary:

Couplet 5: One of the ways in which the poet's friends reproach him is their derisive laughs, exposing their front-teeth that look like stitches. The stitched shirt's breast suggest that, under restraint, he is no longer giving expression to his madness—his passion of love.

---

[1]The mirror is a steel-mirror.

[115]

The pleasures of the world are worthless except consuming lifeblood,[1]
And of that, in my heart, not a drop is left!

Save that the wind carries me away when I turn to dust,
In my wings and feathers absolutely no ability and strength are left.

Who is that of paradisiacal qualities whose arrival is expected
That along the way there's only the splendour of flowers, no dust!

Well, if she didn't, at least I should have taken pity on myself:
Completely devoid of effect are my laments, not affecting me even!

It is the thought of flower's[2] splendour that makes the imbibers drunk,
Otherwise, what is there about the walls and doors of the tavern?

The devastations of the passion of love have put me to shame;[3]
Except for the desire to build, now nothing remains of my home!

Now my poetry, Asad, is only to please my heart:
Excellence in art is treated like dust, this I have learnt!

[116]

It's my heart—not a stone nor a brick—how won't it overflow with grief!
A thousand times I would weep; why should anyone torment me!

---

[1] "Consuming lifeblood," i.e., vexing oneself to death. It is a pleasure because it is for love's sake.
[2] "Flower," i.e., the beloved.
[3] Put to shame because nothing is left to offer to love to work its devastations on. (A sarcasm or regret, or both.)

Not a temple, nor the Kaba, nor an abode, nor a door;
Sitting on a road, why should anyone move me from here?

The heart-illumining beauty, like the midday sun, dazzles the vision;
Why should such a one be hiding behind a curtain!

Your glances' dagger a killer! From your coquetry's arrow no refuge!
Though it is your own face's reflection, why let it look at you?

The prison of life and the bondage of grief actually are the same:
How a human, before he is dead, can from grief attain freedom!

Her trust in her beauty and judgement saved the lustful one from shame;
Confident of herself why should she put the stranger through the test?

There pride of glory and grace, and here regard for good form!
When will she invite me to her party, how can we meet in the street!

Granted she is no God-worshipper, and what if she is disloyal!
One holding his religion and heart dear, why must need he go to her alley?

Without heartbroken Ghalib what worldly business has come to a stop?
Why then weep piteously and why wail and exclaim, "Ah! Alas!"

[117]

Don't show me from a distance a rosebud that it is thus;
For a kiss I am asking, with your lips demonstrate it is thus.

Why ask how she captivates the heart? Without her telling it,
Her every wink and nod shows plainly this is how.

129

At night, having drunk wine, taking along my rival!
I wish to God she comes to me but God forbid not like this.

With the stranger how did it go last night? When I asked this,
She came and sat in front of me and said: "Look, like this!"

In the party, in her presence, how shouldn't I keep silent?
When she is silent, her silence says: "This is the way!"

I said her exclusive party should be vacated of the stranger;
Hearing this, the playful tyrant removed me and said: "Like this?"

When my love asked me: "How do the senses leave someone?"
Seeing me in a trance, the wind started blowing that thus it does.

When did I know how to live in the beloved's alleyway!
The wonderment of the footprint showed me that was the way.

If in your heart lurks the suspicion that union cools passion,
Look at the wave, how restless it is though in the ocean.

If someone asks how can Urdu be the envy of Persian,
Just once read to him the poetry of Ghalib—thus it can!

[118]

If envy makes you depressed, go and watch the world:
Possibly by the plenitude of exposure your jaundiced eyes be opened.

130

In the measure of the heart's desire for sins would be the pleasures of sins:
Only my shirt's hem would they wet if the seven seas' waters were sins![1]

If she of cypress-like stature and graceful gaits comes walking,
Every handful of garden's soil, like a turtledove, would be cooing.

[119]

If to the Kaba I have moved, don't taunt me:
Have I forgotten the claim of association with idolaters?

So that devotion be not for the love of honey and wine,
Let Paradise be moved and with Hell merged!

From the custom and ways meriting reward how won't I deviate?
Askew was cut the pen's nib with which was written my fate.

From my efforts, Ghalib, I am not going to benefit;
If the locusts won't devour the crop, lightning will destroy it!

[120]

I'm delivered from it that why love it shouldn't be;
If nothing else, let it be hostility even.

Grown weak, the strain of socializing I can't sustain;
On my heart even the impress of love is now a burden!

---

[1] I.e., the desire for the pleasures of sins is insatiable. Also see the commentary on couplet 6 of
ghazal 39.

That you speak of the stranger, that is my complaint;
Even if it's by way of reproach, notwithstanding that.

For every affliction there is a cure—this is what is said;
If that's true how come for the pain of love there isn't a remedy?

My forlornness occasioned no dealings with anyone:
If I feel ashamed, it is of none else but my own self.

The human being in his very being is a tumult of thronging thoughts:
It is like I am in company even when alone.

Accepting others' influence is a moment of weakness for lofty aspiration;
Don't take a thing from the world, not even a lesson or admonition.

Freedom from the worldly bonds is no excuse for estrangement:
Neither one's own self nor the others should one dread!

The opportunity called life, will the grief of its loss be effaced,
Even if wholly in devotion this dear life is spent?

From the door of the tormentor I am not going to move, Asad,
Even if the calamity of Doomsday breaks upon my head.

[121]

In a cage am I and even if they don't like my lamentation,
How my being hurts the songsters of the flower-garden?

If intimacy isn't easy, so what? Is not jealousy enough agony?
I wish the desire for my friend God had not given to my enemy!

Not a drop of tear your eyes shed for my wound—the wound
That made blood drip from the needle's eye[1] in my chest!

May God shame my hands that keep in a state of perplexity,
Sometimes my shirt's breast, sometimes my beloved's skirt!

We think the killing-ground is going to be an easy thing:
Your charger swimming in the river of blood we haven't yet seen.

When news of making fetters for my feet spread,
The iron ore in the mine, stirred to its core, impatient became.

What joy if the clouds gather over my farm a hundred times!
I apprehend the lightning is already looking for the harvest to strike.

Fidelity, if strong and steadfast, is the essence of faith:
If a Brahmin dies in the idol-temple, in the Kaba bury him!

Martyrdom was destined for me, so it was given in my nature
That whenever I'd see the sword bared my neck to it I'd offer.

If in daytime I weren't robbed, how so soundly could I sleep at night?
I pray for the highwayman; gone now is the fear of theft!

Can't I write poetry that after gems I would seek!
Don't I have a liver that the mines I would dig!

With my king of Solomon's majesty can't compare, Ghalib,
Faridoon or Jamshed or Kai-Khusrau or Darab or Bahman.

---

[1] I.e., even the insensate needle while sewing the heart's wound wept tears of blood that dripped from its eyes into the lover's chest. The couplet is about the hard-heartedness of the beloved.

Commentary:

Couplet 8: According to the traditions based on the Quranic texts (e.g., chapter 2, verses 125 and 127, and chapter 3, verse 96, besides others) the prototype of the Kaba was built in Mecca by Abraham and Ishmael of the Bible and was the first temple ever established for the worship of One transcendent God. However, at the time of the advent of Islam it housed idols worshipped by the Arab tribes; it was rededicated to the worship of One God by Prophet Muhammad. In a word, the Kaba in Mecca to which the Quran also refers as *al-bayt al-atiq* ("the Ancient Temple") and as *al-masjid al-haram* ("the Inviolable House of Worship") is a place of worship of One unseen God and is not a cemetery and has never been a cemetery, and the Brahmins in India are never buried, always cremated. Obviously, the second line of this couplet with a powerful element of surprise is meant for effect so that what has been said in the first line becomes a part of the readers' consciousness. (For more about the Kaba, so see the commentary on couplet 5 of ghazal 87.)

Couplet 11: The term "gems" has been used both in its literal sense and figuratively for gems of poetry. The gemstones are mined and digging the liver (*jigar kavi*) is an idiom both in Urdu and Persian for hard work that writing creative poetry demands besides inspiration.

Couplet 12: Faridoon, etc. are the names of celebrated Persian emperors, either fictive or real. For example, Jamshed is an emperor of the legend and Kai-Khusrau is said to have succeeded Cyaxares (died 584 B.C.). Darab is Darius I or Darius the Great (ruled from 522-486 B.C.) who conquered Thrace and Macedonia in the West and Sindh and the Punjab in the East. Finally he annexed to his Persian Empire Asia Minor, northern Greece, Egypt, Syria, Iraq, the Arabian peninsula and Afghanistan, besides Sindh and the Punjab. It hardly needs to be added here that the poet, by comparing Bahadur Shah Zafar, the last Mughal Emperor, with these personages, is creating his own fiction for sheer pleasure.

[122]

When I want to show to the radiant beauty my respect and loyalty
From contrariness and obstinacy away she withdraws from me.

How innocently he died! For the mountain-digger I have great regard.
Ah, alas! Why didn't the strength fail the old woman's legs!

To escape, I ran hard at great speed for which I am thus punished:
Made a captive, to the highwayman's legs comfort-pressure I give!

In search of ointment I travelled far and wide;
Now more than my wounded body afflict me my injured feet!

O God, how great was my love for desert-wandering that
Even after death my feet move of themselves in my shroud!

In springtime such is the luxuriance of flowers all around
That the birds in flight in the garden get ensnared!

Was it that yesternight in someone's dream she came!
Today the legs of that delicate beauty ache!

How my poetry won't be enjoyable, Ghalib!
To the sweet-worded Khusrau I do homage.

Commentary:

Couplet 2: For the legend that is the context for this couplet, see commentary on couplet 2 of ghazal 102.

135

Couplet 8: Khusrau (1253-1325), a celebrated Persian and Hindi poet, who was born in Agra and lived in Delhi. His real name was Abul Hasan, but is generally known as Amir Khusrau. His extant works include five Divans (Collections) of Persian ghazals. He was also a maestro-musician, invented new modes of Indian music and vastly improved the performance of the Indian sitar (a musical instrument) by adding a third string to it.

[123]

She is having palpitations of heart and I feel ashamed,
Apprehensive that it might be the effect of my sighs.

See how she delights in tyranny that
For a mirror the eye of her prey she wants to have!

[124]

On reaching her alley I continually swoon and arise and swoon;
This for me is kissing a hundred times my beloved's feet!

I keep my heart and my heart keeps me captive of fidelity;
How great is our mutual pleasure in being prisoners of grief!

From weakness, an ant's footprint would be a yoke on my neck:
To run away from your lane when do I have the strength!

So I have some hope let your indifference show you know me;
Looking past me, as if I were a stranger, is like poison to me.

The jealousy of the similarity of style and the pathos of song!
The wailing of the nightingale is a double-edged sword for me.

When I asked her to repeat her promise to strike off my head,
Laughingly she said: "A vow I have made as regards your head."

Why do I shed tears of blood? Because no other option!
That my eyes shouldn't be without lustre is my great concern.

You are so sensitive that my silence you call lamentation;
I am so exhausted, even your indifference is an affliction.

The reason for my coming to Lucknow remains unclear;
The desire for excursion it can't be for of it I have very little.

This city isn't the end of the journey to the places I want to go;
A visit to Najaf and pilgrimage to Mecca are my goals.

It is a hope that is taking me somewhere, Ghalib!
The attraction of expected beneficence is the highway.

[125]

It is your lookout if with the stranger you continue your association,
But what sin will you commit if to me too you give your attention!

You will not escape accountability on Judgement Day;
Though my rival is my murderer, you are the *witness*!

Are they, too, the killers of innocent people and deniers of justice?
Granted that not a human but like the sun and the moon are you.

I see a thread prominent on her veil; it kills me—
The thought that someone's fixed gaze it might well be!

Now that the tavern is lost, what difference it is going to make:
Let it be a mosque or a monastery or a school or any place!

The praises of Paradise that I hear, all of them as truths I accept,
But God grant that it be the place where you[1] will manifest!

It won't be such a great loss even if Ghalib be no more,
But, O Lord! May the world exist and my king live forever!

[126]

That if I could speak to her what mightn't happen, that thing is gone:
My words had no effect, so what good if I speak to her again!

In my mind, this perplexing thought itself is union,
That if it doesn't happen where to go, and if it can, how?

The dilemma of desire and good manners, what should I do!
Her bashfulness and her indecisiveness, what can she do!

You tell me how could the idolaters pass their life,
If the idols, too, had the same disposition as have you?

Looking into the mirror you wrangle with your own reflection;
If in the town there were a few like you, what would happen!

He to whose lot has fallen the dark days[2] like mine,
If he doesn't call his night day, then what else?

---

[1]The word "you" here can be taken to refer to God or the earthly beloved.
[2]Dark day (*roz-e-siyah* in Urdu and Persian) means, metaphorically, trouble, adversity or misfortune, in which sense it has been used in the first line. In the second line it is used in its literal sense, which adds to the somberness of the picture and thus heightens the feeling of gloom.

For me again to have hopes from her and she to appreciate my worth!
When she pays no heed to me, how is that going to happen?

I wasn't wrong in presuming your letter would bring satisfaction,
But if my eyes, keen to see you, aren't content, what can be done?

Look at her eyelashes and tell me how can they have I peace?
Their sting going deep into the arteries of my life, how can it be?

I am not mad, Ghalib, but, as His Majesty has said,
How is peace possible while separated from the beloved?

[127]

After giving one's heart to someone, why should one wail and complain!
When the heart isn't in the chest, what use has the tongue in the mouth!

She won't change her habit, why should I change my ways?
Why lose dignity and ask why is she ill-disposed to me!

My sympathetic friend caused me disgrace; perish such friendship!
One who can't hold in grief, why such a one my confidante be?

What love? What loyalty? If what remains is to break my head,
Then, O stone-hearted, why necessarily it be at your abode's threshold?

Don't fear, my friend, telling me, encaged, of the garden's incident;
The thing the lightning struck yesterday, why should it be my nest?

Can you say you aren't in my heart? But tell me this:
When you alone are in my heart, why from my eyes you hide?

To complain of my heart's passion is wrong; see who's fault is it!
If withdrawn you don't remain, how between us any tension be?

Isn't it calamity enough to destroy a human being?
When you are a friend, what need has the heaven to be his enemy!

If this indeed is a trial what else is torment?
When you are all for my enemy, why test me?

You say why your meeting with the stranger would bring infamy:
Well said, truly said, say it again that, yes, why should it?

Are you trying to achieve your purpose through sarcasm, Ghalib?
Your calling her unkind, would that make her gracious to you?

[128]

Now I want to go and live at some such place where nobody lives—
Nobody to converse with and nobody who my tongue speaks.

There I will make my home without walls and doors:
There I will have no watchman and no neighbours.

If I fall ill there would be nobody to nurse me
And nobody to sing dirges when I die.

[129]

From the sun to a particle, everything is a heart—a mirror!
In whatever direction it turns, the parrot faces the mirror.

[130]

The walls of my house of sorrows is covered with lush grass:
If this is its spring, what its autumn is going to be, don't ask me!

One can't help wishing one had made a lonely journey:
Of the companions' outrages, besides the way's hardships, don't ask me!

[131]

Hundreds of splendours are there to see if we raise our eyes,
But when do we have the capacity to receive all these favours!

It was decreed that stone be the subsistence of love-madness:
To wit, I have yet to live on the kindness of street urchins.

The wall is bowed under the weight of obligation to the labourers:
O you who are ruined, don't ever accept anybody's favours.

Either don't disgrace my wound of jealousy,
Or the mystery of your sly smiles disclose to me.

[132]

In the neighbourhood of the mosque a tavern is needed:
O preacher, close to the eyebrows the eyes are located!

You, too, have fallen in love with somebody:
After all, some requital for your tyranny there had to be!

If nothing, O heaven, give my grief-adorning heart due appreciation;[1]
For depriving me of pleasure there ought to be some compensation.

For the moon-faced beauties, painting I have learned;
After all to meet them some occasion is needed.

Who is that sinner who drinks wine for pleasure!
A kind of forgetfulness, day and night, is what I desire!

From the root, O Ghalib, arise and thrive the branches,
And from silence emerge words that express our thoughts.

Tulips and roses and eglantines are different in colour,
But the affirmation of spring is in every colour.

The head appropriately be at the base of the flagon when drunk,
And the face in the direction of the Kaba when saying prayers;

That is, in conformity with the revolving cup of His manifestation,[2]
The God-conscious ones always remain drunk with the wine of Being.

[133]

In my wretched state, all I have is my heart, a drop of blood,
And that too, head down as if any moment it may fall.

With the saucy one, displeasure I managed to feign for some days:
Frankly speaking, that too was but a manner of madness.

---

[1] I.e., the grief of unfulfilled desires. The expression "grief-adorning" is in a sarcastic mode and suggests accumulation of grief over a period.
[2] I.e., the manifestation of His attributes.

When can the thought of death give comfort to my grieved heart?
It is just another of many feeble preys in my net of desires!

I wish laments I hadn't made but, my friend, how could I know
That even this be a cause of increase in my heart's anguish?

Don't be too proud of the sharpness of your scimitar of oppression;
It is just one of many waves of blood in my river of perturbation!

Why wish for the wine of pleasure from the heaven's cupbearer?
With one, two and four inverted cups it is sitting there.

In my heart, Ghalib, are the desire for union and complaints of separation:
May God bring that day that I tell her of the one as well as the other!

Commentary:

Couplet 6: One, two and four (they add up to seven) cups refer to the seven heavens. When the cups are placed upside down it means that there is no more wine to be served—a subtle suggestion that the heavens only dispense pain, not pleasure.

[134]

In the beauties' company, of the lips words are weary;
Utterly tired am I of such ones as demand flattery.

Serving wine in cups in turns is to dissipate it:
Put just once a flagonful of wine to my lips!

The drunkards at the tavern's door are insolent, O zealot!
Never enter into dispute with these unmannerly sorts.

See the tyranny of fidelity that life finally escaped,
Although with my lips a long-lasting bond it had!

[135]

So that even for a complaint I am not given an occasion,
She hears out what others say but never mentions me on her own.

O Ghalib, to tell her of your state we will find an opportunity;
That on hearing of it she will invite you we can't guarantee.

[136]

What was in there my home that love's woes would have destroyed?
The desire to build that I always had I still have!

[137]

From worldly woes, if ever I get respite and raise my head,
I see the heaven and instantly of you I am reminded.

O Lord! How will she know what I say in my letters?
My sweetheart has made a vow about burning papers.

To wrap up blazing fire in silk may be easy,
But no way to hide in the heart burning grief!

To go and see her wounded ones was what she intended,
But see her playfulness, a walk in the garden she pretended!

It was my naïveté that at your graciousness I was ready to die:
Your coming here, O tyrant, was nothing but the preparation to go!

The blows of calamities of the world I can no longer endure—I
Who once had the strength to bear the beauties' airs and whims.

What to say of the pleasing ways of the people of the time, Ghalib!
He did ill to me to whom I had done a good turn many a time.

Commentary:

Couplet 2: The use of the expression "a vow about burning papers" instead of a vow to burn papers in the second line has created the possibility of two opposite interpretations. The first, that she has made a vow to burn all the papers, in which case she would never know of the passion, desire and grief the lover had been expressing in his letters. The second interpretation is that she has made a vow that she would never burn any paper—of course she is never going to read them—which is an even worse possibility for the lover, for had she burnt them the fire would have symbolically represented to her the fire of his love and the grief of its non-fulfillment.

[138]

Give up the hope of yield, O you, pursuing your desire!
The heart is a tenant farmer drowned in the torrent of tears!

Like a candle that someone has snuffed out before it burnt up,
I, too, am one of the burnt ones but with the stigma of incompleteness.

[139]

We the oppressed ones, how constrained is our world,
The world of which an ant's eggshell is the firmament!

The cosmos is in motion because for You it yearns:
The particles come to life because of the sun's light!

Though my heart is tulip-coloured from hard-hitting stones,
The heedless ones think my cup is filled with wine!

In the heart of the lustful one she chose to sit;
Why shouldn't she? A cool place is it.

How true, to my rival you didn't give a kiss!
Better keep quiet; I, too, have a tongue in my mouth!

The one sitting in the shade of his beloved's house,
The sovereign of the whole realm of India is he!

The grief has effaced even the notional existence:
To whom to say the burn-mark the vestige of my heart is?

Finally, Ghalib, in my loyalty she has such great trust!
That she is unkind to me, I am happy with that.

Commentary:

Couplet 3: "Hard-hitting stones" is a metaphor for calamities. "Cup" is a metaphor for "heart" in the first line which is "tulip-colored", i.e., red like tulip flower, having been hit by calamities. (Tulip flower is cup shaped.)

[140]

My anguish is making you anxious and uneasy, ah, alas!
What happened, O oppressor, to your nonchalance, ah, alas!

If in your heart wasn't the strength for a torrent of grief,
Why then you became my sympathizer and friend, ah, alas!

Why did you think of commiserating with me?
It was enmity with yourself, your friendship with me, ah, alas!

Lifelong loyalty you vowed, but so what?
Life itself doesn't last long, ah, alas!

The season of life here is like poison to me
Because it did not agree with you, ah, alas!

Whatever happened to your airs and graces strewing flowers;
Now flowers are being strewn on your tomb, ah, alas!

To fend off the shame of notoriety, behind the veil of earth you hid!
In keeping love a secret you were the limit, ah, alas!

With you is gone the good repute of the pledge of love;
Gone from this world is the custom of friendship, ah, alas!

She, the wielder of the sword, can't use her arm anymore:
On my heart it hadn't yet made a mortal wound, ah, alas!

How is one to pass the dark nights of the rainy season?
My eyes had become used to counting stars, ah, alas!

Ears starved of message and eyes deprived of the beauty's sight!
One heart and such swarming despairs, ah, alas!

Love had not yet taken on the colour of madness, Ghalib:
All my desires for love's sufferings remained unfulfilled, ah, alas!

Commentary:

Couplet 1: The poet is in anguish seeing his beloved in a critical condition which, in turn, makes her uneasy, unlike her usual indifference in the past which the poet recalls with regret. The poem is an elegy written on the death of the beloved of whom not much is known. (Couplets 1 to 4 are about when the beloved is in the throes of death, and from 5 to 12 about after her death.)

Couplet 9: "Swords" here is a metaphor for feigned disdain, nonchalance and other ways by which the beloved bewilders, tantalizes and tries the lover causing him the pleasure of pain. "Arm" which corresponds with "sword" signifies the ability to act which is no more there, she having died. "Mortal wound" in the second line suggests that the affair was in its early stage; it had not reached the point when he would have died from the joy of union or pain of separation. (See the last couplet.)

Couplet 10: [1]"Rainy season," i.e., in a state when the tears of grief are pouring down at the beloved's death. "Counting stars," i.e., not able to sleep from a mixed feeling of anxiety and anticipation when the beloved was alive, a counterpoint to "the dark nights" in the first line signifying gloom and desolation when the beloved is no more.

[141]

I am in such distress that hope of life I don't have:
Glad tidings for peace! The hope of death I do now have.

For my lost heart no concern shows she:
Does she think it still is with me?

When can one describe the exhilaration of the fever of grief?
Every hair on my body a tongue of gratitude is!

Her pride in her beauty has made her a stranger to loyalty,
Although she has a heart that knows what is just and right.

On a moonlit night drink as much wine as you can get:
For a phlegmatic temperament warmth is good in a cool night.

It is the master of the house who brings it glory, Asad:
The desert is dim, dull, and dreary now that Majnoon is dead.

[142]

If in silence is the advantage one can hide one's true state,
I am glad people don't understand a word of what I say.

To whom may I complain of my pent up desire for expression?
My heart is a huge record of these that couldn't find articulation.

Behind what veil, O God, are You polishing the mirror?
Grant me mercy! My nonsupplicating lips apologies offer!

Woe to the day! God forbid that she be your enemy!
O abashed love, what thought is this?

Know that musky is the Kaba's vesture from the mark Ali left:
Centre of the earth it is, navel of the musk deer it is not.

For my mad wandering it is a tight world:
The oceans are the sweat of shame of this earth.

Don't get deceived that a real existence it has:
The world is but a loop in the net of thought, Asad!

Commentary:

Couplet 3: "The mirror" is a metaphor for the heart of the speaker.

Couplet 5: According to some traditions, Ali, son-in-law of Prophet Muhammad, was born in the Kaba, which Muslims call the centre of the earth because of its holiness and because they turn their faces in its direction when saying their prayers. The Kaba is covered with black vesture. The real musk is produced in the navel of a male musk deer and is black in color. It also has fragrance.

[143]

About my complaints against you, better don't probe me!
Be wary of my heart for in it is hidden smouldering fire.

O heart! Even pain and grief you take for prizes:
Finally, there neither be the morning cries nor the midnight sighs!

[144]

At one place, the word "loyalty" you wrote but that, too, got erased:
Apparently, the paper of your letter automatically removes mistakes!

How won't it inflame my heart, deficiency in remains my desire for death!
I don't burn up though fire rains my every breath!

Fire when extinguished by water makes sounds:
Everybody in distress cannot but making laments.

He of His own accord grants every particle's excuse for intoxication—
He by Whose splendour are drunk one and all from earth to heaven!

Don't tell me: "You used to call me your life."
These days I am disgusted even with my life!

A picture of the eyes at the head of my letter I have drawn
So it becomes evident to you, to see you how they long!

[145]

When passing by my alley, she won't let the palanquin-bearers
Even shift the burden from one shoulder to the other.

[146]

My being is an expanse of the wonderland of desires;
What is called lament is the anqa of this very world.

What's autumn? What's that called spring? Whatever the season,
It's the same I, the cage, and grieving over the lost wings and feathers!

Faithfulness of the heart-stealers is fortuitous, my friend:
Who has ever seen the cries of aggrieved hearts to have any effect?

The liveliness of my thought won't suffer the grief of despair;
Wringing my hands in regret is a vow of renewal of desire!

[147]

Take pity, O tyrant! What existence a lamp extinguished has?
The pulse of a lovelorn one is the smoke of an extinguished lamp.

It keeps me restless, the desire for the flame of love,
Although to be unlit is to the benefit of a lamp.

[148]

The beauties' eyes say a lot even in silence:
Their collyrium as if were the smoke of their flaming voice.

The lover's figure is made from an unlucky star:
His lament, so to speak, the sound of the planet's revolution is.

See the force of flow of tears of blood from Majnoon's eyes!
The desert is a red welcome carpet from the profusion of roses.

[149]

Even if it is not love but just madness, so be it;
My madness is going to make you famous at least.

Don't break off relating to me;
If nothing else, let there be hostility even!

How is my presence going to bring you disrepute?
Well, if not in the party, let me see you in privacy.

I, too, of my own self am not an enemy,
Even if it be true the stranger is in love with you.

Of one's own self it ought to be;
If not awareness, forgetfulness let it be.

Though with the speed of lightning passes our life,
Yet an opportunity for the heart to bleed it does provide.

Am I the one who would forsake fidelity
Even if love be nothing but a calamity?

Give me something, O unfair heaven,
Be it just the leave to sigh and lament even!

I, too, will develop the habit of being resigned,
Knowing now that indifference is your wont.

Teasing and vexing the beloved has to continue, Asad:
If union can't be attained, at least the regret be expressed!

Commentary:

Couplet 5: It is said that there are three sources of the knowledge of God: revelation, reason, and religious, mystical experience. In mystic experience God discloses some aspect of Himself which is considered as the most authentic and credible mode of the knowledge of God and which, the poet says, can be achieved either by looking deep into oneself (self-knowledge or self-awareness) or through devotional, meditative concentration (self-forgetfulness or self-annihilation).

Couplet 6: "The heart to bleed," i.e., to love passionately with all of one's heart and endure suffering for love's sake.

[150]

For my ease and repose I am justly reproached;
At me laughs sarcastically my country's dawn.

My heart seeks the singer whose flaming voice
Would be for me the flash of the lightning of death.

In the valley of thought I travel in a trance,
So the retreat remains no more my choice.

In the garden so unreservedly you now behave that
Before the fragrance of flowers I now feel ashamed.

How to anybody could have been revealed the affairs of my heart?
The selection of my verses gave me away and notoriety brought.

[151]

When, Ghalib, in such a bad state my life has passed,
How won't I remember that I too had God!

[152]

In her gathering to feel embarrassed wouldn't do;
I sat through though unwelcome gestures continued!

154

After all it is a heart, of the doorkeeper's severity afraid it got,
Otherwise, I and passing by your house without making a call!

Ragged garment and prayer carpet I am trying to pawn for wine;
Since I last celebrated springtime is a long time now.

Futilely it passes even if it be a long life like Khizr's[1];
On Doomsday, what will His Highness say what has he been doing?

If you could answer, I would have asked you, O avaricious earth:
"With those precious treasures entrusted to you what have you done?"

When was it that calumnies my enemies did not invent?
When was it that to excruciating pain I wasn't subjected?

I wonder if in the stranger's company this habit she acquired:
Kisses now she gives without being coaxed!

Obstinacy is one thing, but by nature she isn't bad:
Hundreds of promises she's unwittingly fulfilled!

Ghalib, tell me what response will you get,
Presuming you tell it all and she hears you out?

[153]

Life is moving impetuously in a state of agitation;
Its years be measured by the speed of lightning, not the sun!

---

[1]See commentary on the first couplet of ghazal 69.

From the joy of spring the cypress is a flagon of wine
And the pheasant's wings are the waves of wine!

The heel of my steadfastness' foot has become wounded;
Now neither the ability to flee nor the stamina to linger I have!

The fief of the wine-drinkers is this world;
The heedless ones think it is a worthless wasteland.

When can sight withstand Beauty's flash of lightning
Of whose manifestation the veil is the full-blown spring?

For the satisfaction of my disappointed heart, what should I do?
Granted that on the beauty of your face my eyes are feasting.

Asad has forgone the pleasure of receiving his beloved's message;
The envy of the messenger conversing with her he can't stand.

[154]

See my luck! Of my own self jealous I become;
I want to see her but how can I see her!

If this be the fervour of thought the heart is a lost thing:
The crystal goblet is melting away, so strong is the wine!

O Lord! How can she stop the stranger in his audacity?
Even when she feels the shame of it, she is too bashful to do it.

Desire has got into the habit of always making laments,
And the heart's condition is such that breath even perturbs it.

May the evil eyes be far removed from your party of pleasure!
How wonderful! My wailing becomes a song[1] on reaching there.

Though to hide my passion indifference I affect,
But in her presence I look so lost she finds me out.

On hearing of her colourful parties, my sad heart starts sinking
While the stranger's favourable impression on her keeps deepening.

Falling in love, more delicate the fairylike beauty has become;
Her colour as it is fading to even greater advantage it is showing.

All manners of airs is her picture showing to the painter;
Farther it withdraws, the harder he tries to draw the picture.

O Asad! Like smoke my shadow flees from me!
On fire is my whole being, who can stay near me?

[155]

Seeing beautiful pictures on the quilt, fervent laments I made;
This is how in the cold nights of separation ease I found.

Delayed payment in the next world and prompt here—I know the truth!
My high-mindedness redeemed my self from me by rejecting both.

Gracing many with the Only Being's attributes is worshipping illusion;
They made me an infidel, these imaginary idols.

---

[1]"Becomes a song," i.e., is perceived as a song.

157

No rattling in my imagination even of desire for flowers!
A strange quiet has given me the loss of wings and feathers.

Commentary:

Couplet 4: The metaphor of the nightingale (not specifically mentioned here) and its passion for flowers has been used to describe a human situation. The pursuit of any passion or desire or ideal requires at least a minimum of means—in the metaphor of a bird, its wings and feathers—which, when lost, causes the desire to wilt and die. The poet does not speak of the cause or causes of the loss of wings and feathers: it is left to the imagination and personal or vicarious experience of the reader and his perception of the social and politico-economic realities of his time and place causing the discomfiture. The couplet is in ironical mode.

[156]

The tulip's burn-mark is its chief asset in this world;
For its harvest of pleasure is lightning, the farmer's warm blood!

What means for its welfare has the bud of flower?
In spite of its apparent composure its dream is a nightmare.

The grief and perturbation of this world who can bear?
Even the burn-mark and the flame make humble surrender.

Commentary:

Couplet 1: The tulip's stigma is its burn-mark, a dark spot surrounded by red petals, which distinguishes it from all other flowers and, therefore, is its capital asset. Burn-mark is a sign of grief and pain, the counterpoint of ease and pleasure. The warm blood of the farmer signifies his zeal and the labour he expends on raising the crops and plants, including tulips. But the tulip's chief asset is its burn-mark of grief and pain, the result of its harvest of pleasure being struck by lightning, and the cause of lightning was the farmer's warm blood, his hard work that made the tulip grow and flower, and then got struck by lightning. In a word, to be is to suffer pain and anguish.

[157]

Verdure has covered my home's walls and doors, Ghalib:
I am wandering in the desert and it's the springtime back home!

[158]

To die at her innocence, that remains my heart's desire,
But what to do? In the killer's hand I again see the dagger.

How sweet are her words that whatever she says
It feels as if it is coming from my own heart!

Though it is in very disagreeable ways but nevertheless
Remembrance of me is luckier than I that in her company it is.

O swarming, impetuous hopelessness, enough of it!
The pleasure I get from my fruitless efforts is going to be ruined.

Why take the trouble of moving, tiredness is welcome;
Not a step we would take on the path to the destination!

Granted, in my heart is burning the fire of Hell,
But in whose nature the mischief of doomsday is?

Ghalib's mad heart a mystery of distress and agitation is;
At least have pity on its desire for you as in great trouble it is.

[159]

Piercing through my heart in my liver lodged your glance!
Made them both well pleased, your one amorous sign.

The chest has split open: what a pleasure of freedom from care!
From the trouble of hiding my heart's wound now I am spared.

The days of drunken nights of enjoyment are gone:
Wake up now! Gone is the pleasure of sleeping through the dawn.

In my beloved's alley is floating around my dust;
At last, O wind, wings and feathers I no more covet!

Just watch her steps; how bewitching is her gait!
What a mischief it has caused, her graceful, swaying walk!

Every lustful one has the pretence of a beauty-worshiper;
Gone now is the honour and reputation of the true lover.

Seeing her face, too, did the work of weaving a veil!
Getting drunk on its beauty, every glance got scattered.

The distinction between tomorrow and yesterday disappeared suddenly:
Yesterday, the moment you left, the calamity of Doomsday befell me!

Time has destroyed you, Asadullah Khan!
Where is that exuberance! Whither is gone that youthfulness?

Commentary:

Couplet 8: It is said that our concept of time will cease to have any meaning on Doomsday: there will be no future ("tomorrow") and no past ("yesterday"), only the present. Doomsday also signifies a time of unimaginable trouble, pain, and distress—a calamity.

[160]

For peace of mind I won't cry if what I see delights me,
That is, only if in the houris of Paradise your face I see!

After killing me, in your alley don't bury me;
Why should people, by my reference, find your home?

The honour of being the cupbearer don't you put to shame tonight,
For on all other nights I do drink wine in whatever quantity served.

Nothing against you, but the messenger you recommended,
If you happen to meet him, give him my regards, my friend!

I too would have shown you what Majnoon did
If respite from struggling with my hidden grief I could find.

Not necessary that Khizr I follow as my guide;
True, a venerable companion on my journey I did find.

O you who live on his beloved's street, of him take care
If the love-mad Ghalib you happen to meet there.

Commentary:

Couplet 6: It is said of Khizr that he guides those lost in the way as well as travelers on the spiritual path, seeking after Truth. Ghalib is saying that he doesn't need Khizr for his guide, indirectly suggesting that he is well-versed himself.

[161]

If I am going to live for some more days,
In my heart I have resolved to do something else.

When is such heat in the fire of Hell!
The fire of hidden sorrows is something else.

I have seen her displeasure oftentimes,
But her anger this time is something else.

After handing the letter, the letter-bearer is looking at me;
Some verbal message, too, he seems to have for me.

Often the stars have a sinister aspect that cut our lives short,
But the celestial calamity that she is, she is something else.

All the calamities I had to suffer, I have, Ghalib;
Now only one thing is left—the sudden death.

[162]

None of my hopes has been fulfilled—not a single one,
And to make them come true I see no methods or means.

For death there is a time appointed when it will come,
But why for the whole night sleep does not come!

Earlier, at the condition of my heart I used to laugh,
But now, whatever it be, nothing makes me laugh.

Of the reward of piety and prayer I am aware,
But to them I don't incline by my nature.

Yes, there is something that makes me hold my tongue,
Otherwise, is it that I don't know how to say it?

How shouldn't I cry? About me she asks
If and when she doesn't hear my voice.

If the burn-mark on my heart you don't see, O healer,
Is it that you cannot smell it either?

I have reached that state in which I, too,
Of my own self am I not aware.

I am pining away, longing for death:
In the throes of death but not dead!

With what face will you go to the Kaba, Ghalib?
Is it that of yourself you don't feel ashamed?

[163]

O foolish heart! What has happened to you?
For the pain you suffer where is the remedy!

I long for her and she is wearied of me!
O my God, what is this happening!

I too have a tongue in my mouth,
I wish you ask me, too, what do I want!

When other than You nothing exists
Then, O God, what this ado is all about?

These fairylike beauties, who are they?
Their amorous looks and gestures, what do they say?

Their wavy, scented tresses, what do they mean?
The glances of their mascaraed eyes, what are they?

The verdure and flowers—from where do they come?
The cloud and the breeze—what are they?

See my naïvete! Loyalty I expect from the one
Who doesn't know what loyalty is.

Verily, do good and good will happen to you!
What else than this the call of the dervish be?

My life I am ready to sacrifice for you;
It is nothing to me, just praying for you!

I concede, if you insist, that Ghalib is nothing,
But what do you lose if for nothing yours he is.

[164]

Yes, you all say you pray the scented-hair beauty were here;
Would that, bewildered, one of you just said once: "She is here!"

I am in the throes of death; O my passion of love so affect her
That she comes to see me though not a word I will be able to utter!

Like lightning and flame and mercury it is!
The purpose of coming I don't understand, though came!

Obviously, Nakirain won't run away, flustered,
But only if they smell the wine drunk the night before death!

I don't fear the hangman nor with the preacher I quarrel;
In whatever guise whosoever comes I know who it is.

O seekers after Truth! With the taunt of failure who can live?
Realizing, Him I cannot find I let myself be lost.

To sit idle is not my wont;
Not getting access to Him, to the Kaba I went.

My friends spoke to her in moving terms about my condition:
Earned good opinion for themselves but ruined my reputation!

What a wonderful thing that beauty's assembly is, Ghalib!
We, too, were there and your bad luck we lamented.

Commentary:

Couplet 4: Muslims generally believe that two angels, Munkar and Nakir (together known as "Nakirain"), examine the dead in the tomb about their beliefs and actions.

[165]

In a state of restlessness is again my heart;
Again, the love's deep wound my chest desires.

Again, the heart of the lovelorn one is bleeding;
Again, the season of tulip's bloom is fast approaching.

The object of desire of my supplicating glance
Again is the very same veil of the very litter.

Again my eyes are the brokers for the things of infamy,
Again my heart is the buyer of the pleasure of ignominy.

The one shedding tears a hundred times as of yore,
The other making laments in a hundred ways as before.

My heart, from longing for the beloved's swinging gait,
Again is in turmoil like that on Judgement Day.

Again the beauty is displaying airs and graces,
Again, everyone is offering his life as a price.

Again, for the very same faithless one I die;
Again, it is the very same life as of yore.

Again, the doors of the court of coquetry have opened
And criminal cases are happening in large numbers.

The darkness of injustice has again engulfed the world,
Her curling locks are again administering the court.

Again, pieces of the heart have made a petition,
Crying for justice and sighing and wailing.

Again, the witnesses for love have been summoned,
Again, the shedding of tears is the order of the day.

In the suit between the heart and the eyelashes,
Today, again, is the proceeding of the case.

Your being like one in delirium is not without reason, Ghalib!
Something definitely is there for which it is a cover.

[166]

Madness is not to be blamed for peace if I rejoiced:
Sprinkling salt on the heart's wound the occasional pleasure of life is!

To break free from the jostlings of life, what effort can avail?
For the waves of water, freedom to flow their chains become!

After the mad lover's death, his grave is the youngsters' pilgrimage place!
The sparks flying off my tombstone are flowers strewn on the grave.

He who complains of the beloved's tyranny he be reproached
Lest Judgement Day be for him the day of sarcastic laughter!

In Laila's veins the dust of Majnoon's desert would cause wounds
If the farmer would sow in the desert fleams' tips instead of seeds!

As if the moths' wings were the oars of the wine boat,
By the party's fervour the rounds of wine drinking got started.

How am I oppressed by my desire to fly when can I describe!
The strength was gone from my pinions before I could take flight.

How long to keep crying behind her tent! What a catastrophe!
O God, wasn't a wall of stone decreed for me?

Commentary:

Couplet 2: For Majnoon, see commentary on couplet 1 of ghazal 2. In the present couplet the reference is to the reputed incident in Majnoon's love life when Laila, his beloved, underwent phlebotomy and a vein in his hand, too, started bleeding simultaneously. The poet says that this won't happen in the reverse order: for the dust raised by Majnoon's wandering in the desert to have an effect on Laila is as likely as for a farmer to sow fleams' tips instead of seeds and that, too, in the desert, i.e., not likely at all. The couplet is in an ironical mode.

Couplet 3: See the commentary on couplet 1 of ghazal 50 where the wave of wine empowers the "wine boat." In this couplet "moth's wings" do this as if they were oars. Traditionally, lighted candles were among the concomitants of a wine party, and these lights attracted moths, and moths symbolized fervour.

[168]

From intemperance, respectability I lost with everyone:
As the one was on the rise so the other went down!

Hidden was a trap terribly close to my nest:
Before I could manage to take wing, I was caught.

My existence is the proof of my non-existence;
Effaced to a point where only in name I exist!

Of them who endured love's hardships what can be said?
Going through it all, grief incarnate they gradually became!

How would your loyalty compensate, for, in this world,
Besides what you caused, many other wrongs I suffered.

Blood-dripping stories of love's frenzy I kept writing,
Although my hands were smitten for doing this.

O God! How great is the fury of her temper that from its fear
The laments in my heart went to pieces, consuming each other.

For the false lovers abandoning love's battlefield is triumph;
Lifting their legs to run away is raising the victory banner!

In the state of non-existence with some laments I was entrusted;
Those that I couldn't make there became breaths here.

Even as a mendicant, Asad, love I did not forsake:
When a beggar, in love with the generous ones I fell!

169

Commentary:

Couplet 9: For the expression "non-existence," see the commentary on couplet 3 of ghazal 4. In a word it implies existing as spirit or the life principle in some imagined world "there" before being given the human form and appearing in this world "here."

[169]

If the heart's mohur of burn-mark didn't guard the flame of love
The frigidity of spirit, lurking behind silence, would steal it away.

What expectation can I have from her in her season of youth
Who did not hear my story even when a child!

Just so, to cause sorrow and suffering to someone is not good,
Otherwise, I would say: "O God, give my life to my enemy."

Commentary:

Couplet 1: The heart's burn-mark—its most valued possession ("mohur" or "gold coin")—that its passion of love has created must never be allowed to be lost ("the flame of love" should guard it). The frigidity of spirit is always lying in ambush ("lurking behind silence") to steal the "mohur" (obliterating the "burn-mark" by extinguishing "the flame of love").

[170]

In my dark house is cast the pall of the night of grief
Where the only sign of dawn is the candle extinguished!

No glad tidings of meeting nor an opportunity to see the beauty!
A long time it is since my ears and eyes have been mutually at peace.

Wine has made the proud beauty bold and free:
O desire! Surrendering discreetness is now permissible.

Look at the pearls in the necklace of the beauties;
In what ascendancy are the pearl-sellers' stars!

Seeing her is wine, desire the cupbearer, and eyes are drunk!
The assembly of her thought is a tavern without tumult.

O you newly arrived at the festivities of the heart's desire!
Beware if you lust for music and wine.

Look at me if eyes you have that can see warning signs;
Listen to me if ears you have that can hear good advice.

The cupbearer by her splendour destroys faith and wisdom;
The minstrel by his music robs one of dignity and judgement.

At night I would see every spot of the party floor,
From end to end, a bouquet was.

The pleasure of the cupbearer's gait and the joy of the harp's music—
One the paradise for the eyes, the other heavenly to the ears!

But if to the same party of pleasure in the morning one returned,
Neither that gaiety nor that excitement and fervour he would find.

The only sign of the dispersed night party would be
A candle and that, too, extinguished, leaving a scar.

From the unseen world come these themes and thoughts:
The sound of my quill is the voice of the angel, Ghalib!

[171]

Do come soon; no peace knows my soul;
The tyranny of waiting I can bear no more!

Paradise is given as a recompense for life in this world:
The wine is not in the measure of the pain of hangover!

My weeping is forcing me out from your festive party;
Alas! On sobbing and shedding tears no control have I.

Wrongly you think your feelings I would hurt;
In the lovers' constitution there is no spite!

Let your heart enjoy fully the splendours of meaning:
Other than flowers, there are no other mirrors of spring!

At last she has given her word that she will kill me;
If she doesn't keep her promise, what a pity it would be!

You have made a vow that you won't drink wine;
But the credibility of your vow is suspect, Ghalib.

172

Commentary:

Couplet 5: As the beauty of spring shows itself in flowers so are the splendours of meanings of the poet's work manifested in the hearts of the readers who are invited to fill their hearts with the joy of meaning.

Couplet 6: See the commentary on couplet 9 of ghazal 37 where a similar thought has been expressed in a different context.

[172]

From thronging grief my head is bent to such an extent that
Distinguishing the lines of sight from the shirt-skirt's threads is difficult!

The purpose of stitching the wound is the pleasure of the hurt of stitching;
Don't ever think that consideration for pain the mad one is neglecting.

In whichever flower-garden that beauty shows up, Ghalib,
There the buds burst into blossoms like hearts into laughter!

Commentary:

Couplet 2: The purpose of stitching the wound is not healing but adding to the pain: the stitches are additional wounds.

[173]

I, the desert-wanderer, with my head resting on my knee am sitting:
In my knee's mirror, in its polishing-streaks, my feet's thorns I am seeing.

With you in my arms the condition of my heart is worth seeing!
Every hair of your tresses feels like an intimate glance to me.

My being is a musical instrument of the notes of complaints!
You better don't tease me in the presence of others.

Commentary:

Couplet 1: The seemingly simple imagery of this couplet is not all that simple: there is, in fact, a little complex play of the literal and figurative senses of the phrases used which is typically Ghalibian, besides a few allusions. For example, the mirror of the knee is a metaphor for the kneecap and once the poet uses this metaphor its other possibilities are exploited. First, it is a steel mirror on which, when polishing, appear streaks, the metaphor for the thorns in the feet that got stuck when wandering in the wilderness. Then, mirror is also a metaphor for heart as well as truth, for it reflects everything as it really is. So the thorns seen in the mirror are not the thorns in the feet but in the heart itself. Now about allusions: sitting in a position with the head resting on one's knees is not just about the physical position in its literal sense, it is also an allusion to the position in which mystics sit in meditative devotion, and the term used for the knees or knee-caps in this position is "mirror" in the mystic vocabulary, for it is in this position in such devotional concentration that truth is reflected in the mirror of the heart. Thus, taking the couplet as a whole, it means that the seeker after truth has to go through all kinds of hardships that test the limits of human endurance and capacities, both physical (desert-wandering or wilderness-wandering) and spiritual/mental (meditation). The term "desert-wandering" (or "wilderness-wandering") also symbolizes the restlessness of the lover's soul seeking his beloved (the ideal, the truth, or a woman) and it as well brings to mind the story of Majnoon who wandered in the desert looking for his beloved Laila, never giving up (and there were moments when he did catch her sight). It further suggests that for the traveller on this way there are no signposts, it is no beaten path.

[174]

In any company, in your charming style if you happened to speak,
Into the figures in the pictures on the walls life it would breathe!

Like shadows would follow you the cypress and the pine,
If with your statuesque figure you came walking in the garden.

Only then would the tears' pride of preciousness be justified
If with them come streaming from the eyes bits of heart.

Allow me to make complaints, O oppressor,
So that in tormenting me you also find some pleasure.

If from her enchanting eyes it gets the sign,
Like a parakeet, the mirror would start talking.

The thorns' tongues are parched with thirst, O Lord!
May someone with blistered soles enter the valley of thorns!

How won't I die of envy when her delicate body
Comes in the embrace of the loop of the sacred thread!

If the lust for gold hadn't ruined honour and reputation,
Why did the sweetheart of a flower move to the market from the garden?

O ignorant heart! The tearing of the shirt's breast would be a pleasure
Only if with its every shred came entangled the breath of life.

175

Of my chest a furnace it has made, the secret I keep hidden;
Oh! What an upheaval it might not cause if to it I gave expression!

The talisman of the hidden treasure of meaning it is,
Every word, O Ghalib, that occurs in my verses.

Commentary:

Couplet 7: Sacred or Brahminical thread is worn by high-caste Hindus. The beloved is also known as an idol in Persian and Urdu literature and Hindu idols are often shown wearing a sacred thread. The closeness (embrace) of the loop of the sacred thread to the person of the beloved excites the envy of the lover: he wants his beloved in his own embrace, not in that of a lifeless sacred thread.

Couplet 11: The talisman (in Urdu, Arabic, and Persian, *tilism*, *tilasm* or *talism*) is thought to work in two phases. In the first, a treasure of rare and precious things (here, "meaning") is hidden by the use of some words or phrases of magical charm. This the poet has done by his choice of words, which are also the treasures of meaning. In the second phase, this charm is broken to open the treasure that presents its own difficulty and some hard work. This is what is expected from the readers. But once they have succeeded in this the discovery of the many-faceted meanings hidden in the words of the poet's works will bring surprise and pleasure as would the discovery of a treasure after a hard search.

[175]

Though the beauty of the moon—when a full moon—is pleasing,
But my moon-faced beloved of sun-like splendour excels!

Kiss she won't give but on my heart she always has her eyes:
In her heart she says if for free it comes it is a prize.

One can fetch another one from the market if it breaks:
Better than Jamshed's cup my earthen cup is!

Extra pleasure it brings if He gives without asking:
That beggar is better who isn't in the habit of begging.

On seeing her a glow comes over my face:
She thinks the lovelorn one is in good shape.

Let us see what favours the lovers receive from their beloveds;
That this is an auspicious year, a Brahmin has said.

Farhad's skill with the axe brought him in converse with Shirin:
Whatsoever it be, whoever achieves it, excellence is good.

A drop of water if it merges with the sea, sea it becomes;
That act is good of which the consequence is good.

May God make Khizr Sultan flourish forever:
A fine fresh sapling is he in the King's garden.

I know, Ghalib, what Paradise is!
But to cheer the heart a good thought it is.

Commentary:

Couplet 3: Jamshed is a legendary king of Persia who is said to have owned a rare and precious cup which he used for drinking wine as well as for crystal gazing.

Couplet 9: Khizr Sultan was the son of the last Mughal emperor of India, Bahadur Shah Zafar. This ghazal was probably written in 1831, the year of his birth when Bahadur Shah was the crown prince. Later in life, as a young poet, he made Ghalib his mentor.

[176]

If my dying doesn't satisfy you, so be it;
If some test still remains, ignore this one too.

The prickings of the thorn of longing to see her is very much there;
If the flowers of the garden of satisfaction I couldn't gather, so be it.

O wine lovers! Drinking straight from the flagon is now the way;
If for a day the cupbearer is not in the party, so be it!

Qais is the life and light of the desert;
If he is not the lamp of Laila's dark tent, so be it.

On stir and buzz depends the liveliness of the home;
Let there be sad dirges if merry songs there cannot be!

Neither praise I desire nor for reward I care;
If in my poetry people don't find meaning, so be it.

The pleasure of the company of beauties, take it as a godsend!
If, Ghalib, you don't live the term of natural life, so be it.

[177]

With what lively cheer ahead of the executioner I walk
That the shadow of my head is two paces ahead of my steps!

The recording angel wanted me to be drunk with the wine of love;
Only wrote "drunk" and then the pen wouldn't move any further!

The worldly woes wore off the intoxication of the delights of love,
Otherwise, earlier, I too used to enjoy the pleasure of the pain of love.

For God's sake, take a fair view of my love-madness
That before the letter carrier I arrive at her doorstep.

All through my life, disorder I have suffered because of you;
O curl into curl of tresses, may it come upon you!

The wave of blood fluttering in my heart and lungs
Formerly I vainly used to think the breath of life it was.

Now they are swearing not to attend my funeral, Ghalib—
They who earlier always used to swear by my life.

[178]

"The unkind one gets angry hearing the word complaint";
I can't say this even, for this too amounts to complaint.

Full of complaints am I as a musical instrument with tunes;
Just try to tease me and then see what happens.

Though not aware, but see the beauty of the amends she makes!
If I complain of cruelty, even more zealous in cruelty she becomes!

In the path of love, the star-studded heaven moves at the pace
As would a slow-moving person with blisters on his soles.

How wouldn't I be the target of the crossbow of cruelty?
I myself hand back the arrow if its target it misses.

How nice it would have been had I been my own ill-wisher!
I always wish myself well, and always the opposite happens!

My laments used to go beyond the empyrean,
But now they come only up to my lips, if at all.

My pen that is Barbud of the poetic gathering,
Now thus it sings its song in praise of the King:

O Emperor whose soldiers are the stars and the sun the standard!
Your endless bounties when can one ever repay?

If the revenues of the seven continents were brought together,
Just for the shoeing of the horses of your army that would pay.

Every month that from a full moon it wanes to a crescent,
Supplicating at your doorstep it wears off its forehead.

That I am audaciously breaking the rules of the ghazal is because
Your graciousness heightens my desire for your praises.

O Ghalib, forgive me for this my sorrowful song;
Today somewhat exceedingly aches my heart.

Commentary:

Couplet 8: Barbud was a court singer of the Persian emperor Khusrao Pervez (590-628), and was known for the beauty of his voice. It is also said that he invented new modes of singing.

Couplet 13: This is about this ghazal as a whole, exclusive of couplets 8 to 12 which are in praise of the last Mughal Emperor, Bahadur Shah Zafar, and is a *qita-bund*, which, according to convention, if it occurs in a ghazal, describes something specific that can be different from the ghazal's theme or its dominant mood as in this case.

[179]

Whatever I say, you say: "Who art thou?"
You please tell me what style of converse is this!

The flame doesn't have her amorous look nor lightning her grace:
Will somebody tell me what that hot-tempered, sprightly beauty is?

It makes me jealous that with you converses my enemy,
Otherwise, what fear have I of his speaking ill of me!

Soaked in blood, my shirt is sticking to my body;
What need for stitches has my shirt's breast now?

When the body is burnt up, the heart, too, should have burnt up:
Now that you are scraping the ashes, what are you looking for?

Coursing through the arteries and veins, that means nothing to me;
If from the eyes it doesn't drip, of what worth the blood is?

The thing for which Paradise is dear to me,
Other than the rose-colored, full-bodied wine, what else is?

I would drink wine if a few flagonfuls I would see;
These cups and goblets and glasses, what are they to me?

I am left with no strength to speak, and even if I could
On what hope would I say what my desire is?

Becoming a favourite of the King, he moves around exultingly,
Otherwise, what honour does Ghalib have in this city?

[180]

I tease her and she says nothing!
Had she been drunk beside herself she would be.

A torment or a calamity, whatever you are,
Would that you were only for me!

O God, if so much sorrow was fated for me
More than one heart You should have given me!

One day she would have come around, Ghalib,
If for some days more you had lived!

The strangers in your party are enjoying drinks,
And I remain thirsting for a message even!

For my afflictions why should I complain to you!
It is the sleight of hand of the heavens above.

Letters I would write even if there is nothing new,
For, in very truth, I am in love with your name, too.

At night, wine I drank at the Zamzam,
And, at dawn, I washed clean the stains on my ehram.

See how my eyes have trapped my heart!
As if they, too, are the loops of your net.

The King, it is rumoured, having recovered from illness, is to bathe;
Let us see when the hammam is going to have its day.

Love, O Ghalib, has rendered me a good-for-nothing;
Otherwise, I, too, was a man who could accomplish things.

Commentary:

Couplet 4: The Zamzam is the celebrated well very close to the Kaba in Mecca. The ehram is the garment worn by pilgrims after ablution before entering Mecca for Hajj or Umrah. It consists of two unsewn pieces of white cloth wrapped around the body, keeping the head bare. While in ehram, certain things otherwise permissible are prohibited. But in Islam all alcoholic drinks including wine are prohibited under all circumstances, what to speak of when one is in ehram or at the Zamzam. However, at a deeper level of human psyche, the poet is speaking of man's weaknesses and his efforts to correct them.

Couplet 6: The hammam is a hot bath or Turkish bath; here it means a hot water bath.

[182]

Again with such glory springtime has come
That the sun and the moon its spectators have become.

Have a look, O dwellers of this earthly region!
This is what is called adorning the world,

That the earth has become, from end to end,
What puts to shame the sphere of heavens.

When the verdure could find no other place,
On the surface of water moss it became.

To see the flowers and the greenery,
Sight has been given to the narcissus' eye.

Intoxicating is the air as is wine;
Walking in the air is imbibing the wine!

Why shouldn't the world be happy, Ghalib?
From illness has recovered the righteous King!

[183]

Indifference I welcome; mine is proud humility:
If you avoid me, it is as if you vacate the place for me!

The world is stocked up because the people of liberality it lacks:
The more the flagons and goblets are full, emptier is the tavern!

[184]

When is she ready to hear my story,
And that, too, in my words from me directly!

Of the prickings of your amorous, piercing glances, don't ask me;
Just look at the pure blood pouring from my eyes!

What will my friends remember me for and cry
Other than my distressed, distracted utterances!

In the wilderness of thought I am lost;
That I have been forgotten is what marks me out.

Opposition to me my beloved feigns;
Seeing my wit and eloquence, silence she affects.

Like a stone in the way I am being treated:
Very lightly are taken my weight and worth.

The whirlwind of the path of restlessness am I;
The boisterous wind of desire is the source.

When her mouth I could not find,
Evident it became I knew nothing.

My debility has rendered me so helpless, Ghalib,
That my youth is a shame for old age.

Commentary:

Couplet 8: By Urdu poetic convention smallness of the mouth is considered as an aspect of the beloved's beauty, perhaps suggesting that she is a person of few words or no words, and this arising from her pride in her beauty. In the present couplet the poet takes it to its limit as if she had no mouth, subtly implying his frustration at having no word from her and sarcastically admitting his ignorance.

[185]

The picture of the playful beauty in the embrace of the rival!
The peacock's leg for a brush would Mani need for its portrayal.

You are that ill-disposed whom my shocked silence amuses,
And the story of grief can only be told in distressful words.

That fire of love I desire which, like the candle's flame,
Would spread into the arteries of my heart.

Commentary:

Couplet 1: Mani (216-276) was a celebrated painter. Born in Iraq, he lived a major part of his life in Turkistan and China. While a peacock is an ornamental bird known for the beauty of its plumes, its legs are ugly and odious.

Exceedingly pleasing is your company to the flower garden;
Opening of the arms of welcome the blossoming of buds is.

There, the spire of indifference keeps all the time rising;
Here, the laments keep claiming the reach notwithstanding.

Sorrow teaches the lover the ways in self-possession:
Any fresh wound on the heart is a look of admonition.

[187]

The wound that can be closed and healed
May it be decreed as my enemy's fate, O God!

It is good to imagine her hennaed fingertip:
At least a drop of blood in my heart I can see.

What makes you fear lovers would complain, losing patience?
Even if they do, here nobody hears anybody's cry for redress.

A hundred pities for that disappointed lover, Ghalib, who all his life
Longed for a beloved who on him would turn her killing weapons:

Her poniard never turned its attention on his heart
Nor to his neck her dagger paid any heed!

[188]

To the mirror, mercury gives its poise,
But keeps me harassed my restless heart.

Flowers have opened their arms, bidding each other farewell;
Springtime is about to end, so let us go, O nightingale!

[189]

Union is separation if there is reserve and restraint;
The beloved needs to be playful and the lover passionate!

Those lips would sure be bestowing a kiss one day but, yes,
Exuberant desire and reckless courage are needed for this.

[190]

Beauties are to be desired and desired to the limit!
And if they too desire, what else would one want!

The company of drunkards needs to be avoided;
Instead of emptying the glass the place be better vacated.

Desiring you! What did the heart think of this?
Now it needs to be called to account and duly punished.

Don't rend your shirt's breast till the flowers are in bloom;
Some sign you should get from nature, too.

Behaving like a stranger is a cover for friendship:
Hiding your face from me behind the veil you had better give up.

My rival's enmity against me lost him his own position:
What an inveterate enemy is he is a thing to be seen!

When can the lover on his own bring notoriety to himself?
O yes, if the beloved is passion-inflaming, tumult-exciting!

He who lives on the hope of death,
Of his hopelessness what can be said!

Of beautiful faces Asad is enamoured,
But just look at him, and his desire!

O thoughtless one, for these moon-faced beauties,
The lover, too, is to have a pleasing presence.

[191]

With every step my destination seems receding from me:
Seeing my frenzied speed, the wilderness is running away from me!

Reading indifferently just the title of the playbook[1] is better;
For me my sight lines the binding strings of my eyelids are!

In the lonely night, from the terror of fire in my heart,
My shadow, like smoke, took to flight.

---

[1]Playbook, i.e., the world, in its aspect of tamasha or play providing diversion and entertainment.

189

Mourning their lovers, may not the beauties forsake self-adornment!
How cheerless my beloved's dressing table is when I am no more!

By the blisters on my sole the track in the desert of madness
Like a pearl-string became, making general illumination.

May my trance be a prelude to enduring peace
Now that I fill my bed as I fill my shadow!

If you behead me while I am looking longingly at you,
Like the trimmed off candlewick's light would scatter my sight.

The terror of forlornness of the night of separation, ah, alas!
My shadow is hiding from me in the sun of the Judgement Day.

A revolving goblet of a hundred splendours are you,
And a mirror of bewildered eyes am I.

From my fervent eyes is dropping fire, Asad,
Igniting sticks and straws, illumining the garden!

[192]

A quibbler is she, to tell her of my heart's grief no way I see;
When no chance has the ingenuity of speech, how can one succeed!

I do invite her but, O passion of my heart, so affect her
That except for coming to me no other choice has she!

To her love is just a sport; she may not give it up and forget!
Would that tormenting me she wouldn't be able to help!

The stranger goes around carrying your letter in such a way
That if someone asked what was it, to hide it there wouldn't be a way.

She is a beauty, but damn such delicacy!
One wouldn't be able to touch her even if one possessed her.

Who can say Whose manifestation this universe is!
Such a curtain He has dropped that no effort can raise it.

I shouldn't await death, that which is bound to come!
I should desire you, one who despite invitations won't come!

The weight that has fallen off my head was such that I couldn't endure;
The task that has come upon me is such that I can't accomplish.

On love one has no control; it is that fire, Ghalib,
Which one can't ignite nor can extinguish at will.

[193]

If wildness wants to rend the shirt when bare-chested,
Like the crack of dawn here is my heart's wound instead.

Such is the splendour of your beauty that just its thought
Makes my heart's eye the place of pilgrimage for wonderment.

O my God! My heart has no hope of even being broken!
Till when is this glass to make its case to the mountain?

If the tavern is crushed by the beloved's drunken eyes,
The goblets' hair-like cracks would be their drooping eyelashes.

191

The down on the beloved's face is love's written promise to the tresses:
"Absolutely acceptable to me is whatever disorder you bring."

Commentary:

Couplet 3: "Mountain" is a metaphor for the beloved, signifying her hard-heartedness, and "glass" for the poet's heart. Although showing impatience and frustration, but, in a very subtle way, the poet is also suggesting that his heart, in spite of its sensitivity and delicacy, is not broken—it has not given up.

Couplet 4: The word *shikast* in the original, translated as "crushed" in line one of this couplet, has been used both in its literal sense of "broken" as well as figuratively for "overwhelmed" or "defeated."

[194]

She may come in my dream and calm my anxiety,
But is the agitation of my heart going to let me sleep?

It kills me, your breaking into tears when lovingly I tease you;
Who is there who can sharpen the glance's scimitar like you!

If nothing, finish me off by showing the movement of your lips;
If a kiss you don't give, say something with your mouth at least.

Give in the hollow of my hands, O cupbearer, if me you hate;
If not in the goblet, so be it, give me the wine at least!

Overwhelmed with joy, Asad, paralyzed I felt
When she asked me to give comfort-pressure to her legs!

From restless tossings, in great distress is my bedclothes' every thread:
My head a vexation for the pillow, my body a burden for the bed!

Tears gushing to reach the desert are my shirt's skirt's beloved;
My heart lying helpless is the darling of the bed!

How auspicious is my illness! To inquire after me you have come:
The bed-head's lighted lamp my bed's lucky star has become.

In the lonely night, from the fury of the storm of agitation,
My bedclothes' threads are like the rays of Doomsday's sun.

My pillow still smells of my beloved's musk-scented tresses;
Seeing my love only in dream, like Zulaikha, be a shame for my bed.

What to say of my heart's condition in the beloved's absence, Ghalib?
From restlessness, my bedclothes' every thread is like thorn to me.

Commentary:

Couplet 5: Zulaikha is the name of Potiphar's wife whose passion for Joseph is much celebrated in Persian and Urdu poetry. She is said to have seen Joseph in her dream. The poet prides himself on having the physical presence of his beloved ("My pillow still smells of my beloved's musk-scented tresses").

[196]

The danger is, your being my beloved might make me arrogant:
The pride of friendship be a calamity if my enemy you become.

Know that springtime is wanting in flourishing vigour, Ghalib,
If the flowers don't cover the cypresses completely like a robe.

[197]

Plaint doesn't have any tone or tune;
No need for lament to emulate the flute.

Why do gardeners plant gourds
If the garden isn't a beggar for wine?

Though You are manifest in everything
But there nothing is that is like You.

Yes, don't be deceived that things have real existence;
They don't, however much people may insist they do.

Move past the pleasure so no grief you suffer:
If there were no spring there wouldn't be fall either!

Why refuse the goblet, O zealot?
Wine it is, the bees' vomit it is not.

If there is no existence nor non-existence, Ghalib,
Then, O negator, what are you?

[198]

Of the constituents of the salve for the heart's wound, don't ask me;
Just know that the particle of diamond its chief ingredient is!

After a long time your indifference to me has invented this—
The sideway glance which apparently is less than a full regard!

[199]

Jealousy even of my own self I can't bear;
I die for her but don't desire her!

With the stranger secretly she associates:
Purdah is only apparent, in reality there is no purdah.

A cause of despair for the people of lust it would be;
That you speak ill of Ghalib, no good you do to them.

[200]

From your lips the wine acquires the attribute of light,
And like a florist's eyes light up the goblet's lines.

Sometimes at least this mad heart of mine, too, be treated fairly;
It's ages now that for repose[1] it has been yearning.

Right and proper, the nightingale's laments flowers don't hear!
Filled with dewdrops, as with carded cotton, are their ears.

Asad is in death's throes; for God's sake, go to him, O faithless one!
In this situation bashfulness be forsaken and reserve bidden farewell.

---

[1]Literally, pillow or bolster that provides support and eases pressure and thus brings repose.

195

[201]

Why not, yes, why not the beauties' eyes be indifferent?
Have to abstain from casting a full look, their languid eyes.

Till the last breath will remain unfulfilled my desire to see her;
Ah my discomfiture! So sharp is my killer's dagger!

Seeing flowers, Asad, my beloved's face I remember;
Spring in its bloom excites my longing for her.

[202]

If he lost his heart to her, why blame? He is only human!
If my rival he has become what can I say? He is my messenger.

Obstinately it refuses to come today though come it must!
How to say how great is my grievance against death?

Whatever be the time, in my beloved's alley he is found;
If, then, my enemy's house I don't call it, what else should I?

Excellent! How her amorous glances keep deceiving me
That she is fully aware of my state, why speak of it?

It is in the marketplace that she asks me how am I doing,
Knowing well I would say: "It is a public place, what can I say?"

For the bond of loyalty you don't at all care;
I hold it in my hand but can you tell what is that?

Presumptuously she asserts my request is madness—why quarrel?
Responding to it I have stopped—what good would be that?

Achieving poetic excellence is visited with envy—what to do!
Accomplishment in arts is rewarded with vexation —what to say!

Who is saying that Ghalib is not bad,
But what else can be said except that he is mad!

[203]

Seeing that inwardly I was striving to sever worldly ties,
Incorporeity bound my being to my body and left me thus.

I am the grindstone for my beloved's scimitar of glances:
Congratulations! What a blessing for me my endurance is!

Why she be not indifferent when she feels confident
That, questioning my situation, in my own self I remain lost.

When the decree of fate of my house of sorrow was being written,
I too was counted amongst the causes of its desolation.

Suspicious of me becomes my beloved;
Of the nightingales' song I wish I wasn't so fond!

Ah! Even there, the tumult of Doomsday didn't let me rest;
Though to indulge my desire for comfort to my grave I went.

Be true to your word and come to me—what style is this?
Why have you made me the doorman of my house!

197

Indeed, how great is the pleasure of the coming of spring!
Again, the desire for singing ghazals has revived in me.

To my brother God has given a new lease on life;
Mirza Yousuf is to me like Joseph, Ghalib.

Commentary:

Couplet 6: The first line of the couplet alludes to the general belief of Muslims that the dead will be raised from their graves, as from a deep slumber, on Doomsday, a day of great tumult, and that the time from death to the raising from the grave would seem like a moment. The second line speaks of the toils and pains of life in this world, giving rise to the desire for escape from it. When both lines are read together the poet is making the point that there is no such escape. God says in the Quran: "Verily, We have created man into (a life of) pain, toil and trial" (Chapter 90, verse 4—translation by Muhammad Asad).

Couplet 9: Mirza Yousuf, Ghalib's brother, was two years younger than he. This ghazal was written after his recovery from a serious illness. Joseph is the son of Jacob. His story is told both in the Bible and the Quran; in the latter Joseph is Yousuf, its Arabic form. Ghalib is saying here that he loves his brother Yousuf as Jacob loved his son Joseph and that Yousuf is as handsome as was Joseph. The story of Joseph also brings to mind other interesting comparisons: Joseph's time in slavery and Yousuf's serious illness; later Joseph's freedom and achieving eminence and Yousuf's recovering health and Ghalib's hope that God has granted him a new lease on life.

[204]

Even in the midst of rejoicing I don't forget invoking God;
My smile then is like the devotee's soft chant, glorifying God.

198

The loosening up of my constrained, sad heart depends on words:
This from the talismanic word of the alphabetic combination-lock I learned!

O God! From whom to seek redress for this misery!
The ease and comfort of the captives now I envy!

What to do! For the pleasure of sorrows I am eager by nature:
When I desire something, what I look for is its discomfiture!

Having lost your heart to someone, you too, Ghalib, are like me;
Earlier, Mirza Sahib, from falling in love you used to forbid me.

Commentary:

Couplet 5: Mirza Sahib, i.e., Ghalib, the poet.

[205]

In His Majesty's presence the poets are going to be tested:
In the Royal garden, the garden's songsters are going to be tested.

By their beloved's stature and tresses Qais and Farhad[1] were tested,
But where I am, by the gallows and the rope I am being tested.

Finally, the mountain-digger's capacity for grief shall be tested,
For now, the distressed one's physical strength is being tested.

What friendly feeling could Egypt's breeze have for Canaan's old man[2]?
What it wanted was that the effect of the scent of Joseph's shirt be tested.

---

[1]For Qais and Farhad and "mountain-digger" in the next couplet see the commentary on ghazal 2, though the contexts are different.
[2]I.e., Jacob, Joseph's father; both Jacob and Joseph of the Bible and the Quran.

There she comes! Watch out! Can't say you weren't warned;
Patience and self-restraint of the people assembled will be tested.

Arrow lodging in the heart is good; going through the liver, even better:
My only purpose is that the aim of the beautiful archer be tested.

No hold over them have the loops of rosary and the sacred thread;
It is by their fidelity that the Sheikh and Brahmin are to be tested.

Lie easy, O captive heart! By losing patience what will you gain?
The power of her tresses' curls within curls you again want to be tested!

When grief's poison spreads in arteries and veins then see what happens;
For now, by its bitterness the mouth and palate are being tested.

What promise—coming to my home! Just wait and see, Ghalib,
With what new calamities by the old heavens I am going to be tested!

[206]

If ever the thought of being nice comes into her mind,
Remembering her past cruelties she remains abashed!

O God! Perhaps quite the contrary effect has the passion of my heart:
The more I try she inclines to me, the more she shies away from me.

She is short-tempered and my love narrative is rather long:
Loses his patience even the messenger and begs to make it short.

There is she, full of mistrust, and here am I, grown so weak!
She won't ask me how am I doing and I can't even speak.

O hopelessness, give me some respite! What a calamity is this!
Even the train of thought of the beloved is slipping away from me!

Frankly, though, I would be one of those who would see her;
But that others also would see her, how this outrage can I bear?

In the battle of love it is my foot that has got wounded first:
Now neither can I run away nor can I stay on to fight it out.

What a catastrophe! Travelling with the pretender, Ghalib,
The beloved whom even to the care of God I can't entrust!

Commentary:

Couplet 8: In the second line of the couplet, the poet is alluding to the
social custom among Muslims that when two (or more) friends or relatives part,
each says to the other: "I entrust you to the care of God!" or "May God protect
you!"

[207]

To keep watching the world for amusement is a sign of madness;
For them the opening and shutting of eyelids are shaming slaps.

I don't know how the blemish of bad faith will you erase—
You for whom even the mirror a vortex of reproach is!

By twists and turns of desires, with comfort don't break your ties;
The course of salvation, in taking a humble view of things lies.

The pretence of love face to face with the beloved's loyalty!
It's feigning madness in springtime—a calamity.

[208]

So thin I am grown that if a place you give me in your assembly
None would be able to spot me, this I guarantee.

Seeing me, if she feels compassion a surprise it won't be,
But only if somebody would take me to her on some pretence!

If your face you don't show, don't, but in a manner of reproach
Just show me your angry eyes, removing your veil.

So pleased is she with my being a captive
That if her curling lock I were, in a comb she would entangle me!

[209]

This world I regard as child's play,
A show going on night and day.

Solomon's throne is to me a mere toy,
And mere words[1] the miracle of Christ!

But for the name the phenomenal world I don't accept;
Things have no existence for me except in thought.

---

[1]For "words" see the commentary on ghazal 223 which has only one couplet.

The desert hides itself in dust because of me;
The river beats its forehead against the land seeing me.

Don't ask what's my condition when you aren't with me!
Just see what's your manner and mood when you are with me.

Truly said, proud and self-regarding am I! Why shouldn't I be?
My beloved of mirror-like forehead is sitting in front of me.

You will see the beauty and style of the flowers of words I strew,
But first let someone set a goblet of rose wine before me.

Suspicion of hating her it raises, so jealousy I forsake:
"Don't mention her name before me," this I won't anymore say!

Faith is holding me back while infidelity is inviting me:
The Kaba is drawing me towards it and the Church attracting me!

Though a lover but at beguiling the beloved I am adept:
Compared to me Laila calls Majnoon the villain of a piece!

One is delighted meeting the beloved but one doesn't die like that;
What I had wished on the nights of separation had to happen then!

Surging from my eyes is a river of blood: may that it be the end!
But who can tell how many more calamities are yet to come?

Though my hands I can't move but in my eyes there still is life,
So leave before me for now the goblet and the flagon of wine.

He is in the same calling, has the same taste, and shares my secrets,
Why then speak ill of Ghalib? Well, at least, not in my presence!

Commentary:

Couplet 9: This couplet is about the battle that goes on in one's heart, not only between faith and unbelief (reading the couplet literally), but, in fact and figuratively, between conflicting hard choices that demand decisions.

Couplet 13: Lifeless limbs but yet some sign of life in the eyes suggest approaching death.

[210]

When I speak of my condition you say what is it I want;
Tell me, what can I say if of the all the persons you ask that!

Don't again respond with the riposte: "Yes, I am an oppressor."
I am in the habit of saying to whatever you say: "Right you are."

Well, it is a fleam but when deep in my heart it has lodged,
Why shouldn't I call her coquettish glance my intimate friend?

The slit made by the tip of an arrow can't bring relief;
It's the sword's wound that is heart-expanding, exhilarating!

If someone your enemy becomes, his enemy don't you become;
If someone says unseemly things, unseemly things don't you say.

At some point write of life-diminishing disease;
At another, speak of the adverse effects of remedies.

Sometimes complain of the grief that has settled in the heart,
At other times tell the story of patience that is running out fast.

When life is taken, give blood money to the murderer,
And if the tongue be cut off, bless the dagger!

If the beloved doesn't love you, so be it! She still is beloved;
Speak of her graceful walk and intoxicating beauty and charm.

If springtime is short-lived, so be it: but, then, spring is spring:
Celebrate the freshness of the garden and the splendid weather.

Now that the ship has reached the harbour, Ghalib,
Of the captain's tyranny and injustice why complain to God!

[211]

Weeping has made me bolder and more daring in love[1]:
The sense of shame has been washed away[2] and constraints gone!

With the gears of wine the price of wine I paid,
These were the two accounts that thus got settled.

Though your waywardness has brought you worldwide notoriety,
But clever of disposition it has made you definitely!

Who says that no effect have the nightingale's plaintiff songs?
In the flowers are hidden a hundred thousand torn hearts!

---

[1] I.e., the love affair which heretofore was a secret became generally known when the pain of separation found expression in weeping. The couplet is about what happens once the secret is out.
[2] I.e., there is no more the feeling of embarrassment.

Of the lovers' existence and non-existence what can be said?
Of their own fire sticks and straws they became[1]!

To complain of her indifference I went to her;
Just a glance she cast and into ashes I turned!

Yesterday she got carried Asad's coffin in such a way
That seeing it, even his enemies disconsolate became.

[212]

Drunkenness is at its colourful best, the music is in joyous transport,
And the flagon of wine is a cypress on the bank of the river of song!

O my friend! Don't tell me not to spoil the beloved's festive party;
Don't you know for her my moans are like a melody?

[213]

The display of the beauty of sparkling teeth is for laughter;
The claim they signify unity among friends is laughable.

The bud, in non-existence, taking warning from the flower's fate,
Is in deep contemplation on what lies after laughter[2].

Excitement is a luxury forbidden for the distress of sadness,
Although patient suffering is the basis of happiness.

---

[1] I.e., ceased to exist as matter ("sticks and straws"), but continue to exist as energy ("fire").
[2] I.e., blossoming into a flower.

That inside I am in anguish, my friends deny:
My heart is an ocean of tears, and on my lips plays a smile!

[214]

The beauty, though independent of wants, yet wants self-display:
Looking into the mirror she keeps contemplating some new way.

How long, O awareness, to keep changing the view of the spectacle[1]!
In the time you open your eyes, the splendour bids farewell.

[215]

Unless love makes in one's heart a wound with gaping mouth,
Hard it is to open the channel of communication with you.

Filled with dust is the whole world by Majnoon's[2] wildness:
For how long could one go on minding Laila's ringlets?

Such is my sadness that joy her mere attention won't bring,
But, yes, it can happen only if in my heart like pain she settles!

O my friend! Don't reproach me for crying;
After all, one has to ease one's heart sometime.

When rending my heart didn't attract her caring attention,
By bringing shame to my shirt's breast what would I gain?

---

[1]I.e., the world.
[2]For Majnoon seen commentary on ghazal 2.

My heart's pieces have made of thorns rose-bearing branches,
But how long can one go on planting flowers in the desert!

The failure of vision by itself is the lightning, burning the sight,
But aren't You the One whom one wants to keep gazing at!

The bricks and stones inflicting wounds are pearl oysters:
A loser one is not if with madness a bargain one makes!

For your patience-trying promise inadequate proved my life:
To fulfill my desire for you when did I get the time!

The wildness of the creative nature gives rise to desperation[1],
But this pain is not something that one can will not to happen.

Madness, when nothing is left for it to do, makes laments:
What else can one do when rendered completely helpless?

The beauty of the light of poetry's candle shines much later, Asad;
First, a heart melted by the passion of love one has to have.

[216]

Let someone be the son of Mary, but what of it?
If one can cure me of *my* afflictions, that is it!

True, religious and state laws are the bases of decision:
But what can be done about such a one who kills without weapon!

---

[1]"Desperation" or despair because their creative work often remains unappreciated, and frequently for a long time.

Like an arrow shot from a taut bowstring she walks away;
In such a one's heart, how is one to make his place?

You utter a word and into rage she flies!
Others have just to listen to whatever she says.

Possessed, I am raving about I don't know what;
I wish to God nobody understands a word of it!

Don't hear if ill of you speaks somebody;
Don't speak of it if wronged are you by somebody.

Stop him if astray goes somebody;
Forgive him if errs somebody.

Who is there who is without needs!
Who can then satisfy everybody's needs?

What did Khizr do to Alexander!
Whom then to make the guide and the leader?

Now that all hopes and expectations are gone, Ghalib,
Why and to what good end to complain against anybody?

Commentary:

Couplet 9: Legend has it that Alexander the Great in his search for the water of life made Khizr his guide and leader. But when they reached the fountain of life, only Khizr drank of it, and Alexander, for some reason, didn't. The poet is suggesting that Khizr somehow tricked Alexander—Khizr, who, according to the legend, guides the ones lost on the way, both in the worldly and more in the spiritual sense. So what can one expect from a lesser person? (However, some exponents of Ghalib have read it to mean that if someone is not destined for something he won't achieve it even under the best guide and leader. But the mood and the tone of this couplet don't seem to support this interpretation.)

[217]

Granted there is too much of worldly sorrow but is wine scarce?
I am the servant of Kausar's cupbearer, what do I care!

Of your modes and manners I am fully aware:
If not an outrage then what is it that my rival you favour!

That in his poetry Ghalib's pen pours fire,
That we accept, but when has he now his old vigour?

Commentary:

Couplet 1: According to Muslim belief, although it is not mentioned in the Quran or the Tradition of Prophet Muhammad, Kausar is a river in Paradise through which flows pure water that has the characteristics of wine, minus the intoxication and crapulence. "Cupbearer of Kausar" is an allusion to Prophet Muhammad.

[218]

In my state of emotional disturbance, the garden so frightens me
That the shadow of the flower-branch seems a viper to me.

The streaks of tempering that the sword acquires is at no other fount
Than the poisoned water that nourishes the verdure that I am.

My foiled desire is rapt in viewing the spectacle of my shattered heart
As if someone is taking me through the hall of mirrors.

Lament is the asset of this world; the world is a handful of dust,
And the dove's eggshell is the firmament of this world!

She would remove me from her assembly when I was alive;
Who would remove me from there now that I have died!

Commentary:

Couplet 2: The term "poisoned water" (*zahraab* in the original) has been used in its literal sense as regards "the sword" and in its figurative sense of grief, pain, and suffering with reference to "I." The wound inflicted by a sword tempered by dipping it in poisoned water after heating does not heal. This is in addition to the streaks of lustre with a greenish tinge ("verdure" in the second line) it acquires by this process which is its distinguishing mark. The poet, in a word, is saying that he is the one who survives on pain and suffering of such intensity and persistence that it can only be compared to the poisoned water at which the deadly weapon of a sword is tempered.

[219]

Trampled by the King's procession is it;
Why shouldn't the dust of that path be proud of it?

When to see the tulip garden comes the King in person,
How won't it attract people's attention!

For a walk in the garden I have no craving,
But why not enjoy the breeze of spring!

[220]

Thousands of desires still remain to satisfy each of which I am dying:
Yes, many of my wishes have been fulfilled but they are so very few!

Why be my killer afraid? How will she have my blood on her hand—
The blood that streamed from weeping eyes all my life with every breath.

The story of Adam's expulsion from Paradise we all have heard,
But of the disgrace in which I left your alley, what can be said!

The secret of your tall stature, O oppressor, would be exposed
If the curls within curls of your tresses were straightened down.

So that anyone dictating his letter to her should use my service alone,
Just as the day breaks, with a pen stuck on my ear I leave my home.

In this age, wine-drinking has become associated with my name:
Again the time has come when Jamshed's cup will regain its fame.

Those from whom remedy for my wounds I expected
More hurt than I by the sword of affliction I found.

In love, there is no difference between dying and living:
Seeing her I come to life, the very darling for whom I die!

For God's sake, O preacher, don't you raise the Kaba's curtain
Lest you find here, too, is my infidel idol[1]!

Think of the entrance to the tavern, Ghalib, and imagine the preacher!
But yesterday I saw him stepping in when we were coming out.

[221]

If a sound I become, for the mountain a burden I would be;[2]
O flying spark of fire, unrestrained like you should I be!

Like an egg is this cage—a shame for my wings!
A new life can begin if freedom I achieve.

Commentary:

Couplet 2: The "cage" is a metaphor for the world and "wings" for one's abilities. The imagery of a bird's life (the wings and the cage) has been used to represent in general terms the possibilities and the worldly constraints.

[222]

The cupbearer's joy in her indifference has ruined my drunkenness,
And the waves of wine have become languishing eyelids!

Except for the wound of your coquetry's sword, no desire in my heart!
Now in tatters, because of you, is also the bosom of my thought.

---

[1]See the commentary on couplet 6 of ghazal 232 though in a different context.
[2]I.e., the mountain would send it back as echo.

In my frenzy I see nothing that is of significance, Asad:
The desert, in my eyes, is but a handful of dust!

[223]

The movement of Jesus' lips causes their cradles to swing:
Those killed by the beauties' lips, how wonderful is their deep sleep!

Commentary:

Muslims believe that Jesus used to raise the dead by uttering the words
"Arise by God's leave" which involved the movement of lips. In the case of
lovers killed by the ruby-like lips of their beloveds, the poet says, this
movement of Jesus' lips, instead of waking them from their deep sleep (death),
makes their cradles swing which puts them to even deeper slumber.

[224]

The roaring sound of water the herald of the coming flood is;
The footprint has put the finger of the pathway into its ears.

Whose drunken eyes have made of the wine party an eerie place?
The wave of wine is hiding in the bottle like a fairy's pulse!

Commentary:

Couplet 1: A footprint (which looks like a magnified ear) is washed away by
the flood and the poet is using it as a metaphor for the precariousness of
human existence. The second line thus is an imagery of the terror and
helplessness of the human situation. The cause of terror is the "coming flood"
heralded by the "roaring sound of water." The flood can be any force, within

214

and without, that can be highly destructive, physically and emotionally, individually and collectively.

[225]

I, too, am a spectator of the magic of desire;
But not at all with the intent that I must attain my desire.

[226]

Like ink spilled over the paper at the time of writing
Is the picture of the nights of separation in my destiny!

[227]

O swarming plaints! Bewildered, not a single lament I can make;
My silence is the sign that complete surrender I have made.

Frankly, deadlier is the ill-disposed beauties' favour;
Their bold coquettish look is a sharp, unsheathed scimitar.

My sorrows are legion that have so destroyed my happy state!
The dawn of Eid[1] is to me worse than the torn shirt's breast.

For a deal with the cupbearer bring your heart and faith for ready payment:
In this market only the goblet of wine changes hands on easy terms.

Grief nurtures the lover in the bosom of trials and tribulations:
My lighted lamp[2] is a coral in the sea of raging wind.

---

[1]For "Eid" see the commentary on couplet 5 of ghazal 18; the "torn shirt's breast" signified extreme distress though the appearance of the "dawn of Eid" that heralds happiness.
[2]"My lighted lamp" is a metaphor for the lover's heart.

[228]

In your silence are wondrous, amorous signs:
From your heart's eye come collyrium-anointed[1] glances!

Squeezed by their tight privacy into dewdrops it turns—
The zephyr that strays into the recesses of the flower-buds.

Don't ask the lover's breast how sharp is her glance's scimitar,
Just imagine the breathing wound of the door's aperture.

[229]

Wherever the gentle breeze combs my beloved's hair
Its fragrance it carries far and near.[2]

At whose sign of manifestation is wonderment gazing, O God!
A mirror spread are all the six faces of the waiting world!

By the tightness of space my desire is crushed into a cloud of dust:
The vast desert is going to be a game in its net!

The heart is the plaintiff and has made the eyes the defendants;
The case regarding sighting has been reopened for proceedings.

The dew is sprinkling water on the mirror of the flower-petal;
The parting time for spring is come, O nightingale!

---

[1]For the connection between "silence," "glances," and "collyrium-anointed" see the commentary on couplet 5 of ghazal 58.
[2]Literally, this line will translate as: The brain of the Tatar desert deer a musk bag becomes.

216

A matter of keeping faith with my beloved's promise is it;
Whether she comes or not, I shall wait.

Don't go without a veil, O beloved, to Majnoon's desert;
Every particle there is a reflection of his perturbed heart.

O nightingale, gather a handful of straws for your nest;
Like a torrent springtime is approaching fast.

Don't lose heart; if not knowledge[1], enjoy the sights:
O thoughtless one! This mirror an album of pictures is.

Mindlessness guarantees everlasting life, Asad, and never-ending pleasure!
O sudden death, what is it that you are now waiting for?

Commentary:

Couplet 5: There is an allusion to the Iranian custom of sprinkling water on
the mirror when somebody is leaving, thought to augur a safe return.

Couplet 10: In this couplet the poet seems to be saying that an everlasting
life of never-ending pleasure with no higher purpose would be a life without
meaning, not worth living.

[230]

Why not give you a mirror and watch the wondrous sight?
From where to bring one of whom I could say: "Here is one like you!"

---

[1] I.e., the knowledge of the ultimate truth or truths, the heart considered as the centre of inmost
thought and feeling; it is also a mirror as in the second line of this couplet.

My longing for you has placed in the banquet of my thought[1]
The bouquet of your glances people call the heart's black spot.

O my God! Who has breathed into love's ear
The spell of expectation, in truth desire!

Driven by the impetuosity of the pain of alienation,
Throw on its[2] head that handful of dust called desert!

In my tearful eyes, from pining to see her,
Lies hidden like a river in flood an uncontrollable[3] desire.

For the flower of pleasure to bloom it needs
The dawn of spring—a smiling flagon of wine.

Don't take it ill, Ghalib, if the preacher calls you bad;
Is there anyone in this world whom everyone calls good?

[231]

The dewdrops on the tulip are not without signification:
The scar on a loveless heart, to shame is an invitation!

Here am I, heart bleeding from grief and pining to see her;
There is she, intoxicated, in her hennaed hand holding a mirror!

---

[1]"Thought," i.e., the heart, the centre of inmost "thought" and feeling.
[2]"Its" refers to the "pain of alienation" in the first line of this couplet.
[3]Literally, "with broken rein," used here as a mixed metaphor for the desire that is riding the steed with broken rein, and for the tears that are flowing from the eyes like a river in flood.

The flame[1] might not have done what the desire for flame has done:
At the frigidity of my heart how fiercely with anger I burn!

So playful is your image that, with the greatest pleasure,
The mirror has opened its arms of welcome like a flower!

The turtledove a handful of ashes, the nightingale a cage of colours!
What else than lament the sign of a heart consumed with love is!

Your manner has dampened the ardour of my heart;
A beloved and so cold! A strange calamity is it.

A compulsion and the claim of being a love's captive!
Like the hand caught under a heavy stone the pledge of loyalty is.

Now I know what they went through—the martyrs of the past:
Your sword of oppression is the mirror showing their images!

O world-illumining sun, cast your light in this direction too;
Like a shadow the bad time has been following me!

The regrets for the sins not committed also call for justice,
If, O Lord, for the sins committed one is going to be punished!

If people behave like strangers, Ghalib, don't be disheartened;
If nobody is for you, even so, with you is your God, my friend.

Commentary:

Couplet 1: The dewdrop is a metaphor for sweat—the sweat of contrition
and shame. The scar is the scar of love, a metaphor for the tulip's stigma. In a

---

[1] I.e., flame of love.

word, the tulip is sweating because of shame—shame because it carries the outward sign of love—scar or wound of love—while its heart is empty of love.

[232]

For the revelation of light was chosen your person;
Your stature and countenance was auspicious for manifestation.

A blood-dripping shroud has adornments beyond count;
A wistful eye upon your martyrs the houris cast!

You can't drink it nor to anyone else you can offer;
What to say of your pure wine of Paradise, O preacher!

On Judgement Day, my killer quarrels with me why I arose,
As if the sound of the trumpet she hadn't yet heard.

Spring, it seems, is coming that nightingales are singing;
Told by the little birds, the rumour is spreading.

Though not there but the ones turned out from there they are;
With the Kaba these idols also distantly connected are.

Is it necessary that everybody will get the same reply?
Come on, let me too make a tour of Mount Sinai.

Fierceness in speech let be her way—but not to the extent that
To whomsoever she speaks, he sure makes complaint!

If, Ghalib, the King takes me along on this journey,
The reward for the Hajj I will offer to His Majesty.

Commentary:

Couplet 1: The terms "person" and "stature and countenance" are allusions to the person of Prophet Muhammad. But they can also be read to mean the beloved.

Couplet 6: Before Islam, Kaba housed the idols worshipped by the people of Mecca. They were removed from there after the advent of Islam. "Idol" is also a metaphor for the beloved and the beauties.

Couplet 7: For Mount Sinai see the commentary on couplet 11 of ghazal 61. In this couplet the reference is to only one clause of verse 143 of chapter 7 of the Quran, viz.: Said God: "Never canst thou see Me." This was in response to Moses' request to God to show Himself to him. Ghalib is saying that it is not necessary that everybody will get the same reply so why not try and make a tour of Sinai. Apparently the couplet is in a lighter mood but at a deeper level it is about man's higher aspirations and hopefulness even in the face of not very encouraging past experience, personal or vicarious.

[233]

My disappointed heart is too weak to swallow grief;
That there is very little of wine is most distressing.

Telling this to the cupbearer makes me feel shame,
Otherwise so it is that even the dregs of wine would do for me.

Neither the hunter is in ambush nor is the arrow in his bow;
In a corner of the cage I find great repose!

How can I revere abstinence and devotion even if not hypocritical!
For these labours there is too much of raw greed for requital.

221

The people of wisdom are proud of what special ways of theirs?
Very much bound are they to the common modes and manners.

Leave me at the Zamzam; how can I circumambulate the Haram?
Too much defiled by wine is my ehram.

A calamity it would be if even now I don't succeed,
When she is not refusing and I am so insistent.

O death! The liver hasn't yet turned into blood and dripped from my eyes,
So leave me here; a lot of unfinished business still have I!

Can there be anyone who won't know Ghalib!
True, a good poet he is, but a bad reputation has he!

Commentary:

Couplet 6: For "Zamzam" and "ehram" see the commentary on couplet 4 of ghazal 181. "Haram" is the Sacred Temple in Mecca at the center of which is the Kaba. Here the Haram is a metonym for the Kaba, the circumambulation of which is a required ritual of Hajj and Umrah.

[234]

It is a long time now that my beloved was my house guest
When by the fervour of goblets of wine the party was illuminated.

I am again collecting pieces of my heart;
Much time has passed since her eyelashes were feasted.

My circumspect ways are again suffocating me;
It is years now that my shirt's breast I rent.

Again my breath is fervently making fire-raining lamentation;
It is a long time since I viewed the spectacle of illumination.

Love is again astir inquiring after my heart's wounds,
Making provision for a hundred thousand salt-cellars.

Again my eyelashes are soaking up my heart's blood,
Preparing to decorate my shirt's skirt like a flowerbed.

They are again competing with each other—my eyes and heart—
The one ready to provide for the sight and the other for thought.

Again my heart wants to make the rounds of the alley of reproach,
Making desolate the idol-temple of pride.

Love is again looking for a taker,
The assets of mind and heart and life are on offer.

My thought again roves over tulips and roses,
Providing for the eyes a hundred flower-gardens.

Again I want to open the letter from my beloved,
Offering my life to her heart-alluring salutation.

My desire is again looking for her on her terrace,
Her black tresses falling disheveled on her face.

My longing again wants in front of me my beloved,
The scimitar of her eyelashes with collyrium sharpened.

Again my eyes are keen on seeing the blooming beauty,
Her face, lighted up by wine, glowing like roses.

Again I want to remain lying at my beloved's door
Placing myself under the obligation of the doorkeeper.

My heart again seeks the same leisure that, night and day,
I sit quietly, thinking only of my beloved.

O Ghalib, tease me not, for, again, with tears swelling,
I am in a state ready to bring down a torrent.

Commentary:

Couplet 8: The beloved's alley is ironically called "alley of reproach" being the cause of desolation of the "idol-temple of pride." The key word, however, is *tawaf* that as a general term means the act of going around something, but is a specific term for making the circuit or circumambulation of the Kaba. Thus Ghalib is very subtly suggesting, as poet Faiz Ahmed Faiz perceptively pointed out in his article on this ghazal in the February, 1974 issue of the monthly *Ajkal*, New Delhi, that love for the beloved is the real, central thing in life and making the rounds of her alley is like circumambulating of the Kaba, and pride is an idol-temple, a fantasy.

[235]

Glad tidings for a life of peace is the beloved's tyranny;
No manner of oppression is now left for the heaven to try.

Never mind if the beloved's eyelashes are thirsting for my blood;
Some of it for my own blood-dripping eyelashes is to be saved.

O Khizr[1], we who mix with others are the ones who really live;
Not like you who, for the sake of an eternal life, lives like a thief.

In the midst of other calamities, jealousy too keeps plaguing me:
Life-trying is your bewitching style for so many besides me!

O heaven, don't keep me away from her; why should I be the one
On whom be tried from a distance the killer's weapon of oppression?

The parable of my efforts is the captive bird that,
Though in a cage, would collect straws for a nest[2]!

Taking me for a mendicant, her sentinel kept silent, but,
As ill-luck would have it, I arose and fell at his feet.

In the measure of my desire the ghazal's strait is not:
To give expression to my thoughts, a wider scope I want.

Others too have been provided with, so from an evil eye he be preserved,
Otherwise, for Tajammul Husain Khan were luxuries essentially created.

---

[1]See the commentaries on couplet 1 of ghazal 69 and couplet 9 of ghazal 216. He is supposed to live in uninhabited places, hidden from peoples' eyes.
[2]I.e., to make a nest.

O great God! Whose name has rolled out from my tongue
That in rapture my words are kissing my tongue!

The defender of state and faith, the helper of nation and country!
It was for his abode that the high heavens were fashioned.

In the time of his reign the world is busy adorning itself;
In the firmament new stars would now be created.

The pages are used up but the praise remains:
A ship is needed for this boundless sea.

In a style distinctive has Ghalib written this ingenious ghazal;
To share in it, for my discriminating friends it is an invitation general.

Commentary:

Couplet 8: The poet in this couplet is saying that now he wants to speak of something that cannot be the poetic theme of this ghazal, which, too, he puts poetically, creating a justification for digressing into an ode (*qasida*) to Tajammul Husain Khan in the next five couplets of this ghazal. The couplet is to be read in this particular context and not as the poet's view on ghazal as a genre, which it is not.

Couplet 9: Couplets 9 to 13 are about Tajammul Husain Khan (died, 1846), a well-known ruler of Farukhabad in UP, India. His first name, Tajammul, which means beauty, dignity, pomp, and pleasure, has been used to advantage in this couplet, as well as in couplets 10 and 12. *Naseer-ul-Dawla-o-Deen* (defender of state and faith) and *Mueen-ul-Millat-o- Mulk* (helper of nation and country) were his titles, which find their place in couplet 11. (Tajammul Husain Khan had invited Ghalib to Farukhabad and was very eager to see him, but, perhaps, Ghalib could not go there.)

Couplet 12: New stars would now have to be created to retain the beauty of the sky as the existing ones would be used for adorning the world.

Couplet 13: The word used by Ghalib is *safina*, which means a "ship" as well as a blank book or a notebook, and both of these meanings are relevant: the ship connects with the "boundless sea" and the "pages" with the blank book or the notebook. And the "boundless sea" is a metaphor for countless "praises."

ODES

ODE TO ALI[1]

Nothing in the flower-garden its bounty ignores as of no use:
The spotless tulip's shadow the black spot[2] of spring's heart is.

It is the zephyr's intoxication that has caused this greenness:
The mountain peak's luster is from the wine-bottles' pieces.

Green like emerald-goblets the cheetah's spots are,
And fresh like the veins of orange the flashes appear.

Grief is gathering the flowers of pleasure from the ecstatic clouds;
Maybe the sorrows of both the worlds would be squeezed in their embrace.

Mountains and plains are flourishing with the things nightingales love;
The sleepy paths by the laughter of flowers have come alive!

By the breeze's beneficence, a streak of dust, like an orphan's eyelashes
Comes to possess the power of the water-laden mass of clouds.

Like the crescent it would wax if one cut and threw the fingernail,
The power of growth wouldn't leave even this one idle!

A handful of dust flying in the sky would be a dove;
A sheet of paper burning would be a net and peacock its game!

---

[1] Ali was the son-in-law of Prophet Muhammad and the fourth Orthodox Caliph (656-661 A.D.).
[2] The black spot of the heart is the mark of love in the heart (ref. the commentary on couplet 2 of ghzal 2.

If you wish to gather flowers while in the tavern
Just leave a wineglassful in a niche of the flower-garden.

If you lose your turban in a nook of the tavern
Seek its fragrance in the recesses of the buds in the garden.

If Mani[1], a man of ideas, drew picture of the flower-garden
Like the down on an adolescent's face would its lines turn green.

To sing the king's[2] praises, the green mountain parrot
From the ruby its beak it fashioned!

To build the palace for the king of kings,
Gabriel's eyes became the moulds for its bricks.

The highest heaven, its shoulders greatly bent, was the carrier,
And the thread of eternal grace the mason's plumb line!

The nine heavens' verdure was like a stripe on its parapet's exterior;
The castle's height was where lofty thoughts of man of wisdom could reach.

If from his garden's trash one could get a blade of grass
He would no more be pleased with the fan of fairy's wings.

For the seekers of Truth the dust of Najaf's[3] desert has spiritual worth:
The eyes of their footprints are the mirrors of their fates woken up!

A particle of that dust is for the sun the pride of brightness,
The dust of that desert is for hope the ehram[1] of spring!

---

[1]For "Mani" see the commentary on couplet 1 of ghazal 186.
[2]"The king's" and "the king of kings" in the next couplet are reverential references to Ali.
[3]Najaf is a city near Basra in Iraq where Ali's tomb is.

Seeking from there the intoxication of pride is the whole world;
Asking for creation's enduring reward is every wave of dust.

O candle of spring's chamber[2], it is by your bounty that
The moth's heart is illumined and the nightingale's wings are a rose-garden.

In the likeness of a peacock the hall of mirrors fly
Yearning for your manifestation and eager to see your face.

From grief of your offspring, on heaven's face,
In the string of stars, the new moon a pearl-shedding eyelid is.

Your footprint is the place for prostration in prayer;
For mystical devotions your aspiration is the power.

In your praise is hidden the song of the Prophet's encomiums,
From your cup overflows the sparkling wine of spiritual mysteries.

Your hands raised in prayer are mirrors of the virtue of effectiveness:
The eyelashes have been made proud and the thorns of grief are gone.

The black spots of mourning for the lost felicity may those eyes' pupils be,
The eyes that fail to give reverent honour to your door's dust.

Of this place of merriment[3], for the enemy of the House of the Prophet;
May every arch and cupola and vault become the waves of flood!

---

[1]For "chram" see the commentary on couplet 4 of ghazal 181. Physically it is only a garment consisting of two unsewn white pieces of cloth, but in the spiritual sense it signifies righteous intentions.

[2]"O candle of spring's chamber" is an allusion to Ali.

[3]"This place of merriment" is a metaphor for this world.

From Asad's eyes to his heart is a mirror reflecting his ardour;
Brimful with the wine of meaning is this poet's cup.

[2]

ODE TO ALI

The world is nothing but the manifestation of the Unique Beloved:
How could we be if the Beauty weren't self-regarding!

Ah, dispirited sightseeing! Neither enjoyed the world nor taking warning!
Alas, the poverty of desire! Missing the happiness of both worlds!

It is babbling, singing of existence and non-existence in high and low tones;
It is absurd, making a distinction between dignity and madness.

Creating meaning is all for the sake of of gaining prominence;
Discussing Truth is all a measure of desire for praise!

The boast of knowledge is mistaken and the benefits of worship are none:
The dregs of forgetfulness is it, be it this world and the next!

Like fidelity, the hands touching the ground in obeisance remain empty;
Like a footprint, constancy's head gets trodden and is covered in dust.

Love is an irregularity in the links that tie in the senses;
Union is rust on the face of the mirror of beauty of belief.

The mountain-digger[1] was a hungry labourer of his rival's palace;
Mount Bestun[1] was the mirror of Shirin's sound sleep.

---

[1]"The mountain-digger" is an allusion to Farhad.

Who has seen the people of fidelity's sighs kindling fire!
Who has seen the laments of sorrowful hearts having any effect!

A listener of the chants of the people of the world am I,
But neither to praise nor to reproach incline.

Heaven forefend! How have I been chattering!
Devoid of the elegance of manners and the dignity of address!

O delirious pen, write: "There is no power but with God!"
O human nature, the companion of the devil's temptations, say "O Ali!"

The manifestation of God's grace, the last Prophet's heart and soul!
The king of the House of the Prophet, the Kaba of faith!

He, the asset of creation, where he would walk, there
Every handful of dust would become the disk of a new Earth

The place where his footprint would display its splendour,
That handful of dust would be the custodian of both the world's honour.

Because of its association with his name[2] the Earth has the distinction that
Bearing with its airs, the firmament's back would remain bent till eternity.

It is because of the bounty of his good disposition extending to it
That with the fragrance of flowers is always loaded the morning breeze.

---

[1]"Besitun" is a mountain in Persia, modern Iran, between Hamdan and Karmarshah that Farhad is reputed to have dug through to bring water to the "merriment palace" of Emperor Khusrau Pervez and his Queen, Shirin. For more on this see the commentary on couplet 2 of ghazal 102.

[2]The reference is to Ali's nickname of Abu-turab, which means the originator, protector, possessor and respected of the Earth to which the poet is referring to make the point that the firmament will remain arched forever bearing with the manners and whims of the Earth.

The sharpness of his sword is talked about all over the world;
Be not that the claim of creation is severed by it!

A torch of infidelity is his splendour by whose presence,
Like the colour of a disappointed lover's face, the idol-temple's life fades!

O protector of life! O cause of grace for the heart and the soul! O king!
By the verdict of faith, for you was the last will of the last Prophet!

For your pure person, the Prophet's shoulders a pulpit became[1];
On the highest heaven's was engraved forehead your celebrated name!

Other than the Necessary Being, who can befittingly praise you?
Only the flame of the candle can adorn the candle!

Your abode's stone slab is like a shining steel mirror;
Its wavy lines are scripts that say upon you attends the trusted Gabriel!

These are the things made ready for offerings at your doorstep—
The things God granted to earthly beings: life, heart and the faith.

For your praise are the heart and the mouth and tongue!
For salutation are the pen and tablet, the hand and forehead!

Who can ever sufficiently praise the one who is praised of God!
Who can adorn the Paradise on high!

---

[1] It is an allusion to the tradition according to which after the conquest of Mecca when Prophet Muhammad entered the Kaba he told Ali to stand on his shoulders to reach and break the idols that could not be reached otherwise. It is said that there were about three hundred sixty idols in the Kaba then.

A thing of the market of sins[1]Asadullah Asad is,
No one, other than you, his buyer be.[2]

In my spirited representation of my wishes, I am being audacious,
This because in your high-minded dispensation of grace full faith have I.

Grant to my prayer that position of goodly acceptance
Where acceptance says "Amen" a hundred times at every word of my prayer.

Let my bosom overflow with sorrow for Shabbir[3]
That my eyes always remain red to such an extent.

Grant to my nature such fervent affection for Duldul[4]
That as far as it goes, it should be its step and my forehead!

May my heart remain attached to you and the chest be God's expanse!
May my eyes worship His Manifestation and will choose Truth.

On your foes be spent the efficacy of flame and the smoke of Hell!
To your friends be given the roses and hyacinth of Paradise!

---

[1]"The market of sins" is this world of offences against the law of God; Ghalib is a citizen of this world.
[2]I.e., he will be acceptable to you, his sins notwithstanding.
[3]"Shabbir" was another name of Husain, son of Ali, who was martyred for his belief in high principles and noble acts.
[4]"Duldul" in Arabic means "to put into motion." It was the name given to the mule that was sent by the ruler of Alexandria as a present to Prophet Muhammad who gave it to Ali.

[3]

ODE TO BAHADUR SHAH

O new moon let me hear from you his name,
The only one whom you are bowing in salutation!

For two days you were seen at daybreak,
This very style and this very figure.

Where did you hide for two days?
"The creature is helpless before the revolution of times.

"Where could I fly away?
"The sky had spread of net of stars."

Welcome! O select delight for the elect!
Excellent! O general pleasure for the common people!

As an excuse for not appearing for three days,
You have showed up with the news of Eid.

He should not be called as the one gone astray
If he goes out in the morning and in the evening his is back.

Not only I, everybody has come to know
Your beginning and your end.

Why are you hiding from the secret of your heart?
Do you, perchance, think I am a talebearer?

I know this that today in this world
There's only one to whom mankind turns for hope.

Granted that you are his servant,
But doesn't Ghalib too attend on him?

I know that you know it,
That is why the way I asked you.

O moon, for the radiant sun it may be possible,
Everyday audience with him eternally!

But when have you that position that he would see you
Except on Eid, following the month of fasting!

I know that by his bounty
You want again to be a full moon.

The full moon, be moonlight, what is it to me?
Are you going to share his largess with me?

My own affair is different;
With others' dealing what have I to do÷

I desire a special gift from him
While you hope for a general blessing.

He who would bestow on you the glory of light,
Wouldn't he give me the rose-coloured wine?

The fourteen mansions of heaven,
Moving swiftly, when you have crossed.

And by the beams of your light are illuminated
The lanes, the palaces, the courtyards, windows, and terraces.

Then will you see in my hand, overflowing,
A crystal-glass looking like you!

But now it has taken to the path of ghazal;
My temperament's steed needed to be reined in.

GHAZAL

The poison of sorrow had done its job,
Who then told you, O beloved, to get a bad name?

Why should I not go on drinking wine
When sorrow has made living as sinning?

Who hopes for a king? Even this I take as a boon!
That she isn't aware her calling me names is my pleasure!

To the Kaba I would go and there blow the horn;
For now, while in the idol-temple, I have on ehram!

That glassful of wine is available and circulating in my assembly
From which heaven borrowed some and is in revolution everlastingly!

Kisses she refuses me,
But captivating my heart she won't give up!

I tease her so that she gets angry;
Why else should I give myself the name "Ghalib"?

(Now the poet returns to the ode and again addresses the moon.)

I have told you everything; now you say something,
O fairy-faced, O swift-footed messenger!

Who is he at whose door in adoration prostrate themselves—
The moon, sun, Venus and Mars?

If you don't know, then hear from me
The name of the Emperor of high dignity!

He is Bahadur Shah, veneration for eyes and the heart,
The manifestation of the Almighty, the Most Gracious!

The expert horseman of the path of justice,
The fresh spring of the garden of Islam,

Whose every action is like a miracle,
And whose every word is like a word inspired.

When entertaining, Caesar and Jamshed are his guests,
In battles, he is the instructor of Rustam and Sam.

O you whose kindness is life-erasing!
O you whose reign will have a happy ending!

May God preserve from the evil eye your imperial glory;
All praise to God! How wonderful your devotional compositions are!

Amongst your devotees is Caesar of Rome;
Amongst the partakers of your grace is the spiritual guide Jam[1].

Recognize you as the inheritor of the realm,
Iraj and Toor and Khurauand and Bahram.

Acknowledge the strength of your arms,
Gio and Godurz and Bizam and Ruham[2].

How great is the precision of your arrow!
How to praise the sharpness of your sword!

Your arrow makes the arrow of the opponent the target;
Your sword makes the sword of the enemy the scabbard.

How it overwhelms the thunderbolt,
How it puts the lightning to shame—

The trumpet of your ponderous elephant!
The speed of your swift-footed steed.

In the art of sculpture, if your mace
Complete mastery does not have,

How is it that the head and the body of the one stricken by it
Appear in the form of the one sunk into the other?

---

[1] Jam is Nuruddin Abdur Rehman Jam (1414-1492 A.D.), a saint and an eminent poet and prose writer. His tomb is in Herat in Afghanistan.
[2] Jamshed, Rustam, Bahrum, etc., are the names of the celebrated heroes of Persian epics such as the inimitable *Shahnama* of Firdausi (940-1020. A.D.)

In the eternity, before the beginning of time, it was written
On the pages of nights and days of what was to come.

On those pages, by the pen of the recording angels,
Was entered, compendiously, the decree Divine:

Of the beloveds it was written that lovers-killers they would be,
And, in the case of lovers, that their foes wishes would be fulfilled.

About heaven it was decreed that it should be called
The fast revolving dome of bluish hue.

A definitive order was recorded that we should write
Of the beauty spot on the chickpea and the curling locks the net!

The fire and water and wind and earth,
Were to the disposition op burning, moisture, movement and repose.

The resplendent sun was given the title of Emperor of the daytime;
The radiant moon was named the Viceroy of the evening.

Your empire received the Divine seal of acceptance;
According to established rule, this, too, was written down.

The recording angels, according to the Divine decree,
Wrote that it be an adornment everlasting.

Beginning in eternity, it has come down to this time;
May it continue to exist till eternity!

[4]

SECOND ODE TO BAHADUR SHAH

At daybreak, the door in the east opened;
The face of the world-illuming sun appeared.

The king of stars spent it all:
At night, the treasure of gems was lying spread.

But that too was an illusion, an enchantment;
In daylight the mystery of the moon and stars unravelled.

The stars are something but something else they appear;
They patently deceive us, these conjurers!

On the expanse of firmament during the night,
Lay spread all around the ornaments of pearls.

At daybreak, in the east, I could see
The beauty of a flaming face, the head uncovered.

I was bewitched but when I cast away the spell,
It turned out to be a glass of rose-colour wine!

The cupbearer had brought a golden cup
And served it up for the morning draught.

The Royal Court has been adorned by his presence;
The door of the Kaba of peace and security has opened.

244

The golden crown is more resplendent that the radiant sun,
Appearing to advantage on the face of the ruler of the world.

He is the king with an enlightened mind, Bahardur Shah,
To whom the mysteries of life were made manifest.

He it is by whose creation,
The purpose of the nine heavens and seven stars became evident.

He it is by whose exposition
The mysteries of the Prophet's commands became clear.

Dara's[1] name has first shown up
When the record of his captains' names has been opened.

And where the list of his acquaintances is maintained,
There is clearly given the word-picture of Caesar.

The king's steed has the merit that,
When out of the stable, it puts the hurricane to shame.

Its footprints have such bewitching appearance that
You would say the door of the idol-house of Azar[2] has opened.

To me, through the beneficence of the king's education became known,
The positions, functions and axes of the sun and the moon.

---

[1]Dara is Darius the Great, king of Persia (529-486 B.C.).
[2]Azar is Terah of the Bible, Abraham's father. According to tradition Azar was a sculptor, worshipper of idols, and the keeper of the idol-house of the ancient Sumerian city of Euphrates in the south of the present Iraq.

A hundred thousand knotty problems vexed my heart,
But each one of them, through beyond my power, got resolved.

My unhappy heart was a lock without key.
Who opened it? When did it open and how?

A garden of meaning I would make to bloom
If the poet-king favouringly inclines to me.

The moment I would start reciting a ghazal,
People would think the box of ambergris had opened.

GHAZAL

It is a pity, sitting in a corner, wings spread;
Would that the door of the cage would open!

I announce myself and then it is opened; how can I enter like that,
If I find the beloved's door is open for all?

I feel proud of this that I am keeping her secrets;
By to my enemy my friend's secrets are known.[1]

Indeed, the love-scar on the heart looked pretty,
But the wound, compared to the scar, showed to better advantage.

When did the eyebrow put away the arrow from its hand?
When did the amorous glance remove the dagger from its waist?

---

[1] I.e., died from joy on receiving the letter.

Who minds a free guide and guard?
But, travelling on the way, the – ability was exposed.

To the burning heart, what can do the downpour of tears?
The fire flames as the rain for a moment stops.

When the letter came the message of death[1]:
The opened letter dropped on my chest!

Beware, if with Ghalib anybody wrangled!
A saint hidden and an infidel outwardly is he!

Again, to composing his praise my thought has turned;
Again, the book of the moon and sun[2] has opened.

The pen from the drift of thought received help;
As the anchor was raised the soul spread!

The praise brought into view the grandeur of the praised one
As the form reveals the distinguishing reality.

The sun trembled, the sky went into a whirl,
When the standard of the king's cavalry unfurled.

The king's name is mentioned by the recitor of the sermon;
By this the high position of the pulpit has come to be known.

Of the king's coin an acquaintance it has become:
Now is known the touchstone of the value of gold!

---

[1] I.e., the science of astronomy.
[2] I.e., the poet's ode to the king that has the beauty of the moon and brilliance of the sun begins again.

In front of the king there is a mirror;
Now is understood the ultimate purpose of Alexander's effort[1].

The inheritor of the country, the people have seen;
Now they know of the deception of Tughral and Sanjar[2].

When is it possible appropriately to praise him sufficiently?
Only a hint of the book of praise of the king of the world.

These are good thoughts but the praise remains incomplete;
The helplessness of the miracle-working eulogizer is apparent!

I know that the writings on the guarded tablet[3]
Are known to you, O celebrated king!

May you continue to rule as a great emperor
Till the time the door of the magic of days and nights remains opened.[4]

---

[1] The mirror is reputed to have been first made in the times of Alexander the Great (356-328 B.C.) under his command. It is perhaps this fiction that led to the coinage of the phrase *aina-e-Sikandar* in Persian, adopted into Urdu, that means "the mirror of Alexander," specifically a mirror of polished steel

[2] Tughral was the founder of the Seljuk dynasty that ruled much of West Asia from 1037 to 1157 A.D., and Sanjar was the last ruler of the dynasty,

[3] I.e., whatever is destined to happen in all eternity.

[4] I.e., till the end of time, forever.

SEHRA[1]

Rejoice, O Luck! Today you have the honour of doing something great:
Arise and place on Prince Jawan Bakht's head this sehra.

On his moonlike face, how lovely it looks.
For his heart-charming beauty, an ornament is this sehra.

You look comely on his head, O crown,
I am afraid you may lose your position to the sehra.

They must have been strung from the choicest of a boatful of pearls;
Why else have they brought in a boat-like tray, this sehra?

From the seven seas must these pearls have been gathered,
Only then could have been made such a classy yard long sehra.

From heat, the drops of perspiration rolled down from the bridegroom's face
As if it were the pearl-raining cloud, this sehra.

Impudent it would have been had it exceeded the gown's length;
Just it reached the skirt and there it stopped, this sehra.

So that the pearls don't give themselves the airs of being unique,
There need also necessarily be a flower-sehra.

---

[1] *Sehra* is a garland placed on the head of a bridegroom at his marriage ceremony. In the case of a prince the garland would be of pearls. The poem written for the occasion is also called sehra as this one by Ghalib to celebrate the marriage of Prince Jawan Bakht, son of the last Mughal Emperor Bahadur Shah Zafar. It was published in the March 28, 1852 issue of a Delhi newspaper, *Delhi Urdu Akhbar*. Ghalib is the first poet to use the word "sehra" as a refrain (*radif*) in his poem for such an occasion and most probably is the originator of this genre as a Ghalib scholar, Ghulam Rasul Mikhr, has pointed out in his book *Nawa-e-Sarosh* ("The Voice of the Angel").

If carried away by delight they are unable to contain themselves,
How is one to string these flowers into a sehra!

The glow of his lit up face and the shine of the intertwined pearl strings!
How, then, the moon and stars' light wouldn't the sehra!

It is not the silk-string, it is the vein of the vernal cloud
That may bear the heavy weight of the pearls of sehra!

We understand poetry, the partisans of Ghalib we are not:
Let us see if there be anyone who could write a better sehra.

ON MANGO

Yes, my feeling, singing heart
Why shouldn't it open the door of the treasury of secrets?

The pen moving on the paper
Is like a branch of a flower-plant strewing flower.

O pen, why do you ask me what to write?
Write wisdom-increasing, subtle conceits.

Let there be a brief description of mangoes;
Let the pen be a date-tree shedding dates.

Which fruit dare compete with the mango?
Here are the fruit and branches, the ball and the sticks of polo!

Why should the grapevine's desire remain untried?
Let it come out! This is the ball and here is the field.

Against the mango when can it succeed?
The grapevine only vents its spleen!

When its ability in no way awaited the grape
Into pure wine the grape turned.

But this is self-destruction in desperation;
It is turning shame into perspiration!

Ask me! What do you know about it?
Compared to the mango, what sugar cane is?

Neither has it flower nor branches, nor leaves, nor fruits;
When it is autumn, then is its spring.

What other sally should the imagination make?
Whenever had life the sweetness of mango!

If life had its sweetness,
The mountain-digger[1], despite his sorrows,

And though in sacrificing his life he was unique,
He wouldn't have taken his life so easily.

To me this fruit appears like this,
That in the pharmacy of eternity,

On the flame of flowers, from the molasses was prepared the syrup,
And the thread of this syrup was called the fibre.

---

[1]For "mountain-digger" see the commentary on couplet 2 of ghazal 102.

251

Or, this may have happened that, from kindness,
The gardeners of the garden of Paradise,

By the order of the Lord of the world,
Sent sealed glasses with honey filled.

Or, that Khizr[1] planted a sapling and for a long time
Irrigated it with the water of life.

Only then it became a fruit-bearing tree,
Otherwise, where we and this tree!

A citron of gold had Khusrau[2],
Yellow in color but no scent.

Had he but once see a mango
He would have thrown away his squeezable gold citron.

The mango is the ornament of the garden,
The pride of the vegetable kingdom!

It is the provision for the traveller on the way to Paradise,
It is the darling of the *tuba* and the *sidra*[3].

Blessed with flourishing branches, leaves and fruits is mango tree,
Lovingly and delicately nourished by the raining season.

---

[1]For Khizr see the commentary on couplet 9 of ghazal 216.
[2]The reference is to Khusrau Pervaiz, the ancient Persia king, who is reputed to have a squeezable gold citron.
[3]*Tubu* and *Sidra* are the fruit-bearing trees of Paradise.

The specialty mangoes which are easily available
Are freshly picked from the tree of the garden.

The prince[1] who is the crown prince of the realm,
He who is the patron of justice in his time.

Fakhruddin is honour for religion, power and majesty,
He is the beauty of character and prettiness of perfection.

He is the administrator of religion, state and destiny;
He is the adornment for the crown and the throne.

His shadow is the shadow of Huma[2];
For the people, he is the shadow of God.

O Bestower of bounties on the shadow and the light!
So long as the shadow and light exist —

Make His Lordship the cherisher of dependents,
The inheritor of the treasury and the throne and the crown —

Make him happy, gladden his heart, give him joy
And let him be always gracious to Ghalib.

---

[1]Suggesting that the gift of specialty mangoes have come from Mirza Fakhruddin, the Crown Prince, as mentioned in the next couplet.
[2]See the commentary on couplet 3 of ghazal 50.

QIT'AT[1]

---

[1]*Qit'at* is plural for *qit'a*, literally " a cutting, section, segment." A qit'a can be written within a ghazal as its part in which case a series of these couplets is read as a "connected sequence." If it stands independently it is generally given a title, and it has a minimum of two couplets; there is no prescribed maximum.

‘

1

TO HIS MAJESTY THE EMPEROR

O Emperor of heavenly presence, you are peerless, unlimited!
O bounteous ruler of the world, you are matchless, incomparable!

The throne in fealty touches your feet;
The crown on your head feels fortunate.

Your way of speaking is like a comb for the revelations' curling locks;
The movement of your pen is the movement of Gabriel's.

Your person makes plain to the world Moses' nearness to God;
The table of your generosity spread all over the world.

By your writing and speech you raise the dignity of world and meaning;
By your bounty you put to shame the Nile and the Red Sea.

So that, in your time, pleasure and enjoyment are maximized,
So that, in your reign, grief and sorrow are minimized.

The moon has stopped its passage for Taurus,
The Venus has given up movement once it is in Pisces.

Your wisdom is the surety for the correction of my faults;
Your generosity is the security for attaining to my purpose.

Your kindness is for me a glad tiding of life;
Your indifference towards me be an indicator of my death.

My propitious luck wanted me to have no peace;
The heavens' adverse moves wanted to bring me to ignominy.

First, the device that unties the knot with a nail was impaled,
Then in the circumstances of my life a knot was tied.

The agitation in my heart is not unrelated to a fear great,
Drawing breath is not unlike the law of drawing a heavy weight.

The pages of my poetry, from the perils of meaning, are like Laqa's beard,
And like Amar's bag is my chest from the sorrows of the world![1]

My thought abounds with many-faceted gems of constructs;
My pen teaches by writing pithy poetry.

To my ambiguity the clarity pays homage;
From my succinctness exude details.

If I were in a happy situation I wouldn't trouble you,
If my mind were at ease I wouldn't hasten it.

The qibla[2] of the world, such delays in caring for the distressed one!
The Kaba of serenity and security, such slackness in untying of the knot!

---

[1]Laqa and Amar are fanciful characters of the famous Urdu fiction *The Enchanted Story*; Laqa used to adorn his beard by stringing its hair with pearls and Amar's bag was limitless in its capacity. Also see the commentary on couplet 7 of ghazal 23.
[2]Qibla is the Kaba in Mecca; also "an object of veneration or reverence," and the one when one looks up for "the attainment of (one's) necessities."

2

TO HIS MAJESTY THE EMPEROR

O Emperor, whose throne is on the high in the sky!
O ruler of the world who as the impress of the sun.

I was a recluse and had no riches;
I was the one afflicted, wounded in the heart!

But when you bestowed honour on me
Such a great fame it brought

That such a worthless particle like me
Became an acquaintance of planets and stars.

Although, from the shame of having no skill,
In my own eyes, I am so contemptible

That if of the dust I call myself
I know insulted would feel the dust.

But there is this gladness in my heart
That of the king I am a servant proficient.

A devoted servant, a disciple and encomiast
This supplicant ever was.

And, thankfully, now that I am also an employee
Four distinctive bonds have been established.

If not to you then to whom should I tell
Of the needs that must need be told?

O my spiritual guide though I have no desire
That my head with a turban be adorned[1],

But, after all, for winter I do need something
So the Arctic mind may not afflict me.

How wouldn't I need some clothing?
I, too, have a body, though lean and weak!

I have not purchased anything this year,
I have made no preparation this time around.

The fire in the nights and the sun during the days!
Let such nights and days to the fire be consigned!

For how long can a human being warm himself with fire?
For now long can one go on basking in the sun?

The heat of the sun and the heat of fire!
Save me, O my Lord, from the torment of hellfire!

My salary which is a sum fixed by Your Majesty,
I receive it in a way strange.

The custom is to commemorate the dead once, six months after his death,
This is the norm that people observe.

---

[1] I.e., the desire to be decorated with a medal or award.

And here am I, though alive, a prisoner of life,
Yet my commemoration is held in a year twice!

I have no choice but to borrow money every month,
And this keeps compounding the interest amount!

In my salary, to the extent of one-third of my salary
The moneylender has become the sharer.

Today there is none like me in this whole world—
The one who writes poetry of rare beauty and is pleasant of speech.

If you hear from me the tale of a battle,
My tongue is like a well-tempered sword.

And when I write of your convivial gatherings
My pen is like a cloud raining rains of pearls.

It would be unjust if you deny my poetry the appreciation;
It would be calamity if you withhold your affections.

I am your servant and I move around naked!
I am your employee and I live on money borrowed!

Let my salary be paid on a monthly basis
So that life may not be so hard for me.

Now I end this with a prayer;
It is not poetry that concerns me here.

May you live in health and peace for a thousand years
And of fifty thousand days be each of the years!

[3]

TO HIS MAJESTY THE EMPEROR

O King, the conqueror, the bestower and ruler of the world,
You keep receiving hundreds of glad tidings from the unseen world.

The troublesome knot that no striving can untie
You undo that knot by just making a sign!

Is it possible Khizr[1] would mention you name to Alexander
Unless with the water of life he cleansed his lips.

Asaf as Solomon's vizier exalted became;
Solomon would be proud of him your vizier you make!

Receiving the stamp of your acceptance as a disciple is by God's will;
Being bounded as your slave is receiving the royal signet of nobility:

If water you deprive of its ability to flow,
If from fire you remove its power to flame,

No search would discover waves in the river,
And no heat would remain in the fire!

Though for writing subtle conceits I have a passion,
Though in writing poetry of enthralling beauty I excel,

---

[1] See the commentary on couplet 9 of ghazal 216,

But why not end this encomium with a prayer
When words are failing short of praise!

Today is Nauroz[1] and it is that day
When insightful people watch the wonderwork of God.

On this day may you be blessed with the glory of the world-illuminating sun!
And may Ghalib be granted access to your abode on high!

[4]
CELEBRATING THE LAST WEDNESDAY OF OF SAFAR

It is the last Wednesday of Safar[2], let us go!
Let us place in the flower-garden a pitcherful of wine of musky bouquet!

Whoever comes, let him drink glassfuls of wine and get drunk;
Let him trample the grass and leap over the flowers.

O Ghalib, what is all of this you are talking of?
Other than King's encomium no writing or reading I relish now.

---

[1]Nauroz was celebrated by the people of ancient Persia as New Year's Day, the first year of their calendar year which fell on March 21. They still celebrate March 21 with great fervour but not as New Year's Day but rather as the first day of spring. Also, on March 21 the sun enters Aries which in astrology is considered auspicious. This idea of auspiciousness of the sun's position is carried forward to the next couplet.
[2]Safar is the second month of the Islamic lunar calendar. The Islamic era dates from September 24 of A.D. 622 when Prophet Muhammad and the converts to Islam moved from Mecca to Medina to escape persecution by the Meccan idolaters. This event, called Hijrah (Hejira or Hegira), turned out to be the rise of Muslims as a world power and a great influence worldwide in all the significant aspects of human life. the last Wednesday of the month of Safar is the 11th Hijrah was the day when Prophet Muhammad recovered from a serious illness; Muslims of Indo-Pakistan sub-continent celebrate it every year by distributing alms and giving presents, a tradition that started with the Mughal emperors.

In the Royal presence are distributed rings of gold and silver
Compare to which gold and silver of the moon and sun look dull.

Or visualize these rings like this that emptied from the centre
Are in innumerable moons and hundreds of thousands of suns!

[5]
IN PRAISE OF NUSRAT-UL-MULK

O Nusrat-ul-Mulk Bahadur, tell me this:
Why such great faith do I have in you, why?

Although you are the one that if an assembly is called in the sky,
It would be apparent the sun's and moon's splendour is because of you.

And I am the one that if ever I think of myself,
What to say of others, I myself come to hate my state.

Blessed be my wounds because of which, for the present,
There is some connection between your hand and my heart.

May you always have your grip on the rein of the state!
Evening and dawn, that is my prayer to God Almighty.

You are Alexander for me and I feel proud meeting with you,
Though I also have the honour of meeting with Khizr[1].

On no account he be suspected of guile or hypocrisy;
From amongst the people of a tavern[1] is humble Ghalib!

---

[1]It is not definitely known to whom this is addressed. It could be Emperor Bahadur Shah, the last
Mughal Emperor, or some prominent noble (*nawab*) of the time.

[6]
THE POET'S STATEMENT[2]

The purpose is to narrate the true state of affair;
It is not a statement about the goodness of my nature.

For generations soldiering has been the calling of my forefathers;
In no way has poetry been the source of honour.

I follow my own path; peace with all is;
Ill will towards anybody most definitely I never bear.

Is it a small honour that Zafar's slave am I?
Granted that no high rank nor office I hold nor wealth have I.

That with the King's *ustad*[3] I would be in contention,
Such ability or daring of power don't have I.

A world-reflecting mirror is the Emperor's heart;
A statement on oath or a witness don't need I.

---

[1]People of a tavern, i.e., the genuine people; honest and open, no contradiction between thoughts
and actions, outwardly and inwardly same.
[2]See the last couplet of The Sehra which reads as follows:

We understand poetry, the partisans of Ghalib we are not:
Let us see if there be anyone who could write a better Sehra!

Shaikh Muhammad Ibrahim, pen name Zauq (1789-1854 A.D.), a famous Urdu poet who was eight
years senior to Ghalib and the mentor in poetry to Emperor Bahadur Shah Zafar, took umbrage at
it thinking it was directed at him and adopted an adversarial attitude towards Ghalib to which this
qita is his response, clarifying his position. Essentially it was a diplomatic move on Ghalib's part to
pacify Zauq and thus propitiate the Emperor whose mentor he was. (In 1854, at Zauq's death,
Ghalib became the Emperor's mentor in poetry.)
[3]Mentor in the art of writing poetry.

What have I to do with Urdu poetry but, yes, it does have a purpose
Which is, part and all, to give joy to His Excellency's heart.

The sehra was written by way of compliance with the order;
I could see that there was no way but to obey.

In the closing verse a poetic conceit found its way;
The purpose could never be the severance of the ties of love.

If it was directed against anybody disgrace may overtake me;
I am not mad, I am not possessed, and wild am I not.

True, afflicted by bad luck bad by nature I am not;
It is a matter for gratitude that no complaint have I against anybody.

It is the truth I am telling, O Ghalib! God be my witness!
I always speak the truth, for telling a lie is not my wont.

[7]
THE BETEL NUT[1]

This betel nut that is on the palm of your hand
It woud be becoming of it however it be praised.

Astonished, the pen is wondering what to write;
Challenged, the speech is contemplating what to say.

To a seal on the revered friends' letters it be likened
Or an amulet adorning the beauty's arm it be called.

---

[1](See at the end of this *qita*.)

As the missi[1]-tinged tip of the comely one's finger it be described
Or a wound on a distraught lover's heart it be called?

Similar to Solomon's signet ring it be depicted
Or like a fairy's nipple it be described?

To the burnt-out star of Qais's[2] fate it be compared
Or the black mole on Laila's attractive face it be called?

Like the black stone in the Kaba's wall it be supposed
Or the navel of the musk deer of Khutan's[3] wilderness it be called?

In shape as the letter C of the theriac it be considered
Or, in colour, as the down on Jesus' face it be described?

In a cloister if with the spot one's forehead touches in prayer it be identified
In the tavern, the seal of the bottle of wine it be called.

Why describe it as the lock of the door of the treasure of love?
Why call it the centre of the compass of desire?

Why imagine it as a rare, unprocurable pearl?
Why call it the pupil of the eye of the Anqa[4]?

Why paint it as the button of Laila's dress?
Why call it the footprint[5] of Salma's[6] camel?

---

[1]"Missi" is a powder made of various ingredients that women apply to their teeth with their ring finger.
[2] For Qais (and Laila in the next line) see the commentary on couplet 1 of ghazal 2.
[3]A region in Chinese Turkestan famous for musk deer.
[4]See the commentary on couplet 4 of ghazal 1.
[5]A camel's footprint is round in shape.
[6]Salma is the name of the heroine of Arab literary legend.

Why not just assume that your honour's palm of the hand is a heart
And consider as its core this smooth betel nut?

Commentary:

About the occasion of composing this *qit'a* there is an anecdote. Ghalib was in Calcutta in 1828-29 in connection with his pension case (see Section XII of the Introduction). While there, in one of the gathering of friends and acquaintances and lovers of poetry somebody profusely praised Faizi who had become Emperor Akbar's court poet. Ghalib commented that Faizi was not all that what people make him. Then arguments followed and the one who had extolled Faizi said that when Faizi first presented himself before Emperor Akbar he composed impromptu two hundred and fifty verses in praise of the Emperor. Ghalib countered that there were still poets who, if not two hundred, could compose quite a few couplets extemporaneously on any subject at any occasion. At that Faizi's fan took out a betel nut from his pocket, put it on the palm of his hand, and asked Ghalib to say something on that. Ghalib's's response was this *qit'a* which he composed extempore there and then.

[8]

Calcutta

Now that you have mentioned Calcutta, my friend,
An arrow you have shot in my chest!

Those verdant meadows of rare luxuriance
And those elegant, proud beauties –how I miss!

Their patience-trying glances! May they be saved from the evil eye!
Their perplexing signs and gestures—how I reminisce!

Those sweet and fresh fruits—how delightful!
And those neat rose wines—how agreeable!

[9]

Gram-flour Bread

About its true significance don't ask me—
The buttered gram-flour bread His Majesty has sent!

Hadn't he eaten wheat he wouldn't have been expelled;
Had but Adam eaten gram-flour bread instead.[1]

[10]

The Strangers' Loyalty

Gone are the days when you, oblivious of the truth,
Would speak highly of the strangers' loyalty and I would keep mum.

Now that they have failed you why feel ashamed, rejoice.
I swear I will never say: "Didn't I tell you?"

[11]

Ghalib's Partner

I am accursed, my name nobody should utter
If victory and gain he seeks in this world.

Dominance over anybody I never attained:
Whosoever joined me Ghalib's[2] partner he became!

---

[1]Wheat is supposed by the populace to be the forbidden fruit.
[2]Ghalib besides being the poet's pen name, has been used here in its literal sense of being predominant.

[12]

Fasting[1]

If one has the means for the repast to break the fast,
It is required that such a one should fast.

But if one has nothing to eat after breaking the fast
What else that helpless one can but not to fast.

[13]

Note of Excuse[2]

Taking the purgative was easy but this great difficulty now I face
That, not being in attendance, how would I pass all these days!

Three days before the purgative, three days after the purgative;
Three purgatives and three coolants—they all add up to how many days?

[14]

The Courtiers

Although they are the servants of the same king,
The courtiers are not familiar with each other.

---

[1] I.e., total abstention from food and drink from dawn to sunset for the 29 or 30 days of Ramadan, the ninth month of the Islamic lunar calendar ordained by the Quran, that permits exemptions in certain circumstances (Chapter 2, verse 183). But Ghalib's lines are in a lighthearted spirit. As he wrote in a letter to his friend Nabi Bakhsh Haqeer, he recited this qit'a before Emperor Bahadur Shah Zafar who greatly enjoyed it. It was 7th of Ramadan, 1271 A.H. (June 3 of A.D. 1854).

[2] It is addressed to Emperor Bahadur Shah Zafar. The interesting thing is the jolly description of the regimen of purgative and refrigant and leaving the calculation of the days of absence to the addressee, the Emperor.

They place their hands on their ears[1] while greeting:
By this is meant: 'We don't know you.'

[15]
Mirza Jafar's Wedding

Blessed is Mirza Jafar's marriage party
Seeing which everybody's heart is happy

.

Having taken place in such an auspicious year, Ghalib,
Why not the chronogram of this year of the Christian Era be "happy."[2]

[16]
Mirza Jafar's Wedding

When Mirza Jafar was married
The Venus danced at his wedding party.

Ghalib was asked what its chronogram would be;
He said, "The festivity at Jamshad's feast."[3]

---

[1]This *qit'a* is a satire. It has been a long-established norm to greet the king by touching one's forehead with one's right hand. To greet others in the same way in the presence of the king was considered improper, so they greeted each other by placing their right hand on their right ear. But the phrase "placing (one's) hand on (one's)_ears" means, in Urdu, denying or disclaiming acquaintance, hence the satire.

[2]"Happy" is "*mahzuz*" in Urdu and Arabic that as a chronogram expresses 1854 of the Christian Era.

[3]"The festivity … feast" is "*Inshrah-e-jashn-e-Jamshed*" in Urdu and Persian that as a chronogram expresses 1270 of the Islamic Era which corresponds with 1854 of the Christian Era.

RUBAIYAT[1]

---

[1]*Rubaiyat* is the plural of *rubai* (quatrain). The meters of rubai are prescribed by tradition and the rhyming is usually AABA.

[1]

After the end of the hilarity of childhood,
In the days of youth I remained drunk on the present.

And now that the environs of non-existence I have reached
O life that has slipped by, come forth to welcome me!

[2]

At night, I grieved imagining her tresses and perspiring face;
How to describe my condition that was strange beyond description!

I wept with a thousand eyes till the day-break,
Every drop of tear becoming a weeping eye!

[3]

As firework is an amusement for children
So are lovers' aflamed hearts for beloveds.

The inventor of love was also a mischief-maker;
For the sweethearts what a sport was invented!

[4]

Verily, my heart began its life in pain;
Yea, it was restless with jealousy and longed for your sight.

But, alas, it is the very same I that am[1] dispirited, O Light!
Let it be a new manifestation if repetition is ruled out!

[5]

People, from envy, are ready to fight
Seeking their purpose in this wild world, they fight;

That is, everytime, like paper kites,
Those rascals meet only to fight!

[6]

My heart has become very sad, I would say,
It is full of complaints against her, I would say.

And, in the presence of the beloved, not a word I can say,
O Ghalib! My mouth is sealed again, one would say.

[7]

The grief has become agreeable to my heart, Ghalib;
The heart has gradually got exhausted, Ghalib.

By God, I can't sleep the whole night,
As if sleep were under oath not to come, Ghalib.

---

[1]The allusion is to God showing Himself to Moses for which see the commentary on couplet 11 of
ghazal 61. The lover is asking here for a new manifestation, repetition being closed out.

[8]

No doubt, my poetry is difficult, O my heart,
Listening to which, the poets accomplished

Ask me to write simple verses;
Now saying something simple is difficult and not saying anything difficult!

[9]

The King with Jamshed's grandeur has sent me this split pea dish;
Of the King's courtesy and favours an indication it is.

The dish, being the King's favorite, is indisputably the focus
Of the rays of light of state, religion, wisdom, and justice!

[10]

In the King have gathered attributes divine—
The one of dignity and the other of beauty.

Why wouldn't both the nobility and the commoner be happy?
This time came together the Night of Power[1] and the Divali[2]!

---

[1] "The Night of Power?" (*laila-ul-qardri* in Arabic or *shamla-ul-qadri*) is the night when Prophet Muhammad received the first revelation of the Quran in the last months of Ramadam, the ninth month of the Islamic lunar calendar, corresponding to July or August of A, D. 6111. Mulsims celebrate it on 23rd or 27th of Ramdan every year by spending the night in devotions. (The Prophet Muhammad received the last revelation eighty-one days before his death, i.e., on June 8, 630 A.D.)
[2] "Diwali" literally means a row of lamps. It is a Hindu festival celebrated on the 15th of Karrtik, the seventh month of the Hindu solar caldendar, October-November of the Gregoian caendar. At the Diwali night the Hindus worshp Lakshmi, the goddess of wealth, illuminate their houses and streets, and spend the night gambling.

[11]

May God grant the King a long life, making the people happy;
And the King continuing dispensing wisdom and justice!

This knot that has been added in his life string
Is a zero on the right side that multiplies the number.

[12]

May the life-string have a hundred thousand strands and even more!
May as many years as be counted as the strands and even more!

Let us assume each hundred year as one-knot,
May there be a thousand such knots and ever more!

[13]

She is more an afflicter, it is said,
Showing concern for her lovers she is not ashamed.

The hand that might have withdrawn from oppression,
How to believe that she is not holding a sword in that hand?

[14]

Though I salute them and acknowldge their spirituality,
The transactors of affairs keep procrastining.

Good gracious! They tell me to invoke God for help,
The one who turns who turns day into eve into day!

[15]

The means for prosper meal and reposeful sleep when do I have have?
The things of comfort how can I provide?

Gasting is fundamental to my faith, Ghalib,
But a cooled room and cold water when can I afford?

[16]

 Who can know the significance of these beans
That, as a rarity, His Majesty the King has sent to me!

A hundred times I would invoke God's blessing on the King;
A rosary's beads of turquoise are these beans!

THE END

Printed in Great Britain
by Amazon

46694022R00199